Praise for **Joseph D**

"The author can break your heart recalling the most romantic memory of his life or make you laugh out loud."

—*Kirkus Reviews*

"Di Prisco delivers thoughtful contemplation of the human condition and plenty of self-examination that reveals how he made it to where he is, and why he survived when others didn't. His sharp wit and hard-won wisdom make *Subway to California* a story that anyone who's risen out of a hard-scrabble life with the odds stacked against them will love and learn from."

—Diane Prokop, *Foreword*

"Di Prisco's latest is part Mafia thriller, part comic farce, part lament about the anguish of dementia—and all hyperkinetic…fast-paced and often charming."

—*Kirkus Reviews*

"Though Di Prisco takes a heartbreaking look at the scars left by pedophilia, and some readers will surely feel anger at the sins, the tale unfolds, bravely [and] with much humor, thanks to Brother Stephen's bemused narration."

—*Publishers Weekly*

"The novel's surreal tone, Brother Stephen's drily acidic worldview, and the enigmatic portait of a pedophile all combine to deepen this thoughtful look at the heartbreak left in the wake of child sexual abuse."

—*Booklist*

"Along with Joe Di Prisco, I rode that same sweaty *Subway to California*. But somehow, his was a local, with every stop an adventure: crime, passion, gambling, drugs, all the tantalizing stuff we goody-goodies missed."

—Leah Garchik, columnist, *San Francisco Chronicle*

"Joseph Di Prisco writes with humor and a great sense of character, poking fun at things that would leave a lesser author cringing. Think *Cuckoo's Nest* meets *The Godfather*. He interweaves all these elements with the skill of a master writer."
—Anne Hillerman, *New York Times* bestselling author of *Spider Woman's Daughter*

"Great funny lines on every page. Am I recommending *The Alzhammer*? As the protagonist Mikey might say, 'Eggs ackly.'"
— Jack Handey, author of *Deep Thoughts*

"A brilliant portrayal of a wise guy who faces his biggest arch enemies… time and Alzheimer's. The last tango of power, fear, loyalty, and love is beautifully danced for us right to the very end."
—Vickie Sciacca, Lafayette Library

"A beautiful, heartfelt, sometimes funny, occasionally harrowing story of a man making his way through the minefield of his own family history. Di Prisco has lived more lives than most of us, and managed to get it all down in this riveting book."
—Jerry Stahl, author of *Permanent Midnight* and *OG Dad*

"Brimming with humor, heartbreak, and at times the feel an old-time Catholic confessional, *Subway to California* is a one-of-a-kind read."
—Kathleen Caldwell, A Great Good Place For Books

"A book replete with all the rich unfolding and poetic reflection of a novel, and all the focused research and unsparing truth-seeking of biography."
—Laura Cogan, Editor in Chief of *ZYZZYVA*

"What Di Prisco has written here is likely to become the standard-bearer for all future memoirs. This *Subway* ride is the real deal."
—Steven Gillis, author of *The Consequence of Skating*

"An attention-capturing cliffhanger."
—Judith M. Gallman, *Oakland Magazine*

"Told with enough tenderness and humor to elevate his pain-filled recollections to poetry at times, pure fun at others, Di Prisco brings us home—grateful our family is less volatile, or feeling less alone if we, too, survived a wild childhood."

—Lou Fancher, *Contra Costa Times*

"A heartwarming and hilarious sharing of his dysfunctional family adventures, Joe said it best when he wrote: 'Stories happen...to people who can tell them.'"

—Ginny Prior, *Oakland Tribune*

"A very fine novelist and poet who has now written a moving and actually quite funny memoir about life with two parents who should never have married, and once they did, should never have had children. But then we wouldn't have Joe to tell us their story."

—A. R. Taylor, author of *Sex, Rain, and Cold Fusion*

"People struggling to find their place in the world often search for answers in a psychiatrist's office, in love affairs, religion, illegal drugs, gambling, social activism, academia, work, and vicariously, through their children. Di Prisco visited all those places, and then, coming up short, found himself by writing a memoir."

—*Mercury News*

"It's rare to encounter a book so heartfelt and compassionate and yet so incisively hilarious at the same time."

—Heather Mackey, author of *Dreamwood*

"Throughout *Subway*, Di Prisco evokes the past with vivid, often hilarious, prose, describing his Italian-Polish upbringing in Brooklyn, the flight to a strange world called California, his doomed and dramatic love affairs, and his colorful parents—the kind of parents you enjoy reading about and are grateful they were not yours!"

—Anara Guard, author of *Remedies for Hunger*

"What makes Di Prisco's novel work is its narrative voice—poignant, rueful, and wise-crackingly sardonic…Readers of J. F. Powers' *Morte d'Urban* and Alice McDermott's *Charming Billy* should find their way to *All for Now*."

—P. F. Kluge, author of *A Call from Jersey* and *Gone Tomorrow*

"It is especially moving to read a book that looks so broadly at the ubiquitous issue of Roman Catholicism and pedophilia…Di Prisco has given us a brave, bumbling, soul-searching hero whose wry humor only enhances his honesty."

—Jan Weissmiller, Prairie Lights Books

"Catholic or not, religious or not, *All for Now* is accessible to everyone because mistakes and forgiveness are universal."

—*Seattle Post Intelligencer*

"*Confessions of Brother Eli* fairly sparkles with humor that ranges from sophisticated to slapstick, in what some believe to be the most difficult writing to carry off."

—*Tucson Weekly*

"With dry, sardonic wit, Brother Eli questions his faith and vocation, while recounting adventures that take place at his school…The writing and narrative voice in this book is some of the best I've come across."

—*Akron Beacon Journal*

"With a wit that questions as it embraces, *Poems in Which* provides us with a strong, original voice."

—Carl Dennis, author of *Practical Gods* and winner of the Pulitzer Prize

Subway to California

Joseph Di Prisco

Subway to California

Joseph Di Prisco

AUTHOR OF

The Pope of Brooklyn

A VIREO BOOK | RARE BIRD BOOKS
LOS ANGELES, CALIF.

A Vireo Book | Rare Bird Books

453 South Spring Street, Suite 302

Los Angeles, CA 90013

rarebirdbooks.com

Set in Bembo

Printed in the United States

10 9 8 7 6 5 4 3 2

PAPERBACK ISBN: 9781945572531

A part of *Subway to California* appeared in an essay by the author, "Head Fakes in Ho Chi
Minh City," published in *The Threepenny Review*.

The author has changed names and altered details where appropriate in his memoir, to
safeguard the privacy of some whose lives intersected with his.

Publisher's Cataloging-in-Publication data

Di Prisco, Joseph, 1950—Subway to California : a memoir / by Joseph Di Prisco. p. cm.

ISBN 9781940207353

1. Di Prisco, Joseph, 1950–. 2. Di Prisco family. 3. California—Biography. 4. Brooklyn
(New York, N.Y.)—Biography. 5. Gambling and crime —Biography. 6. Addictions. I. Title.

CT275.D481 S8 2014

979.4/092—dc23

For my son, Mario

PART ONE

I too lived, Brooklyn of ample hills was mine,
I too walk'd the streets of Manhattan island, and bathed in the waters around it,
I too felt the curious abrupt questionings stir within me.

—"Crossing Brooklyn Ferry," Walt Whitman

Brooklyn Transfer

WHEN MY FATHER RAN away, he said, "Go back to Grandma's house and don't take no shit from nobody."

If I'd had a camera that Sunday afternoon, I might have snapped a picture of his backside when he made a mad dash for the tree line, plunged into the thickets, and disappeared. I was ten years old the day he left my younger brother and me on that Long Island country road. Not that I knew it at the time, but that was only the beginning of a long journey for him—and for me.

Soon after, my mother rounded up my brother and me and we hauled out of Brooklyn.

We weren't the first family to skip town and we wouldn't be the last. Nothing awaited us elsewhere, but elsewhere did have one big advantage: It was not Brooklyn. Brooklyn, however, was not the problem. As I would one day find out, the FBI was on my father's trail. Who wouldn't call that a problem?

★

HIS FLIGHT BEGAN ONE peaceful day in the late spring or early summer of 1961, while my family was visiting my grandparents' farm in sleepy, suburban East Islip. Though I loved the farm, I didn't appreciate missing Mass that Sunday. I was a pious child.

A tiny train station stood within walking distance of the farm, but it was more convenient to drive, despite the bumper-to-bumper weekend expressway traffic, and that is how we traveled to spend occasional Sundays. Nowadays, where my grandparents once lived, tract homes stretch as far as the glaucomaed eye fails to distinguish. Back then, there were trees and dirt roads, wild pigs plowing the brush, hawks soaring, wild turkeys gobbling. Frayed signs were nailed up in the forests we roamed, warning *No Hunting No Trespassing*. Shots rang out from time to time in the distance. I had no idea what anybody could be hunting. Maybe wolf, maybe fox? That depended on the movie or the fairy tale disturbing my dreams. My father and uncle took me out into the woods a few times, armed with shotguns and .22s so we could take aim at the quarry of soda cans and wine jugs.

Before the old man scooted off, he blurted out those parting instructions: "Go back to Grandma's house and don't take no shit from nobody." Old man? *Old* man? He was in his thirties. Still, he spoke his piece and didn't stick around for discussion and explanation—neither of which he was big on under any circumstances, including those apparently less urgent than the present.

Not that the man was auditioning for street mime. He had his opinions. We never had a question as to where he stood on the subject of shit-taking. He was anti. We didn't fully understand what he meant by that bromide, but we knew it was his all-purpose take on life.

My father invoked memorable counsel on other subjects as well: "Don't count your money in front of no windows." Seems there once was a rash fellow in Brooklyn who did such a foolish thing and lived to regret it. My father didn't say how or why somebody was conducting surveillance on said man, but he also didn't say he was a disinterested party. And he didn't exactly admit that *he* stole the guy's money or that anybody he knew stole the guy's money. The guy had it coming, though, because he was stupid enough to count his money in front of a window, which, in case there was a question, nobody should do. For the record, my brother and I didn't have in our possession any rolls of cash to count in front of a window or anywhere else. Still, the notion was weaponized and loaded into the memory chamber for later discharge.

I watch my father vanish that Sunday, quickly enveloped by the trees. I turn to look down the road, and I instantly understand what has clipped wings onto his shoes. My grandparents' house is surrounded by black and white police cars and other official-looking vehicles unmarked yet easily detectible as chariots of law enforcement. Lights flash on top of the cruisers parked in ominous, threatening diagonals.

John and I wander back to the house. I do not recall being frightened for myself, though there must have been some element of fear. Wouldn't any child have been afraid to see his father run for his life? At the same time, I also do not recall being intimidated by the spectacle of the great blue line. My childhood fantasies failed to run toward a career in the well-compensated and respected field of criminal justice. More than anything, what I recall is that it all felt normal—or at least not particularly strange. It's the sort of thing I intuited my father was capable of doing. He *would* run into the woods and *would* flee into the wind.

What were the odds that my father would be taking a walk with his sons when the cops showed up to not find him? A long shot. My father has been a gambler forever and he would have said the odds were too steep to take. What an amazing piece of luck. Luck isn't the word.

We come in through the back door, go down the steps into the cellar past the canned sweet tomatoes and the jarred red and green peppers and the half-gallons of reedy red wine, which we had to sip on during Sunday supper for no other reason than to validate our boyhood. Everybody is standing around, only now their standing around has a solemn function. They are seriously smoking cigarettes, looking highly pissed off. This condition applies to everybody, from my grandparents to my mother to my uncles to the guys in the suits whose jackets flare open, revealing weaponry. If they are saying anything, they aren't sharing recipes, and they are all talking in English, not Italian.

★

IN THE 1920s MY grandparents arrived in America, passing through Ellis Island like many Italian immigrants. They had left Fontanarosa, a lovely hillside town of diminishing economic prospects famous for its high-quality stone, in the region of Campania, forty minutes these days by car outside Avellino, more than an hour away (by horse cart, who knows?) from Napoli. Giovannina Ruzza was born on May 5, 1896. Pasquale Di Prisco, September 18, 1897. They were married on November 27, 1919, in their home town. She was twenty-three, he was twenty-two. Pasquale became a naturalized citizen of the United States of America in July 1929. Their four children, three boys and a girl, were born in Brooklyn.

Giuseppe Luigi Di Prisco was the second child, and he was born on March 18, 1925, about thirty-five years before scooting into those woods. He was usually called Joe, but his street name was Popey. That was Pope-y, not as in Popeye, but as in of the Pope, or Pope-like or -ish. So it was pronounced "Pope-ee." Popey's wife, my mom, was a Polish girl from the neighborhood, and she used to say they called him Popey because, in her words, he "never shut the fuck up." That was a difficult for me to understand, because my father never expatiated at length, preferring the aphoristic, like about not counting your money or taking shit. Then again, if my mom was in attendance, she commanded the floor. As for the street name, my dad testified they called him Popey because his crew caught him coming out of a church one time. How he lived down the embarrassment he never did explain, and what he was doing in a pew he never said, either. Truth is, I had only few faint recollections of his ever being inside a sanctuary.

My uncles normally speak to their parents in their Napolitano tongue, because the immigrants speak hardly any English. This dialect is rough, considered low-class in Italy, and easy to pick out. It's reminiscent of the "Italian" in '50s pop songs that people who don't speak Italian believe sounds Italian. At every opportunity, closing vowels are severed. Ricotta becomes ricott', spaghetti spaghett', manicotti manicott'. The English "ch" sounds in Italian become "sh." "Diciamo," let's talk—"di-CHA-mo"—sounds like "di-SHA-mo." "Scopa," the delightful Italian card game, "SHH-copa." And so on.

Meanwhile, on this farm in New York, the grandchildren are on the monorail to cultural assimilation. None of us grandchildren spoke Italian at the time, and it would take decades for that misjudgment to be corrected. Nobody wanted to be outed by speaking Italian and being labeled a wop. Everybody assumed Italians were mobsters who preferred wife-beater T-shirts—that day being a case in point.

★

THE CELLAR WAS WHERE my grandparents lived, with stove and sink and fridge and lots of cupboards for canned tomatoes and peppers, tools and weaponry and so on, the usual comestibles and combustibles. That's where they rolled out the pasta, made the family dinners, did the TV-watching, the yelling, the drinking of their homemade red wine, the crying, the chestnut-roasting, the anisette-pouring, the card-playing, and still more of the crying and yelling. The bathroom was upstairs, though my grandfather preferred the outdoor sink for his morning toilet and the water pump by the garage and the outhouse on the farthest edge of the property. If he was out there at six a.m., he had overslept. I loved the water that came out of that pump. It always tasted sweet and cold.

The stairs leading to the upper floor obeyed no rational twentieth-century building code, constructed at about a sixty-degree angle, just this side of a ladder. Upstairs, there were bedrooms and a living room and another kitchen—a more conventional domestic arrangement. They never cooked or ate up there. Up there, genteel codes prevailed. Furniture had plastic covering and walls were painted dusky brown and lime green. The halls reeked of mothballs, amazingly, considering that twenty, thirty feet downstairs no garlic bulb was safe from the olive oil in a spattering hot pan. The real living went on downstairs, in what they called the cellar.

Entering the cellar, you had to pass a pole. This pole was painted that very same lime green as the walls upstairs, a color signaling an alert—perhaps to prevent grandchildren from running into it after sipping on that Sunday supper wine. It must have functioned as a sort of structural support, because the aesthetic enhancement was dubious. Whenever I saw this pole I remembered something my mother said a hundred times: "When your father was a boy, your grandfather used to tie him to a post in the cellar, beat the shit out of him with a belt, and leave him crying in the dark. They're all fucking barbarians, these Italians."

My mother also had iron-clad culinary views that clashed with Italian traditions and my father's native-born food preferences. Herbs and spices were practically banished from her board. Salt and pepper were tantalizing rumors. Cinnamon was around, for toast or to garnish rice pudding, and of course all types of sugar, granulated, brown, or powdered. Sure, she used plenty of sour cream and whipping cream, but for her, everything tasted better with one special ingredient. Later on, when my father was getting word on his elevated cholesterol count, he often could be heard shouting about it: he accused his wife of killing him—with butter.

She hated garlic. She hated garlic almost as much as she hated the Italians, and for obviously related reasons. It seems perhaps incomprehensible and almost insanely impressive that she waged a one-woman crusade against garlic her whole life, but it is true. I don't know what she could eat on Sunday at my grandparents' given that position, and now that I think about it, I have no recollection of her eating anything on Long Island. Her indictment of garlic was absolute. I couldn't buy her contention that garlic made her physically ill, a claim underscored with grotesque facial contortions and nauseating sound effects. I would not have had the vocabulary to articulate that her argument was symbolic or passive-aggressive, but that was my take. How could anybody not like garlic? Whenever we went to restaurants, she would interrogate the waiter about every item on the menu: "Any gah-lick?" A naked swinging light bulb over the waiter's head couldn't have added to her efforts of intimidation. If the waiter swore, "No garlic, lady," she would size him up to see if he was fucking with her. I can imagine her proposing to snoop in the kitchen, to check if any garlic bulbs were lying suspiciously around. Despite her vigilance, dishes with supposed garlic were dangerously served up to her. I lost count of how many times she sent back her plate. The garlic phobia was not rooted in sensory reality.

"Mom," my brother Eddie would say to her, "you can't eat garlic?"

"Makes me want to puke."

Eddie would lift up a bottle of kosher pickles. She loved her dills.

"Says here, right on the label, there's garlic in these pickles. Want one?"

When she did not have a leg to stand on, she strutted: "Never mind."

Despite the fact that her previous husband—with whom she had three children—and her current husband—with whom she had two boys, me and my brother John—were both Italian, or maybe because of it, she never relented on her garlic antipathy or on her position that Italians were all fucking barbarians. She often reminded everybody of her anti-Italian worldview when she was angry with my father, as if she were clearing up doubts as to why he was a fucking barbarian, and why he couldn't help it, the motherfucker. Sometimes, rarely, she said this in a sympathetic tone of voice, as if to convey how much adversity he'd overcome, or would have overcome if he were capable of overcoming adversity, which so far the fucking barbarian had not managed to do.

My mother's frightening accounts of cellar beatings made for an indelible image: my father prostrate on the cold cement floor, shivering in the darkness, welts all over him from the belt buckle. My mother was doubtless relaying what she believed to be accurate information—she must have gotten the details from her husband. My father, for his part, never once mentioned this ordeal, but he was never less than deferential to his father, fearful even.

More than anything, perhaps, what my mother had to say about my father and the fucking barbarian Italians showed that she was continuing the pattern of abuse my father had experienced since childhood—not that I ever made that connection at the time. Maybe my father found in my mother the perfect mate to abuse and love him. She wasn't tying him to a pole in the cellar and leaving him in the dark. She was tying him to herself and leaving him in the dark.

I find it curious that her observation about Italian parenting customs never really did the trick of making me feel intimidated by my grandfather, which was, I assume, at least one strategic aspect. He was difficult enough on his own terms, so I kept my measured distance, in case he got any ideas of tying me up and leaving me in the cellar. I didn't believe he would do that to me, his prized oldest grandson—yet how was I to know for sure after taking into account my mother's vast wisdom on the barbarian subject? But when his face turned tomato red and he wanted to show affection, he would nuzzle my cheek, and his grizzled face would amusingly scratch my face and the scent of the wine would please and terrify me. My grandfather yelled at my younger brother a lot, which, to tell the truth, just about everybody did. But he never yelled at me, not even after the time we were searching around in some cupboards—for what, I cannot recall—and I came across, fifteen feet from the dinner table, three or four loaded rifles and shotguns along with plenty of rounds and buckshot. When the breach of security was analyzed, the guns were moved and never stumbled upon again.

My grandfather's eyes crossed, so sometimes it was hard for me to face him. Which eye to look at? Left or right? Maybe focus on the nose, a target prominent as a Roma tomato? When I was very young, my parents noticed my own eyes would drift when I got tired, a gift from the family genes. My eyes would still be crossing if at age twelve I hadn't started wearing glasses with prisms in the prescription, as I still do.

Thick, broad-chested, florid of complexion, and squat, my grandfather resembled a blushing turnip. On a good day he was five feet tall. He was comically bow-legged. This last observation seemed connected to another of my mother's choice observations: "Pasquale was a cavalier." She enjoyed enunciating the word "cavalier." The truth was, he was a Cavaliere dell'Ordine di Vittorio Veneto, and served in Ethiopia in the cavalry. My mother found worthy of mockery this family military history, especially the part about Ethiopia. She would say he should go back to Ethiopia, because he was a fucking barbarian, and I was forced to conclude Ethiopia was another country full of barbarians, like Italy. At which point my father would counter by saying something inscrutably laudatory about somebody named Haile Selassie, whoever he was.

I remember going to church one Sunday with everybody in East Islip. The priest's homily was delivered in Italian. My grandfather was wearing his brown work shoes that had never been afflicted by a coat of polish and a blue suit, topped with a grey fedora that was too small, so he looked like a cartoon character bloated into a Pez dispenser. He had put on a starched white shirt stiff as cardboard with a tie wide as a flag, a tie whose knot, from the look on his red face, was constricting his oxygen supply, the shirt collar flipped up as if he had a set of wings under his chin. If he were a horse in that church, he could not have appeared more skittish.

When he was in high spirits, and his nose turned beet red from the wine he had been drinking all day, he used to beam and warn he was about to break into the tarantella. He would strike a pose like some Sicilian dancer, hands over his head, snapping his fingers, kicking his heels, threatening some imitation of the flamenco. But as much as his grandson wished for this star turn to take place, my Nonno never did break into the tarantula dance. That would have been something to see.

By the way, how did we know what they were saying though we did not speak their dialect, or any Italian? I don't know, but we did. Somehow I inherited a good Italian accent, which I discovered when I learned to speak the language many years later.

As for my grandmother, like every Italian boy of literature and lore, I adored her. She must have been a ravishing beauty in her youth, for she had that gorgeous mocha Southern skin and high cheekbones and a ready sparkle in her eyes. My mother wanted me to dislike her because, according to my mother, Giovannina was pitting my father against his siblings and his own father, while she elected to play the role of martyr and saintly matriarch. It was implicit, from my mother's point of view, that my grandmother was devious. I am not saying my mother did not have a point. She may well have, for my mother could have received a graduate degree in deviousness. Still, my grandmother trumped every argument made against her by being herself. She wept for joy a lot—joy is my guess—when she and I chatted at the table, though I never knew why she wept, or what the joy, if it was joy, was about. She had big feelings and she showed them. Then she would pat my hand and slip me a twenty-dollar bill. The money smelled nutty and woodsy, a lot like shaved Parmigiano cheese, which should have been a clue as to where she secreted her cash.

Don't tell your father about the money, she would communicate in broken English. I got the message and squirreled away the loot. What nobody needed to know nobody needed to know. *Acqua in bocca*, as they say in Italian. Water in the mouth— which makes it hard to talk, you see, and which amounts to "Mum's the word." Well, if it was important to her that nobody needed to know, okay. Anything for Nonna—anything.

★

WHEN MY DAD RAN off, he didn't bother to say: "If anybody asks you something, especially a cop, don't open your mouth." Every child borough-wide is hard-wired. You don't talk. You don't answer questions. Answer a question with a question, buy some time. And volunteering information? That was something that could get you smacked. You take every opportunity to shut the fuck up.

Still, the uniform might be asking questions—but then again, I had an overactive imagination and a bustling fantasy life. Probably the cop didn't ask me anything, but his disapproving scrutiny amounted to something like this:

Where's your old man?

Where?

So it's gonna be like that.

Like what?

Where. Is. Your. Old. Man?

My old man?

That's the greaseball I'm axing about, chubby.

My mutha says I am stout.

You're a punk, orange ya, like your old man. Stout means fat, did your pretty Polack mutha tell you that, too?

She takes me shopping for clothes in the husky section.
You know, husky is another word for…
Also she says I have big bones.
Yeah, you got lotsa big bones all right. In your freakin' head.

★

WHEN MY FAMILY IS finally reunited, it's a long time from now and a long, long way from here, in an airport on the other side of the country. It would take longer, much longer, for me to have a clue as to what the FBI wanted with my father and what it was that drove us far from home.

Brooklyn in my past, as a boy I would come to discover I had arrived in a place where oranges grew on the trees and shiny convertibles glided along the expressway, which they called a freeway, and a different ocean—and also the Brooklyn Dodgers, only they weren't the *Brooklyn* Dodgers anymore. This was a strange and beautiful place. There were redwood trees and brown hills. The food was different, too, including the pizza, which barely qualified. They didn't know from chicken parm, either. The rain was not the New York rain, rain that gave off attitude: *You want a taste of this? I got your rain right here.* And the snow…what snow?

I would soon find out the people who lived here talked weird. They would snicker when you said didjuh and shoulda, wautah and fawk. They would correct you and say *did you* and *should have, water* and *fork.* Your mudda, fadda, and brudda were a source of amusement as well. At the movies, everybody waited in line, and not on line, as they shoulda. Yes, they thought they wuz pretty smaht, only they said *smart.* It was enough to put the kibosh on the whole friggin ding. The only sport I had played was stickball in the middle of Humboldt Street in Greenpoint, when we yelled *fuck you* at the drivers whose cars interrupted us. Here they had gorgeous green fields for baseball, and perfect black asphalt courts for a game known as basketball. I had never touched a basketball before. The whole landscape was sad and dazzling, lit up by the unyielding, bleaching sun. Over time, I might get used to it all, maybe, but I doubted it.

The place was called California.

February 4, 2010

CHILLY, CHILLY, CHILLY NIGHT here in Greenpoint, which is in Brooklyn and which is where I was born. I don't often come back to Greenpoint, except for weddings and funerals.

So far, no weddings.

Tonight's forecast is a blizzard.

Bring it on, I say, even as the sparkling black sky makes me doubt the meteorologist's crystal ball. I like the toasty, tinny taste in the air. Maybe that means the flu is coming on.

I'm here in Greenpoint to see my mother. It has been almost two years. A lot has happened. But first, I am going to walk. And walk. And walk some more. Though it is freezing, I need to prepare. Fortunately, the sidewalks are mostly empty, the way I have preferred my sidewalks and, for longer than I would care to admit, my romantic entanglements.

Greenpoint is toying with me. Brooklyn, my mother's appearance, the imminent blizzard—the puzzle pieces of the past, my personal history, are shifting around on the board when who knew there was a game to be played? Bless me, Father, for I have obviously sinned, it has been a long, long time since my last confession, but if it please the court, there are two observations I would like to observe at this time: As far as I am concerned, nothing has changed in Greenpoint since I was ten years old and was transplanted in California, and everything looks completely different.

★

ONE DAY MY WIFE had a routine medical appointment. This was many years before tonight and three thousand miles away.

I had never met Dr. Smith, though other relatives as well as friends were Dr. Smith's patients. At the time I was traveling, and when my wife called, she sounded tentative, wary. She does not do tentative or wary. She is more like standing on the bridge in bungee-jumping school and then leaping: *Wheee!* This was the exchange she related:

Dr. Smith, she said to her healer, you and I have a mutual acquaintance.

Oh, really, her doctor asked, who would that be?

That would be Kay Di Prisco, your patient.

How do you know Catherine?

This was a legitimate query on the doctor's part, because his patient did not take her spouse's last name in holy wedlock.

She is my mother-in-law.

That means you're married to that writer, Joe Di Prisco?

Yes, he is my husband, she admitted, like that casually throwing away her constitutionally protected right not to incriminate herself.

Faster than you could spit out First, do no harm, Dr. Smith declared: You know, if she was my mother, I would have committed suicide.

★

I SHOULD HAVE SEEN that one coming. That doctor's point of view was one with which I sympathized, though sympathized is not the word. My reaction to the doctor's wisecrack was to laugh. Not because it was funny, though it *was*, in an awful way, something like funny, but because—what else was I supposed to do?

If she was my mother...

Who knew members of the healing profession were licensed to say stuff like that?

...I would have committed suicide.

It would be tempting to observe that the doc's harsh remark reveals more about the doctor than his patient. But no, that's probably not so. And how did he know Kay Di Prisco's son was a writer? My literary career has been the publishing world's equivalent of an unmanned drone zipping under the radar over the polar cap. Truth is, my mother's doctor had a point, because if you knew my mother—well, the doctor had a very interesting point.

So I'm walking around Greenpoint and it's so cold it hurts to breathe. I shouldn't have given up cigars. Smoking a Dominican Robusto would be a warm comfort, if not a consolation. I look over to where the dry cleaner used to be, where my mother worked fifty years ago. That was where I would keep her company in the back after school or during the summer, when the fan boxed in the window whirred like a mosquito. The fan was an exercise in futility. It was never anything but insufferably hot in the store. Even so, she inhaled her Lucky Strikes and sipped on her green-tinted glass bottles of Coca-Cola while I threw down icy cold Yoo-Hoo, the partially hydrogenated soybean oil-rich chocolatish drink that might as well have been laced with laudanum, it was so addictive. Down the block from the dry cleaner's there is the funeral parlor, on the corner of Humboldt Street and Driggs Avenue: Stobierski's Garden View Funeral Home. Nobody in Greenpoint has ever captured either the elusive unicorn or the view of any garden in the vicinity of the establishment.

That's where my mother is tonight, at Stobierski's, after the plane ride. She has been living in Florida with my father for the last eighteen months. My father's poor health wouldn't allow him to accompany her, so she made the trip alone.

Tonight, her journey has come to an end. It won't be long before somebody is telling her only living son that his mother looks beautiful. She herself heard that a million times. Tonight she won't. She is lying in a casket.

★

IN THE 1930s THOMAS Wolfe wrote a story called "Only the Dead Know Brooklyn." It's a famous work first published in *The New Yorker* and narrated in the argot reminiscent of a favorite television program, "The Bowery Boys," starring a smart doofus and a softie wise guy, off whose tongues rolled lots of *dese* and *dose, duh* and *dem bums.*

I must have first read Wolfe's story in an anthology when I was eleven or twelve, and I read it over and over, not because I was obsessive-compulsive (though I was and obviously still am), and not because it was short (though it was), and not because the writer was illustrious (who knew?). This was the reason I was awestruck: The guy put the name of Greenpoint, or *Greenpernt,* where I was born and which I had left, and its lingo into a story. I couldn't get over this. It made me appreciate that Greenpoint was real, as in real enough to be put inside the pages of a *book,* and books, which were rare and precious, I loved more than I loved Greenpoint itself.

Wolfe's last lines go, "It'd take a guy a lifetime to know Brooklyn t'roo an' t'roo. An' even den, yuh wouldn't know it all."

I might have thought that a bit overstated, if *overstated* were a word in my working vocabulary when I was eleven or twelve, which I did strive to expand through stacks of personal index cards, tough or big words scribbled on the front, dictionary definition on the back. I loved reading around in the dictionary, a mental amusement park. I hated the thesaurus, because it seemed out of control, indiscriminate, manic, suggestible. Another problem was, the thesaurus had no pictures. But my dictionary, the battle-torn hardcover Webster's held together by Scotch tape, was an instrument—no, it was an exotic vehicle, like Aladdin's lamp. The skillful, dogged use of the dictionary gave me most of my knowledge of, for instance, sex education, which was a term never heard in school. Unbelievable the words the dictionary defined, right there in plain sight, often employing handy sketches and (not nearly enough) instructive photos. Words like, say, *masturbation*. Maybe there was not enough description to give a how-to-visual, but that was okay, because I would never never never never never commit such an act, consciously anyway or while completely awake, whatever the dictionary said it was, because that deed was proscribed. As Sister advised, "Don't do anything you wouldn't do in front of the Blessed Virgin Mary." This image of the party-pooping Virgin was scarier than any vampire movie, because vampires were less likely than the BVM to pop up while you were possibly doing something that would elicit, if not a hardworking vampire's, certainly the Virgin Mary's sorrowful disapproval.

Yes, to anticipate a reasonable-enough question likely surfacing: I was a boy who spent a lot of time by himself.

Brooklyn t'roo an' t'roo? That was the issue. At eleven or twelve, though, I thought I was done with Greenpoint and with Brooklyn, and there was nothing worth knowing t'roo an t'roo about it that I didn't already know. One thing that famous story did not do was make me feel nostalgic, now that I lived in California. At its Greek root the word nostalgia refers to that profound, intrinsic desire that people supposedly have to come home. Greenpoint, I felt sure, would never have qualified.

Nowadays, Greenpoint has become very hot: trendy restaurants, soaring real estate prices, hit television show locations, big-ticket events covered in *The New York Times*. But Greenpoint as recollected in childhood memory: row houses upon row houses, East River waterfront, penny bridges, diesel fumes, air thick as pencil lead, abandoned factories, Polish bakeries, Italian tough guys, bars and grills, churches and churches and churches. That's not a home to be nostalgic for, that's a movie set. As it happened, good mob movies like *Donny Brasco* and *The Departed* would come to be filmed in Greenpoint. The latter became a favorite of my dad's, though he never got the name quite right.

He called it *The Deported*. He did this sort of thing with words, which he mangled marvelously. Like with Pennsylvania. For him, the Keystone state was pronounced Penn-slyvania.

Then again, maybe Thomas Wolfe got it right. Maybe it's only the dead who can say they knew Brooklyn, once they aren't able to say anything anymore. Tonight I might make progress finding out if that's true. Tonight is the wake for my mother, so, if Wolfe was right, she would theoretically be in a position to help. They won't start the ritual of the wake till her only living son gets there, so I keep walking the neighborhood. Timing is everything in life. In death, too.

Brooklyn t'roo an' t'roo. What could that mean?

★

THE POSTED SIGN READS **McGOLDRICK PARK**. Back then, nobody called it McGoldrick Park. Everybody called it Winthrop Park. There is the pseudo-Classical stone portico and there are the columns of the building dedicated to veterans of foreign wars. I spent a lot of time in that park. I was fascinated by cocoons and caterpillars and asked to hear again how that chrysalis thing works. One day in 1960 I was at the park after school because I had an appointment to fight Stephen Somethingski. I did not want to be there. But did I have a choice? No. My buddies showed to root me on.

Stephen Somethingski's father reviewed the rules of engagement:

No uze rasslink. We does boxink.

The man was an idiot. Stephen was a moose, so nobody with current brain function was going to wrestle him—all he'd have to do is fall on you and it would be over.

No locks off head.

He was a regular Marquis of Queensbury, only with a Polish accent and a trucker's cap and plaid flannel coat. Headlocks? You'd need a ladder to get up there to grab Stephen around the neck.

No scratch witt nail, scratch like girl.

Okay, the man might truly be an idiot. And what was he doing here, anyway?

One gray wintry school day Stephen Somethingski had called me out. Stephen was a head taller and maybe fifty pounds heavier than me, which was saying something. Stephen told me to meet him at the park after school to settle our "differences." I did not like Stephen much, make that not at all, and I didn't know we had anything called differences or if they could be settled via fisticuffs, or any other way. Words would have worked, maybe. Words worked except when they didn't, like, evidently, now.

I must have done something terrible to provoke Stephen, but I have no recollection. Maybe you don't need a rationale to fight when you're growing up a boy in Brooklyn. So I arrived that day after school, full of something like excitement mixed with dread and nausea. Then Stephen appeared. Only Stephen's father was with him. Another enormous, beefy Polish guy, this one reeking of barely suppressed anger and the Pabst Blue Ribbon *piwo* he drank for lunch. As I prepared myself for fisticuffs, I was not afraid of Stephen—I was afraid *for* Stephen. And also for myself. But not because Stephen was going to beat me up. That seemed unlikely, especially after he showed up with his old man. There was no good reason for this fight to take place, no principle to uphold, no dignity to protect. What felt worst of all was that there was no way to stop it from happening.

The other guys showed, too, witnesses and pals standing in as the scrappy entourage. It would have been hard for anybody to cheer on Stephen because nobody liked him. Being the biggest kid in the class—maybe the school—is not easy to live up to, not that anybody had empathy to spare. For another thing, he smelled. And his grades were so-so. And he was huge and clumsy and so unsure of himself he got in everybody's way. And he had that needy look that conveyed a pushy insecurity.

Did the dad even like his son? It was debatable. The dad seemed to be present to send a message that his son had something to prove, either to his dad or to himself, or possibly to the other boys in the class, one of whom had been handpicked for fighting.

If Stephen's father hadn't shown up, the adversaries might have had a chance to talk this through, or call each other names and leave it at that, and maybe not have to throw hands after all. But maybe the dumb dad did not want that. The dumb dad being dumbly present meant nobody stood a chance of retaining a shred of dumb self-respect.

So he and I circled each other, acting as if we kind of knew what we were doing. We watched boxing on television, we had a clue. We threw out small fists at the end of arms that had the tensile force of rope.

It was easy to mix it up in the neighborhood, because that's the way it was. I had all I needed to operate: If you know you're going to be in a fight, throw the first punch, ideally in the nose, which will spurt scary blood and convince most guys it's not worth it. I adopted wholesale this M.O. I was not a tough guy and never would be, but you never walk away from a challenge, and that meant you prefer taking a beating to walking away a coward. A simple, brutal, and dimwitted logic, unquestioned by everybody.

Today's fight was not going to cover anybody in glory, because we were fighting over nothing—nothing to win meant everything to lose. We ducked, we bobbed, we weaved, we sadly mimicked courage and resolve. Stephen and I kept circling. Stephen was so tall that I couldn't get an angle, and Stephen was so slow that his telegraphed punches either never landed or had the impact of sunflowers brushing my face. This was a mismatch. I punched Stephen in the face, and again in the face, his doughy face, because I didn't know what else to do, and I saw fear flicker like church candles in Stephen's eyes. Fear observed brings out the worst in people, especially in boys fighting in a park.

It dawned. It was simple.

Stephen Somethingski was trying to impress his dad. That was an objective nobody else could help him achieve, and futility would be his prize. There was a chance there was something more insidious at work. Dad needed Stephen to impress *him,* to defend himself as being the dad of a boy who could hold his own in a fistfight.

Hulking, shoes-in-the-mud Stephen could not fight a lick, and at some point his discouraged dad realized as much and threw in the towel. Stephen wasn't physically harmed. But he had to deal with his father. Then we all walked off—here's the stunning part—*together.* We went to a water fountain and bent over and greedily drank, politely waiting our turn.

You boys, punks.

So much for being gracious in defeat.

Stephen started this, he had it comin'.

So much for being gracious in whatever the semblance of victory would be.

The old man spit on the ground. Then he walked off with his son. He didn't put his arm around him. He walked alongside, insisting on separation. It was the picture of loneliness. If appearances were predictive, a bad night awaited them both.

What happened in Winthrop Park long ago when I was ten, on a gray wintry day after school, was simple. That was when two boys, nostrils flaring, breathing hard, hopelessly fought to earn the respect of Brooklyn and, more important, the respect of their fathers, only one of whom was stupid enough to be present. The other may have not been physically on the scene, but he was ever-present in the imagination of his son.

★

THE NIGHT OF MY mother's wake, a metropolitan bus cut me off in the crosswalk near my old grade school, St. Stan's, as in St.

Stanislaus Kostka School. Greenpoint is Polish as kielbasa, and the smell of cooked cabbage seems to insinuate its way through every stairwell and corridor and nasal passage. The big brick St. Stan's school building squats, imposing, at the corner of the block: bleak and bland, with all the charm of a bank branch, though this was an institution dedicated to another type of saving.

I was a schoolboy, and one of the principal requirements for being a schoolboy was being in school. This was where I became the idea of myself. It wasn't a particularly great, original, or inspired idea to have of oneself, but it was mine. Or maybe it was everybody else's idea of me and I had no choice but to live up to it.

I was a schoolboy the way my dad was a gambler, the way my mom was a beauty and a flirt, the way John was a future felon and tragic fuck-up, the way Bobby was a juvenile delinquent and heartbreaker, the way Eddie was closeted gay and the most generous person in the family, the way my sister was…I had no idea who she was. I never lived with her. My mother's having three children with a man who wasn't my father made for complications later on when I grasped the truth—but her other two boys I always considered my brothers, just like my father's other biological son, John.

In any case, as a schoolboy, I was different. Neither of my parents had graduated, and none of my four siblings would graduate from high school, and high school graduation was an academic breakthrough far, unthinkably far, in my own future. I would get a PhD someday, but being awarded the blue and gold doctoral hood barely registered on the family Richter scale. No, it was high school graduation that shook them. It was the prime social separator.

Once a schoolboy turned seven, life became a much more serious proposition, a life-and-death moral proposition. At age seven, so the Church theologically stipulated, I had the faculty and the obligation to make life-altering decisions. This was called the "age of reason." Theologians have struggled over such issues for centuries, and though I did not know their names and did not have the Latin or the German, I took the point. I was responsible. I had arrived. This was the Big Leagues.

Children were served their theology without a dollop of sugar or spice. They got it whole and cold as a hardboiled egg from a blue booklet called the *Baltimore Catechism*. As with a plate of hardboiled eggs, you shouldn't consume too much dogma in a single sitting. Thus these propositions were advanced in bracing question and unforgettable answer form, and addressed systematically.

Q. 150. Why did God make you?

A. God made me to know Him, to love Him, and to serve Him in this world, and to be happy with Him forever in the next.

Q. 197. What is a mystery?

A. A mystery is a truth which we cannot fully understand.

Q. 198. Is every truth which we cannot understand a mystery?

A. Every truth which we cannot understand is not a mystery; but every revealed truth which no one can understand is a mystery.

The *Baltimore Catechism* was also a guidebook for doing good, works of charity, for so-called corporal works of mercy, as well as a handbook useful for forgiving your neighbor, even theoretically a neighbor named Stephen Somethingski. It was like the *Boy Scout's Handbook*, only without the kites and the forts, the knots and hitches, the birds' nests, and bows and arrows. The *Catechism* didn't treat camping without a tent, or building a fire, or what to do when you got lost in the woods, but, even if merit badges never come up in the *Catechism,* in some respects these works were similar.

The *Baltimore Catechism* helped a boy wend his way through those existential problems that corresponded to being lost, if not in the woods, then in the explorable spiritual world. It was a field guide to mortal existence, Hell, Purgatory, Heaven, and the afterlife. It was about how Jesus was "begotten, not made," about how Mary was a virgin, about how there were three persons in one God, about how Jesus was not fifty percent man and fifty percent God, like some super divine 50-50-bar creamsicle, but one hundred percent God and one hundred percent man—and if you don't get that, you don't get anything important about being Catholic. I never pretended to understand that one about Mary's being a virgin, in fact *the Blessed* Virgin with a capital V. How could I, when I did not grasp what the opposite of virgin was?

"Sistah, is God so strong that He can make a rock He can't pick it up?"

Sister addressed that question to her complete and total satisfaction.

"Sistah, is God so smaht He can make up a math test He can't pass?"

She addressed that question to her complete and...

The resurrection of the body, a big subject. After you die, at the Last Judgment, the physical body is resurrected. Okay, that makes sense, Sistah, and is really fascinating. Or so we somehow absorbed this Baby Church Father version of Tertullian's *Credo quia absurdum est*: "I believe because it is absurd." So, the physical body rises from the grave and goes to Heaven intact and beautiful, your jellyroll or pompadour hair perfect?

"Sistah, what if you was fishing out there on duh ocean in a boat and there was a big wave and you got knocked into the watah and you were et up by a bunch of sharks, your leg went here and your head went there and your body was all over the ocean..."

With a sigh, Sister wordlessly conveyed confidence it must have been time for recess, if not a cocktail.

The big philosophical kicker in all this study and reflection (not to mention the memorization of the *Baltimore Catechism*) was that without free will, there was nothing but predestination. And predestination was an odious, vile, sacrilegious Protestant concept—which translated in my mind as *case closed*. Sure, free will was a part of dogma, but it wasn't dogma for me. It was beyond dogma, it was true, it was the case, it was something you could have by heart like the Pledge of Allegiance.

Around the corner from my apartment was a Lutheran church. I would avert eyes when passing the red brick edifice, on high alert, on the lookout for any gratuitous onslaughts on my soul, avoiding any chance I was going to be sucked into traitorous Martin Luther's vortex. I also used to walk by a Jehovah's Witnesses storefront, an apparent base camp for heathen reprobates who strutted round town, sweating in white shirts and black ties. Those guys were scarier and sillier both, with their pathetic handouts in their clammy grasp and their work-boots-at-the-sock-hop sense of misplaced self-assurance that Catholics were ridiculous dumbbells. I kept a sharp lookout for their heretical asses and would not hesitate to jaywalk to avoid contact.

I did more than subscribe to doctrine, for doctrine had limited appeal. And before I was in college, and certainly during college and after, I understood that the Church could not be more wrong in its doctrines with regard to an all-male priesthood, contraception, sexuality, and all the interrelated issues. These ecclesiastical positions were determined in and by history, and they would be reimagined someday, or so I thought when I was a full-of-myself college student. Change would come in the Catholic Church eventually, and that could mean a few hundred more years, but it was inevitable—because finally the Church testified that it was on the side of the truth, not on the side of power. That was the message the Church was soon to be delivering via the great Pope John XXIII and the Second Vatican Council.

Nonetheless, from early on, the Church led me to one wonderful conclusion: that a life without free will would be too dull for words. Free will was the ticket that needed to be punched for the celestial railroad. So I ponied up. Maybe I was fated to pony up—but if that were the case, let the idiots and the Greek gods argue it out, it was not my problem. As far as I was concerned, I could choose, I could decide how to live—not to mention where to live, including maybe with any luck somewhere other than Greenpoint.

★

MY BUDDIES WERE ANTHONY and Tommy and Michael. Anthony was so stylish and good-looking we figured he could become a lounge singer, like Dean Martin. We called him Antny. Tommy, alternately serious and madcap: maybe he could end up a pizza parlor owner, maybe a lawyer, whatever a lawyer did besides wear a suit and tie and live anywhere except in the neighborhood. Michael, the glamorous one, maybe priest, maybe movie star, maybe shortstop on the Legion team.

Despite my devotion and commitment to showing up at school, one fateful afternoon we made a break for it in broad daylight from St. Stan's—that is, my three buddies and I cut school, midday, during lunchtime, when there was slack in the monitoring of children—maybe the nun shifts were in transition, graveyard to day to night. It was not exactly my *Ocean's Eleven* moment, but I was readily recruited—though there's also the possibility that I could have been the ringleader.

Being on the lam was thrilling, skulking around the streets of Greenpoint in our non-camouflage Catholic school-issue uniforms, green cardigans and salt-and-pepper corduroys, paranoid about being pursued, doing all we could, like hiding behind cars, to evade authorities. One of my big brothers, Bobby, used to speak forbiddingly about truant officers, how they were like cops and how they would catch kids out of school, and how bad things happened as a result. Bad things like so-called reform school where equivalents of *West Side Story* (not that the movie had appeared yet) would break out, albeit without all the great singing and dancing. My big brother cared a lot about the truant officer problem, because he and high school never mixed, and he was destined to do time in a so-called reform school, which sounded like another way to say *prison junior*.

I visited Bobby once in reform school. It was somewhere vaguely "upstate," at the end of a long steamy cigarette-smoky car ride with the windows open, and there were lawns and trees, and my brother had a pack of cigarettes rolled up in his white T-shirt sleeve, revealing a bicep, which was impressive. Coveys of semi-incarcerated teenage boys swarmed the hills on their best behavior for visiting day.

Ultimately, did such an institution reform my brother? Well, he never did go back, or go to prison in the future. In the present, the experience paid off, too. As a result of his stay, Bobby sported a badge of honor. He became identified as a *juvenile delinquent*. To an admiring little brother like me, and to the girls in the neighborhood, JD was the equivalent of rock star. Snap your fingers, it was the fifties, man.

Maybe Anthony, Tommy, Michael, and I played hooky because we had a dose of spring fever. We were not consciously aspiring juvenile delinquents. We went to a diner, where at the counter we drank cherry Cokes and poured cream into warm bowls of rice pudding. We walked around the park. We were friends. This is what ten-year-old boys do, when they are not playing stickball or breaking windows in abandoned factories or walking around looking for somebody to have a problem with them. We never started a problem, let's be clear about that, but sometimes it seemed like we could never fail to find it. *You gotta problem? Yeah, I gotta problem, a problem wichoo, and your sistah too on account she keeps suckin' my dick.*

One paradoxically fascinating aspect about flight from school was that it was truly, deeply, terminally boring. The breaking of rules and the flouting of expectations was exciting, because isn't it always? But we replaced the blind following of rules with walking around aimlessly, looking for something to experience—something to fill in the precious time we had freed up by cutting school. It seems to be reminiscent of the mobster life, which, so they say, consists mostly of waiting around for something to happen, for somebody to show up, for some phone to ring or some car to drive by, a span of incredible boredom interrupted only occasionally by sheer terror when the call or the car or the guy arrives. Was playing hooky possibly a gateway to racketeering? My mother would have a theory.

Cutting school was exciting, but the experience of being outside school was in and of itself tedious. It was exciting to plot escape, not so hot to experience the successful achievement. If there is a moral to this story, it is too obvious and doesn't need to be stated—or, for that matter, overstated. These days we take for granted so much when it comes to the fascinating reports of brain research, but perhaps in my case there was not much development in the marvelous, color-coded, mapped part of my brain responsible for understanding that when you skip out of school in the fifth grade in the middle of the day, everybody will know you qualify as a moron.

We have established the obvious: that maybe I wasn't the smartest kid in Brooklyn. But the evidence is mixed. As for smart, there must have been a mix-up somewhere, since after I finished the first grade, I went directly to the third, thereby skipping the academic travails and rigors of the second. That administrative determination led to all sorts of complications later on, particularly in high school, when I graduated at sixteen years old, roughly the hormonal equivalent of a newt.

When my mother came home the day of the breakout, she radiated irritation that truancy was the first step toward a life of crime. She informed me that the Mother Superior had been in touch. The Mother Superior's name evoked more terror than Carlo Gambino's or any other head of the Five Families. She implied that the similarly disgusted Archbishop, currently heating up caldrons of oil for inquisitional purposes, and several of the twelve Apostles if not Jesus Christ Himself, would be following up. How would she know? She never went to church, which she should have done, not that I found myself in a position to remonstrate with her regarding her soul's prospective damnation, given that my own moral standing was severely compromised.

I recall the crushed, angry look on my mother's face, the anger that trembled like a spiderwebby halo around her head. My mom did disappointment like some movie star. She would fluff up gigantic pillows on an enormous beautiful couch of dismay and settle right down and preside. She could have won a prize. And another prize for saying *I told you so*, which she often told me after the fact, when, in reality, in advance she had done no such thing. I knew that to be the case, because if she had told me so, I would have done as she suggested, as I was mostly a very good boy.

"Joseph," she pleaded, "what the fuck did you do?"

Joseph had no fucking idea. Not that I used such a bad word.

One of my older brothers piped up: "Jo Jo's a fuckin' hoodlum, Ma."

"Bobby and Eddie, the two of yas, shut the fuck up."

My two big brothers had fallen out of their chairs, laughing. The fact remained that Joseph, perfect schoolboy with perfect attendance, was being disciplined. That night, they couldn't stop cracking up over Jo Jo, perfect Jo Jo, being suspended. That's right. Jo Jo was not permitted to go to school for a day in punishment for skipping out of school, thereby instilling in him a confusing message about the value of attending school. Willfully not attending was punishable by enforced non-attending of school.

Almost from the first, the perfect schoolboy handle never did feel right. As it would turn out, in the course of my school career, in elementary school, in high school, and in college, I would be at some point disciplined to the point of suspension, and was actually expelled from one institution, for a few minutes, anyway. Call me a schoolboy, if that's the way it had to be, but I didn't want everybody to think of me that way—as perfect. Maybe that was why I played hooky.

I was nowhere near perfect. My shoplifting habit would prove as much, an activity I perfected at the five and dime on Manhattan Avenue. With my angelic demeanor, I could get away with murder under the nose of the blue-haired clerks who chain-smoked and stood behind counters and never glanced my cherubically chubby way as I pocketed trinkets and toys and chocolate cigarettes.

Catholic schoolboys were encouraged to perform their "examination of conscience," to regularly review their behavior and scour their thoughts for transgressions and failings. For me, this examination of conscience became an all-consuming activity, because I always found in my soul evidence of behavior lacking in sanctity, purity, and obedience. I thought continually about the increasingly high probability I might go to Hell for all my sins, which were numerous and depraved. For example, the sin called "bad thoughts," meaning impractical and vague meta- or para-sexual fantasies about girls like lovely Elaine F., the best student in class, whose status was for me a major turn-on. In terms of sexual information, the dictionary would only go so far, unfortunately.

These days, decades later, I still perform routinely the examination of conscience, but I do so reflexively, an aspect of my obsessive-compulsive tics.

★

TONIGHT, WALKING AROUND GREENPOINT, my first-rate attendance performance continues apace. A semester of perfect attendance, no problem (except for that fifth-grade suspension glitch, for which any reasonable person should grant a mulligan). How about a year of perfect attendance? How about two years of never missing school? Attendance might have been my best subject. It's an underrated subject. Penmanship was a glaring problem, because my cursive was legible as espionage-encrypted Cyrillic, but I couldn't help it—my fingers didn't work that way. Then again, maybe I missed acquiring cursive by evading the scholarly juggernaut of second grade. Still, I could show up like nobody's business. Like tonight. I'm there for the wake when my brothers and father, each for very different reasons, are unable to be.

Near St. Stan's is where the candy store used to be—peddling jawbreakers, egg creams, 50-50 bars, cherry Italian ice, the *News* and *Mirror*, Sunday papers I used to go get for my parents. Over there's where the local Made Guy operated a slightly upscale dive of a bar. When the door swung open, somebody who'd had too much to drink stumbled down the block and you could hear Frank or Elvis on the jukebox and be washed over by the soapy smell of a tide of beer while the neon signs in the window blinked obscure messages about the wages of sin, probably ads for Lucky Strikes and Crown Royal. My father used to work there as a bartender.

My dad was a compulsive gambler—or as my mother would deftly massage the delicate phrase, "a degenerate losing gambler fuck." "Degenerate" was a very big word in her working vocabulary, along with "antisocial," which she also employed with frequency to refer to her husband, but who knows what she might have come up with had she expanded her vocabulary by employing index cards as skillfully as her least-favorite child. Countless times she would pound the table, screaming that she was "going to divorce the motherfucker," which was an interesting word choice whose literal meaning never quite dawned on her two youngest children, the pet audience for her monologues. Once she informed us that she had called Gamblers Anonymous to get them to intervene: "Your father is a degenerate fucking gambler." Her entreaties fell on deaf ears. Gamblers Anonymous probably told her that her husband needed to want to change before they could do anything. She just wanted Gamblers Anonymous to incarcerate the degenerate fucking gambler.

Psychoanalytic thinking connects gambling with masochism. One gambles in order to lose, because a gambler's destiny is foreordained. Every gambler unconsciously grasps and denies this fundamental verity. You gamble, you lose. Psychoanalytic thinking can function at times as an elegant metaphor for understanding experience, even to some degree in these days when Freud has been discredited by his critics as a quack. But it is usually incomplete and simplistic when formulaic, especially when the parts seem to click together like Lincoln Logs. In the case of my father: parental abuse ► gambling ► marriage to controlling, abusive wife ► gambling ► misery ► degenerate fucking Italian. The repetition complex, again according to psychoanalytic thinking, is about a death wish. Keep repeating and repeating and repeating, you beat death. Only you can't beat death, for the same reason you can't win at the track.

There is no joy in gambling: I can testify from painful personal experience. Strangely, there is not much joy even when you are winning. You bet because you know the right side, even if you don't *know* such a thing. Of course, winning beats losing any day, but here's the catch. The high you get from winning does not counterbalance the low you get from losing. In fact, losing feels worse than winning feels good, which makes no sense logically, but makes perfect sense psychologically.

Sometimes my dad liked to preface some prediction of his with "If I was a gamblin' man…" Upon the declaration of this absurd hypothetical, everybody would blink to get the fairy dust out of their eyes. Presumably in the service of his vocation, he once tried to borrow money from the loan-sharking Made Guy, but his informal application was denied. Apparently, he was told he would not be lent the money for the following reason: "Because I like you, Joe." Believe it or not, a loan shark's first job is to talk you out of borrowing money. This episode was related with pride. It took many years for me to understand why he was proud that somebody would not lend him any money, at which point it was transparent to the son that his father either liked playing with fire or was not savvy enough to think up an alternative capital investment strategy.

To a boy of eight, or nine, or ten, what did *gambling* mean? I knew horses were involved, and heard the word "track" a lot, as in one-half of the phrase that often echoed off the walls at home: the "fucking track." I myself had an early and appalling experience with what I construed to be gambling. There was a bazaar in the school basement, and the children brought money and played for rag dolls and balls and tried to knock down pins to win some worthless bauble or ceramic saint. My father gave me a few dollars. I went around the bazaar losing at every juncture. I was mortified. I won nothing, absolutely nothing. And when the last of the money was gone, the five or ten bucks I had been given now up in smoke, I ran out of the bazaar and covered the three blocks home, eyes stinging with disappointment and humiliation and rage. I would tell nobody. It still constitutes one of the bitterest memories in my life.

★

MY NEIGHBORHOOD WALK THIS February 2010 night takes me to the schoolyard where my buddies and I once played. That's where my beloved first dog, a pretty white-chested boxer named Princess, romped and chomped on the snow, and nearby was the toy store, where I used to look longingly into the window, especially around Christmas, at the train sets and the trucks and the cars and the board games and the yo-yos and the Spaldeens and the harmonicas. Not far from here is where the movie house used to be, the Winthrop, right across the street from the park of the same name.

After Saturday matinees, I would scoot home from the Winthrop by myself, sometimes with my little brother, in the early winter dark, terrified and breathless after watching eyes-wide-open those vampire-uprising, veggie-Martian-contagion-takeover, mad-scientist-bug-chemistry-experiment-that-took-uh-oh-a-very-bad-turn-in-the-desert movies. In some weirdly unforgettable horror movie, some sadist with a British accent jimmies up binoculars such that when the viewer attempts to adjust the focus, his eye sockets are stabbed. To this day, this grotesque image lingers, and it may explain why an invitation to a bird-watching expedition makes me reach for excuses.

My all-time favorite movie was *The Thing From Another World* (1951), produced and directed by Howard Hawks. This is the ideal fifties horror movie, and I could watch it every year. It features snappy patter and a vegan-ish monster in the North Pole, not to mention a classy broad dressed in a lab coat and possessed of an advanced academic degree. Nonetheless, she continually walks around with a fresh pot of coffee and says to everybody in the Quonset hut, "You look like you can use a cup." She reports to the head honcho scientist, who is a dangerous wimp with a telltale goatee and his Nobel Prize citation (Nobel? Really?) practically stamped on his forehead, even while she develops a crush on a wise guy Air Force officer in a leather bomber who is brave and expert at making witty repartee and issuing crisp, wry instructions to devoted gung-ho underlings. The scientist almost gets them all killed, the way scientists always manage to do in these movies. In the end, the officer gets the savvy babe and the monster both, not in the same way to be sure, though both ways involve the use of electricity, only one type of which comes from a generator. That is, he fries the vegetable monster sent from outer space who has a taste for blood (logic was another casualty of the narrative) and he can't keep his hands off the barista girl from the academy. *Keep watching the skies!* goes the voice-overing journalist at the end of the movie while symphonic strains elevate endorphin levels in the movie-going audience.

Keep watching the skies!

I was watching, I was always watching.

★

THROUGHOUT THE BROOKLYN YEARS and even long afterward, I watched closely my brothers and father and admired them and secretly reveled in their hotshot behavior and big-shot attitude. There was a part of me that wanted to be like them, even if that meant I was taking a chance on punishment and risking a life of criminality, not to mention eternal damnation. But the good boy who got good grades must have begun to sense early on a way to address the tension, the internal conflict.

I could split, I could compartmentalize.

Gambling like a wise guy provides a useful metaphor. Sometimes the spread in the betting line of a game makes for a golden wagering opportunity when the line drifts, and you can play what they call a *middle*. Say the Jets start out three-point favorites against New England, and you bet them: that means New York has to win by more than three points for you to win the bet. But let's say that big action comes in on the Jets and the line moves, and by game time New England is no longer a three-point but a five-point dog. That is a huge swing, and this sort of opportunity doesn't occur often, but it happens, especially when you are gambling with more than one book, as wise guy gamblers do, because betting lines can be different with various books. Then you bet the Patriots, too. If the game ends up a 28-24 Jets' victory, you win both ways—because the Jets win by more than three (winning your first bet) and the Pats lose by fewer than five (winning your second bet).

Life can feel beautiful for the wise guys who play the middle.

When I split and compartmentalized, I was in effect betting both sides. Somehow I developed the notion—which I never articulated to myself but which stayed with me far into my adulthood—that I could *middle* my whole life.

Joy of my Youth

DIRECTLY ACROSS THE STREET from Stobierski's is the beautiful church of my childhood, where I used to perform altarboy duties Sunday mornings, sometimes early weekday Mass, which was of course the Tridentine, or Roman Rite, Mass. The Latin responsorials would fall trippingly off my tongue, preadolescent piety backlighting me whenever I genuflected and fantasized qualifying for admission into Heaven. I do not recall what I imagined Heaven might be, other than not-Greenpoint, and maybe full of gleaming light and music, along with the generalized suffusion of continual bliss that enveloped me in a gauzy, sweet cloud.

My mother would pack a breakfast for consumption after Mass: it was always a scrambled egg sandwich, wrapped in aluminum foil, which she would hand me as I hustled out the door for services. When I opened the sandwich afterward it was still Wonder-Breadishly, white-doughy warm and delicious. That was a nice thing she did. This was back when you fasted before Communion, so serving at early Mass could sometimes involve enduring a woozy, lightheaded moment or two. This lightheadedness was not related to spiritual epiphany. Although it was not exactly unrelated, either.

In my altar boy memories it is mostly the dead of winter, and it is still dark, with a few cars on the street, steam coming off, exhaust smoke coming out of the mufflers of cars of men going to work, the bakeries not open yet for business. In the armoire near the overheated sacristy, you find your black cassock and the pure white starch-stiff surplice to be worn rakishly on top. You light the candles on the altar, you position texts and cruets, and you assist the priest with his sacred vestments. Lots of times the priest can be grumpy, but that is all right. Sometimes you tag team with another altar boy, but just as often you are flying solo. Mass begins and you process onto the altar. There you do everything according to script, including the Latin recitals. I knew by heart a whole lot of Latin, including the priest's Latin. That's the job.

Priest: *Introibo ad altare Dei.* "I will go up to the altar of God."

Little could I imagine the day would come when I would read the first page of a famously terrifying and erudite book called *Ulysses* and have no need of the glosses.

Server: *Ad Déum, qui laetíficat juventútem méam.* "To God, joy of my youth."

The priest's back was to the altar, pre-Vatican II, and the Communion rail separated him and the altar boy from the congregation. At crucial times in the service, the server had the grave task of ringing the sanctus bells, waking any sleepy people out there for the big sacramental moment. This would happen when the host was raised for the congregation to venerate, and you would ring the bells to call attention to the biggest abracadabra of all time, as far as believers were concerned, the magic that was the presence of the divine. The bells themselves were challenging devices, and you were instructed to avoid any slovenly shuddering and tinkling. The trick was, you had to snap your wrist and finish off the ring crisply. Nothing worse than a rogue *ding* resonating throughout the church. And the goal was to be not too loud and not too soft with the bells. How do you get to Carnegie Hall and Heaven? Practice, practice, practice. And highlight the miraculous, buddy boy, don't try to be the talent.

At Communion time, people come up to genuflect at the rail, and you assist the priest as he dispenses the sacrament. As the altar boy, you hold the paten under each gaping maw. The paten is gold or silver, with a handle, like an old-fashioned holy stovetop popcorn popper. And you are required to place the paten carefully under the chin so you can catch the host in case it is dropped or spit out by a reprobate. Or in case a renegade wafer crumb is falling. Check that. No wafer. That was Jesus Himself. Consequently, you had to be light on your feet, like a volleyball player stretching out for a tricky serve, ready to dive on the floor in case there was an emergency.

I never witnessed anything remotely as profane and precarious as that, but that didn't mean altar boys weren't drilled to be on high alert. I was indeed frightened something would happen on my watch that would constitute degradation of the body of Jesus Christ. And to be clear, the doctrine of transsubstantiation held that this host was the real body of Jesus. It was no symbol. As Flannery O'Connor, the frighteningly great writer and appealingly nutty Roman Catholic, wrote of the Host, "If it's a symbol, to hell with it."

O'Connor's name was much in the Catholic school air of my youth, and the nuns and priests were justifiably crazy about her. Later in life, I loved when I came across what she had written about Catholicism, like this vinegary tonic in a letter to a non-Catholic friend: "I know what you mean about being repulsed by the Church when you have only the Jansenist-Mechanical Catholic to judge it by. I think that the reason such Catholics are so repulsive is that they don't really have faith but a kind of false certainty. They operate by the slide rule and the Church for them is not the body of Christ but the poor man's insurance system. It's never hard for them to believe because actually they never think about it. Faith has to take in all the other possibilities it can. Anyhow, I don't think it's a matter of wanting miracles. The miracles seem in fact to be a great embarrassment for the modern man, a kind of scandal. If the miracles could be argued away and Christ reduced to the status of a teacher, domesticated and fallible, then there'd be no problem. Anyway, to discover the Church you have to set out by yourself."

"You have to set out by yourself"—that was what the great Catholic author said. That was a thought worth holding onto for the rest of my life.

As for the distribution of the Eucharist, it was oddly educational and borderline entertaining in a clinical sense to be looking into people's mouths. I was fascinated by dental work or absence of teeth, and also by shapes of tongues that stuck out there. When during class we went through dry runs practicing taking Communion, we extended the tongue and kept it flat. That was the key part—the flatness. Flatness guaranteed safe passage for the trans-substantiated body of Jesus. Nonetheless, as an altar boy, you had to cope with the mouths that gaped. You had tongues rolled up like soft tacos, which were challenging for the priest in depositing the host. You had big lolling tongues: that notorious Rolling Stones album cover was far in the future, but that was the idea. You had sweet, demure tongues of girls in your class. Their tongues barely broke the goal line of the lips, and this required extra-delicate insertion of the host—and extra-special voyeuristic attention on the part of a paten-holder like me. You had rosy tongues, charred tongues, mossy tongues. And people often coordinated their tongues with their eyelids. Tongue out, eyes would close, synchronized. Some people did fluttery eye-closing, some determined eye-shutting, and some brave souls kept their eyes wide open, like people who elected surgery without anesthesia.

Another altar boy chore I liked was accompanying the priest for the ritual chalk-marking of the lintels on the feast of the Epiphany. I wore the cassock and surplice under a heavy coat, helping the priest as he entered parishioners' homes for this January ritual. The altar boy would hold the priest's coat and steady the footstool, while he, using blessed chalk, would write above the lintel, for instance:

19 C + M + B 58.

This stood for the names of the Magi, the first three wise guys, Caspar, Melchior, and Balthazar, their initials separated by crosses (not plus signs), and bracketed by the year—in this example above, 1958. There would be a ritual and prayer at the door with the family, in which the Three Wise Men would be implored to intercede for this family and bless this home. Those Magi understood the value of a safe home, having found Jesus in a risky manger. The priest would be offered a shot of something fortifying for the cold weather, and then he and his altar boy would trudge through snow to another parish home. The parishioner would usually tip the altar boy. One time I came home with thirteen bucks, a fortune. I may have enjoyed better, longer-lasting epiphanies in life, but none ever beat that one for pure financial upside.

Being assigned Requiem Masses was like batting cleanup. That altar boy's cherry assignment said you hit a grand slam. Funeral services during the week had obvious advantages. Since these Masses usually began at ten o'clock in the morning, you got out of class. Then you were chauffeured in limousines or hearses to the cemetery, where you wore the black cassock and snowy white surplice to play your dour role in the sad pomp as you handled the incense, burned in a censer, suspended by a mechanism of chains, so it could be swung dramatically by the priest and permeate the air with intoxicating bouquets of sanctity, which was when holy lightheadedness might kick in. The smoke symbolized petitions and prayers for the dead rising up to Heaven.

I was mesmerized by the spectacle of lamentation and sorrow. What accounted for the differences among mourners? How come torrents of tears flowed from the bloodshot eyes of some, while stoic resignation rigidified the countenances of others? I felt sorry for everybody, though I paid closer attention to stoics, because they showed no emotion. In addition, I liked to keep the stoics in my sights because they were the bigger tippers. To a boy like me, the rituals of mourning and the demeanors of loss were not merely profitable. They were breathtaking, sad, and beautiful.

★

THE ENCOMPASSING SUBJECT HERE, of course, is how Catholicism imbued this boy's life with meaning and purpose. But that sounds timid. The Church saved me. There's no understating this reality. And that was the beginning of my often rocky and tortured lifelong relationship with the Church.

In my youth, Catholicism fashioned a coherent view of the otherwise seemingly fragmented world, by which I mean my mashed-up, confused version of family life. Why was I so alienated from the family? I had no idea, but it was true. Maybe God knew. Maybe God would help. Catholicism filled me with art and music, images and stories, myths and metaphors, fables and parables, gorgeous suffering and heartbreaking joy. It gave me poetry, psalms, cries in the wilderness. It encouraged me to struggle over paradox and mystery. It gave me Latin and, more than that, a total cultural reference map that I would find nowhere else in the borough of Brooklyn.

Suffering was a particularly exquisite gift. Through suffering the mundane experience of unhappiness was miraculously transformed into something incredibly intense, as in a daily struggle with sin and temptation, with the Devil and with evil. Life was infinitely precious, but it was a gift I would give up in a heartbeat if necessary. What greater love hath a man than he give up his life for his friend? Good question. Then again, sex and romance were not yet on the horizon.

The stories of the martyrs as related by my teachers, the nuns, fascinated more than *The Thing From Another World*. That was the key to religion: It was from another world, but it had something to do with this world. These martyr tales told of magnificent Catholics impaled or beheaded, burnt or drawn-and-quartered, succumbing for their faith with a smile on their face, mocking and simultaneously forgiving their torturers, rising above the pain and the scorn and the ridicule. The main culprits were Indians and Protestants and Infidels.

I myself had never come across wicked Indians, Protestants, or Infidels except in musty history textbooks, but I rehearsed many times what I would do or say if I was forced to choose between, let's say, spitting out the Communion host onto the desecrating ground or having my throat slit or having boiling oil poured down my gullet or having my eyes gouged out or… The images kaleidoscopically multiplied. The hagiographical pictures of St. Stephen and others who had hatchets in their hearts or arrows in their heads featured marvelous haloes. Who couldn't use one of those handy headpieces? I thought about what I would do if asked to give up my life to save another, including a stranger. I hoped to have the strength and faith. Funny, considering how much I used to be interested in martyrdom, that I hated all the self-satisfied martyrs I ran into in real life.

The battle for my soul went on. And on. Like the battle with the dreaded Soviets of that day and age, only for eternity. Conveniently if not inevitably, the Ruskis were atheists, and they tormented Catholics, and they drank boatloads of vodka and were terrible drivers in their stupid-looking cars, and Khrushchev hated Kennedy and pounded on the UN table with his shoe, looking like a Russian idiot, like somebody capable of dropping an atomic bomb right on St. Stan's, not giving it a moment's thought before blowing up me and my buddies to kingdom come. Such thoughts coursed through my mind during the regularly scheduled air raid drills, when I ducked and covered, realizing this tactic was not going to help when all of Greenpoint was reduced to cinders and ash next week, or the week after, by the Red Menace.

Jesus, the Church, the Bible, and the rituals gave me purpose and hope, and the unconditional love I never quite felt at home. This would be my bulwark, given, as it appeared, the very high likelihood bordering on certainty that I would be incinerated by an atomic bomb. As important—if I wasn't to be blown up anytime soon—the Church gave me closets of weirdness and troves of the forbidden, along with the absurdity and the theatricality that logically followed.

Weirdness is important for a child. A certain sort of weirdness, that is. Not abusive Church weirdness, no, not that, because I had no experience with that. But weird smells and weird gestures, weird clothes and weird rituals. *Weirdness* weirdness.

The hunched-over black-veiled old ladies, raven-like, worriedly worked their rosaries, their heads pecking, their mouths mumbling.

The snorts and sighs from the back of the church, which echoed like a sewer-damp prison in a fat library book called *The Count of Monte Cristo.*

Big sad Polish sighs like wings flapping.

The ostentatious genuflection. When did this church turn into Lourdes?

An old man's eye-rolling piety and his ripped, soup-stained cardigan, shuffling down the aisle to receive Communion.

Big black hats on the ladies, which made them look like perches for bats.

Weirdness, indeed. To a ten-year-old no one is weirder than a priest. Oh, sure, a ten-year-old like this altar boy also revered the priest, aspired to such a life as this priest, and would have collected his baseball card if it existed. Nonetheless, a priest is weird from the top of his black tufted biretta to his wingtip shoes. Weird in his inflections, in his gait, in his uplifted eye-rolling gaze. All that weirdness was, to this altar boy, safe to contemplate. By the time I was an adult, the distressing, tragic news came out about what had been going on in the Church, about how children had been molested in massive numbers, betrayed not only by sexual predators in soutanes but also by the powers that be in the Church, who facilitated crimes and criminals. But I knew none of this from personal experience, and at that time I never heard anything like it, either.

For all that, however, the principal weirdness was within myself. I knew I was perceived that way by family and others, and sometimes by myself. I never felt superior to the rest of my family. I never stopped hoping that they would not go to Hell. I prayed for them. I had no choice. But that came with a huge benefit. For me, Catholicism was pure. It was pure solace and comfort when life seemed precarious, and for an extra bonus it provided a father figure, too. A Father in Heaven, unlike my real father, who was at the track, wherever that was and whatever that meant. Funny how Heaven felt more real than any earthly destination such as Ebbets Field, now abandoned and soon to be torn down, or the Empire State Building, which I had heard was the tallest skyscraper in the world. I never visited. But I had been to Mass and Jesus had spoken to me and given me the prospect of eternity. I talked more to God and to Jesus than I did to my family.

Well, not quite. I talked to my brother Johnny a lot, if only to bust his chops. He was the identified scamp, and he richly earned this identification and attention.

One day we were walking over the penny drawbridge, and Bobby lifted up Johnny under his armpits and held him over the edge of the rail, with nothing between him and the slicked water below. Down there, tugboats tugged and barges barged along with their garbage loads and birds fished and factory fumes oiled the air. Cars droned on the bridge, zzzzzzzzzzzzz. It is easy to imagine that Johnny was being impossible as always, bugging Bobby, and maybe his big brother had had enough aggravation— or maybe he thought this was amusing in a Coney Island sort of way. Bobby might have been fourteen, and I might have been five or six, and Johnny might have been four or five, and Johnny was skinny, so presumably easy for Bobby to hold. And maybe there was a catwalk below, some safety landing between Johnny and the deep not-blue sea, but in the moment the worst seemed possible.

And while he was hanging there in midair, Bobby was cackling as he asked *Jo Jo, should I drop him?*

Johnny didn't dare move a muscle, like a rabbit held by the ears. *No, no, no, don't. Don't. Don't, Bobby, don't. Stop, c'mon, stop.*

★

THIS WAS CATHOLICISM'S PRECISE import: I was loved. I was loved by God. Me. The one who answered to Joe or Joseph or Jo Jo— that one boy who was beloved. Not that I deserved to be, but that was another issue—and then again, who does deserve to be loved, all of us being sinners? As a consequence, my mystifying life and my inevitable death were rendered, if not meaningful, at least not meaningless.

It followed therefore that God was looking out for me and that the world possessed ultimate coherence, even though such coherence might be unknown and perhaps unknowable by me. This notion constituted a tremendous relief, because to my eyes that crossed the world looked jumbled, a crazy puzzle viewed through cracked lenses. But what an advantage that I could talk to Jesus. And talk to Jesus I did. That would be between us, until it wouldn't be.

Theologically speaking, the life of a Catholic formally commences with the sacrament of Baptism. My baptism took place on September 17, 1950, at St. Stan's, when I was almost three months old. Back then, if you didn't get baptized and you happened to kick the bucket before attaining the age of reason, then a mythologically fascinating concept would kick in. Under those circumstances, you would be shuffled off not quite to

Buffalo, but to Limbo—that is, no chance for Heaven, but also no risk of Hell. Limbo has its own zip code, and nothing gets forwarded, *stasis qua stasis*. Dante would weigh in on the Classical sages and the Hebrew prophets who were assigned their places there, and it was a sad spectacle. In Limbo, time goes and goes, a river emptying into the ocean of eternity. No, all the clocks stop. Limbo: not a horrible place, not a great place, sort of like parts of Staten Island.

The godparents listed on my Baptism Certificate were Michael Di Prisco, my dad's oldest brother, and Regina La Mana, my mom's best friend. That day at the baptismal font may have been the single peaceful moment of my relationship with Uncle Mike, for he and I would come to have a complicated connection. I found it morbidly fascinating that he had one arm, the other amputated after a car accident. And I liked his daughters, my first cousins, and his wife, too. Aunt Ruthie was Jewish and had a buoyant personality, a soft body, and a sweetly maternal temperament. Her Jewishness set her apart, no question, and it was a scandal, so the story goes, when the Italian boy prince of the family married the Semite. Poor Ruthie. She would die miserably, of cancer, when my cousins were teenagers.

Uncle Mike remarried, and that time he got it wrong. The new wife was a shrew. I think my report cards were circulated in her vicinity perhaps by my grandmother, and Mike's new wife made a point of telling everybody she was (sniff) not impressed. As a college student, I would relish arguing with Mike about politics, about the war, about Nixon. Those were the days. He was pro-Nixon and I was—not. The day Nixon resigned I was at my grandparents' and Uncle Mike was there, too. He was crestfallen, and I took no delight in his pain. His kids loved him, and that says more than any criticism I had of him. In any case, that night, a sad night for the nation, I felt sorry for my uncle, not the president. Uncle Mike had made a mistake in judgment, that was all. These things happen.

Then there was Jeannie, my godmother. She and my mother would drink coffee and smoke and have a grand old time for hours and hours. She was a raven-haired delight, with a gravelly voice and a big presence. In her personal life, unfortunately, she had lots of trouble. All four of her children were beautiful, dark, charismatic, and a mess. Truth is, I envied them their dangerous, intense lives. Rumors of heroin addiction attached to three of them. Her daughter was a serial bride—I gathered she was up to three or four divorces before I was ten. Why she kept getting married over and over was a mystery. Each scruffy husband looked interchangeable with the last leather-jacketed, T-shirted loser. She was so pretty and they were so creepy. What gave? I was still under the impression that pretty girls intrinsically knew better, under which insane delusion I would remain for about the next forty years, give or take. Two of Jeannie's boys did serious prison time upstate. The last time we saw one of them was in California. He was driving a new white Cadillac convertible, red leather interior, and he was working some scam that involved payphones, which I didn't comprehend. Jeannie's boys evaporated, assumed to have been murdered somewhere on the open road when they tried to swindle the wrong guy, or maybe they shot up bad stuff.

Jeannie's youngest son became a Jehovah's Witness. My clearest memory of him goes back to a little lake that will come to serve as the scene of a crucial experience. He was carrying on in a determined, serious, philosophical way, arguing without sign of imminent letup the following demented proposition, to wit: "A guy is supposed to love himself, right? Right. Okay, then he must love his own dick." This was an idea in which he had obviously invested a lot of thought, and undoubtedly hands-on practice. It was his Pensées. His categorical imperative. I recall my father staring at him as if the teenager had a propeller spinning on the top of his head. In the moment, though I believed the guy was nuts, I gave him points for being comfortable in his own canary cage and willing to sing his full-throated song for all to hear. I was hardly surprised when he became a door-to-door guy with a pamphlet vowing everlasting gloom to anybody pretending not to be home on the other side of the unanswered *knock knock knock.*

Jeannie did something good when she married John, her second husband. I loved that guy. He was kind and smart. He was a physical specimen, too, athletic and square-jawed handsome, and a weightlifter and a chiropractor, which sounded an awful lot like a doctor. When we spoke I learned things. I thought of John as my godfather for the following reason: my mother never failed to refer to him, and not Uncle Mike, as my godfather.

Baptism is an immersion and a purification. It is about water, about dying to sin and being reborn in Jesus. Baptism symbolizes the beginning of a new life and a death to the old. Here, again, the handy *Baltimore Catechism* comes to the rescue:

Q. 315. What is Baptism?

A. Baptism is the sacrament that gives our souls the new life of sanctifying grace by which we become children of God and heirs of Heaven. "Amen, amen, I say to thee, unless a man be born again of water and the Spirit, he cannot enter into the kingdom of God." (John 3:5)

As the ritual demands, I vicariously experienced the sacrament through my godparents, who spoke for me, as all godparents must. The rite would have been enacted in Latin, with some English responses here and there. The central drama was clear: christened child is dying to new life, being reborn in the water. Death is more than a subtext here, as the anointing with oil demonstrates. Three times the priest explicitly banishes the Devil.

V. N, abrenuntias Satanae?	V. N, dost thou renounce Satan?
R. Abrenuntio.	**R.** I do renounce him.
V. Et omnibus operibus eius?	**V.** And all his works?
R. Abrenuntio.	**R.** I do renounce him.
V. Et omnibus pompis eius?	**V.** And all his pomps?
R. Abrenuntio.	**R.** I do renounce him.

★

I DON'T REMEMBER MY first baptism, of course, but I do recall my second. That was the time I whispered in God's ear.

Whispered? More like gasped.

My mother and my little brother and I were at a dismal beach on a scruffy lake in the part of New Jersey not appearing in the opening credits of *The Sopranos*. I say my brother was there, because he always was, but I don't have a sharp memory. I am certain my father was not present, as usual. This was a Polish resort village where they served kapusta (that is, sauerkraut) soup with sour cream and pumpernickel bread and the relentless mosquitoes were the size of sparrows.

I was in the middle of the lake, lying on an inflated raft, face up to the microwaving sun, drifting away from shore. It was hot, and I must have had a desire to cool off—I was always getting sunburned, which I hated. So like an idiot, I slipped off the raft. I went down like a rock. Now, I had always loved the water, and I thought I was a pretty good swimmer. Nonetheless, I panicked when my feet hit bottom and the cool sandy floor gave way like a soft pillow. I don't know how long this struggle went on, but I was not gaining any traction, and I frantically tried to gain my footing. The more I kicked, the more I was digging myself down into the muddy, mucky bottom. And when I realized I could not push off to come back to the surface, I began to realize something fairly astonishing. I started swallowing water and I believed that I was going to drown.

Yes, I was going to die.

These were the last moments of my life.

I needed to make the most of them.

My life did not pass before me. I had heard of such a thing taking place, so I kept an eye out. Then again, being eight or nine, maybe I didn't have enough life to work with. I wouldn't say that imminent death was at first a friendly vision. Still, imminent death was familiar—and for this I give thanks to the priests and the nuns and the examples of the slain martyrs and particular thanks to the Q and A of the *Baltimore Catechism*. After all, God made me to know Him, to love Him, and to serve Him in this world, and to be happy with Him forever in the next. And the next was fast approaching.

So was that it? That was my life?

I didn't panic. No, honestly, if strangely, I did not panic. I felt suffused by an inner warmth. A preternatural calm. I felt an otherworldly welcome. God was calling for me, waiting with open arms. It was okay, and I was ready, I was ready to die. I started praying and my feet sunk deeper and deeper into the mud. I started saying the words in the Our Father. I meant wholeheartedly every single one of them.

Our Father, who art in Heaven, hallowed be thy name. Thy kingdom come, thy will be done, on earth as it is in Heaven. Give us this day our daily bread, and forgive us our trespasses as we forgive those who trespass against us. And lead us not into temptation but deliver us from evil. Amen.

Was this a suicidal moment for me? At eight or nine? A case could be made, I suppose. Why was I so ready and willing to give up, why didn't I keep fighting and fighting to survive? Was it because I knew that this world, this vale of tears, was nowhere as important as my eternal home? Nothing like what anybody would call abstract or philosophical reasoning was taking place inside my brain. But let's be clear about something else: At that age, I was fully accepting the inevitability not only of death, but of my death. I was not the least bit sad for what I might miss if my life were to be cut short, and I didn't think about what anybody else would feel if I were to die.

But maybe a sort of bargaining was taking place. Did I take advantage of this last-second opportunity to cash in my chips and call myself a winner in the salvation sweeps? And the Lord's Prayer? Being a schoolboy, did I want to make sure I was impressing God at the last moment, so I would maybe be forgiven for my sins and have my ticket automatically punched for paradise? That would have been cynical on my part, yet there is an element of truth there, too.

I can still see myself down at the bottom the lake, looking up to the unreachable surface. I was exhausted. There was sunlight above. A bright light trembled through the surface of the lake. God was above. I was below. Maybe not for long.

I didn't manage to reach the end of the Lord's Prayer, but I have a really good excuse.

For suddenly all around me there is a rush of displaced water, an enormous whoosh. The lake seems to split apart, like when Charlton Heston parts the waters as Moses in the movie *The Ten Commandments*. I cannot see anything in the turbulence. Maybe I am losing consciousness. It takes an instant to understand what is going on. Now I am not alone down here at the bottom of the lake anymore. I am being lifted up out of the water, and I crash through the window of the water's surface and point my head toward the sunlight. I am gasping and gasping for air. I catch my breath. Then in a moment I am thrown onto the sand. People are standing around, looking.

It is my godfather, John. He has saved my life. Of course, that is what a godfather does in the sacrament of baptism, where he stands up for me against evil when I am an infant in swaddling clothes before the baptismal font, getting my head doused while Latin is spoken over me. Only this is different.

Soon I am dragged to the beach blanket and seated next to my mother. I don't recall anything she says. I cannot hear anything. I know there are people on the beach, but I cannot look them in the eye. I recall thinking *I have embarrassed myself and my mother, I have made a spectacle of myself in public.* I was horrified by this result. I wanted to hide.

How sad, how miserable must I have been to be so geared up to die—at eight or nine years old? What was I so sad and miserable about? Why was I so willing in that moment to give up my life? Had I lost hope in the world or in my life, or was I seeing things clearly? And what did that experience foretell? Was I going to be ready forevermore to slough off this mortal coil upon invitation?

Was I weak or was I strong? Was I staring with clear eyes into the infinite—something that does not come around often? Or was I throwing away my life—something which happens every day for somebody somewhere? Was I a sad and pathetic little boy, or was I somebody who already preternaturally grasped the truth about the meaning of his life? How pious was I to believe that God was welcoming me into his arms? Or was this God's testing of me, to see if I did believe in Him when push came to shove? And how would I know the difference, in the moment, in the instant when my lungs were filling with water and I was giving up and giving over to eternity, where I belonged, where I wanted to go?

The answers continue to elude me. And so do the questions. Sweet, easeful death, or the fight till the bitter end?

What does it mean that somebody, in this case my kind, brave godfather, was watching me close enough to recognize when I slipped beneath the surface?

Afterward, I lay on the beach blanket for what must have been a long time. I still wonder what I was thinking about. The fear may have kicked in finally in the aftermath, but I have no recollection. There is a towel over my head. My mother is nearby. I don't recall anything she says. Maybe she was in shock, which was why she could not articulate her fear, why she felt no need to say that she would have been devastated had I drowned, that she was so upset she could not find the words. At least she didn't say *I told you so*. Her silences were never eloquent. They were, to me, merely silences, inscrutable withdrawals, tactical evasions, punishments. Maybe she was pissed off, I have no idea.

And where was God now—now that I was on dry land? The God I was speaking to, who was reaching out to me a few minutes before, where did He go? Was I destined to be alone now and without Him, or was He still there?

The Jersey summer sky was pale blue, the pine trees across the lake were still, and children's voices on the lakeshore gradually filled the air again—though not my voice, if, that is, I was still a child, having gone through what I had gone through. I might have slept. All over again, I was amazed to find myself still alive. Was life worth it? And how would I know—or when?

625 Humboldt Street

MASS IS TO BE said tomorrow at ten o'clock for the repose of the soul of my mother. St. Stan's is a Polish church, and this is a Polish part of town—Polish funeral home, Polish school, Polish butchers, Polish bakers, Polish priests. Polish on the street signs. There were a few Italians, like my father, who married hubba hubba Polish babes like my mother. These sorts of marriages they called mixed or, in other words, mistakes.

My Polish grandparents made no bones about disliking my father, and my Polish grandmother extended her distaste to his offspring. She typically appeared as irritated as a Polish general who had misplaced his steed. I have zero recollections of any expressed warmth on my grandmother's part, and nobody would use the word "bubbly" to describe her demeanor. If I try to recall her smiling, all I see is somebody sucking on a lemon. She was about the sourest woman I ever met, mirthlessly prune-faced and bilingually embittered in fluent Polish and minimal English, a woman whose chief companion was a Pomeranian, meaning in this case not an inhabitant of that former Baltic country, but the canine species. The dog nipped at every opening.

They say people look like their dogs. It was true in my grandmother's case. The dog was probably not fed choice morsels of kielbasa in a silver bowl, but it seemed that way. I really liked dogs, but that wasn't a dog, that was a wig with a snarl. That whole Polish family spectacle was unbearable, and I yearned to spend as little time as possible with them.

★

THE STREET WHERE I grew up is one-way, and tonight there are no available parking spaces. The wind is picking up ferociously, and I reposition the scarf and flick up the coat collar. It's my favorite coat, a window-plaid long grey-black topcoat, bought in my early thirties during a shallow decade of American life, when I myself was shallower, when labels meant more than they should have. I bought the coat—charged it on a chic department store credit card sent to me and other ne'er-do-well label-chasers during an epidemic of corporate insanity or diabolical craftiness—when I didn't have the money or the credit to justify such confidence. At least I hope it was paid off. There are few occasions to wear such a garment where I live in Northern California, where a light dusting of snow happens every few years and melts immediately, where I have lived most of my life since we took off from Brooklyn.

What I remembered learning about Greenpoint in elementary school was that it was the naval shipyard's birthplace of the USS *Monitor*, and that during the Civil War there was a battle between two iron-clad, crocodilean, dinosaurish ships, the Union *Monitor* and the Confederate *Merrimack*, a battle that revolutionized ship design and ushered in a new age of naval warfare. They fought to a draw in the vicinity of Chesapeake Bay. Greenpoint was also where I learned firsthand about different sorts of war tactics, and how unsatisfying it could be to fight to a draw.

I halt in front of 625 Humboldt Street, my only home address in Greenpoint, and look up. I don't have to crane my neck up to the third floor, because it is a small walk-up. It looks cleaner, tidier, fresher than it ever appears in memory. And a lot smaller. I walk around to the side, which is exposed, and neatly aluminum-sided. Undoubtedly there are new landlords responsible for sprucing up the building. I get a sense of how cramped, how narrow the apartment was. I study the upstairs window, top floor, on the right. That's where I used to sit and look out at what was going on, down in the world. It seems incomprehensible that this space could accommodate two adults, two youngsters, and two teenage boys. In my corner of a bedroom shared by four boys, a room painted algae green, I pinned up maps and studied them for hours. I wanted to know where elsewhere was. I wanted to expand my world, and though a map is not a place, it's a step in that direction.

On the street to my right, behind the gate, there is access down to the basement. Down there was where my big brothers created what they called The Clubhouse. Their friends would come by and sculpt their Brylcreemed pompadours and jellyrolls before the cracked, cloudy mirrors while tiny transistor radios cackled in their ears. They wore Banlon shirts and white buck shoes, though Bobby was also called Bootsy because he liked to wear, well, boots. There would be lots of desperate bragging pertaining to fingering and rubbers and blowjobs, whatever any of those terms meant.

"Hey, Bobby, get your frickin' kid brudda outta here for Chrise sake."

"Leave'm lone. Jo Jo ain't boddering no frickin' boddy."

★

My mother, Catherine Di Prisco, used to be Catherine *Palermo*. She married her first husband on June 12, 1941. His name was Edward Palermo, and I met him once. He was a middleweight pug who sounded like a churning cement truck when he talked out of this side of his mouth, like *dis* and like *dis* and like *dis*. He obviously wanted people to think he was a tough guy, and there is a high probability he was.

The couple had three children: Alice, Edward, and Robert. Catherine was pregnant at seventeen and gave birth to her first child and only girl. She became the plaintiff in divorce proceedings, and, on October 16, 1948, in Brooklyn, she was granted an interlocutory decree based on "the defendant's adultery." She received sole custody of Eddie, age five, and Bobby, age four. He was awarded sole custody of Alice, age six. Her alimony was $10 per week, in addition to $10 per week in child support. As the court documents stipulate: "…the said sums, totaling twenty ($20.00) per week, be paid by the defendant by check or post office money order at the residence of the plaintiff." Divorce was decreed final on January 24, 1949.

Then there was the matter of the daughter, whose father was granted sole custody. Custody in 1949? A father getting sole custody of a daughter? Seems a shocking development. Alice was raised by her father and her father's mother. Nonetheless, being abandoned by her mother was something she never forgave, and in her own family that moment attained the status of myth: how Alice was cast off. For which her own congenitally infuriated daughter regularly vowed revenge.

The divorce was the secular cleanup. On the ecclesiastical side of the ledger, my mother's first marriage was annulled by "Thomas Edmundus Episcopus Brooklyniensis." On June 7, 1949, her "matrimonium" was deemed never to have justifiably existed in the eyes of the Church, or in the Latin: *praefatum matrimonium nullum irritumque coram Deo et Ecclesia decernit atque declarat.* In other words, in church Latin, the marriage never was, in the eyes of God and Rome, a valid marriage. Annulments were practically impossible to come by back then, and they took years.

It was impressive to contemplate that my mother was able to marshal the resources to pull this off. And impressive, too, to have the church sign off on an annulment of a marriage that had produced three children. It is also more than slightly remarkable that she had the support of three other luminaries of Brooklyn Diocesan history, their signatures affixed to the decree: Father Edward B. Brady, who became an official of the Chancery;

Father Raymond A. Kearney, an auxiliary bishop who served as Chancellor; and Father John J. Carberry, who went on to become Archbishop of New Orleans and a cardinal.

News of her annulment came as a complete surprise to her fourth child, me, when I discovered the official documentation in 2010. In her lifetime, she had never breathed a word of such an event to me. By then of course I knew that she had been divorced, but the ecclesiastical move was a bombshell.

Bottom line: She got off on an ecclesiastical technicality with time served and lots of babies in tow. Those are the facts. But why was it important for her to obtain an annulment? She wasn't looking to become an active, cupcake-baking, churchgoing member of the parish.

About a year after the annulment, on June 28, 1950, she had another son: me. Joseph Patsy Di Prisco. Fifteen months after, on September 13, 1951, my brother, John Louis Di Prisco, was born. The name of the father on the birth certificates was Joseph Louis Di Prisco, and the four of us claimed residence at 625 Humboldt Street, along with sons and stepsons and half-brothers, Bobby and Eddie. Joe Di Prisco, my dad, was no pug like Palermo, though, according to Bobby, who mixed it up with his stepfather more than once, "Your old man is a piece of work. He packs a punch."

Joseph Patsy—that was a name my mother didn't seem to approve of, especially the middle name. Joseph was the name of her father, in Polish *Josef*, and she often used the Polish pronunciation to refer to me. The Patsy might have been a signal of respect for my Italian barbarian grandfather, named Pasquale, so Patsy could have been a compromise—and a name the boy always resisted, for obvious reasons. My mother said she wanted to name me Jerome, but my father wouldn't go for it. For a long time, the name Jerome would hold an exotic appeal. I wished I were named Jerome.

My mother dated my father for a year before she told him she had three children from her previous marriage. I believe this to be true because my mother retold this story many, many times, in those simple terms, and always with a wicked smile. Story is not the right word. There was no buildup, no suspense, no satisfactory narrative conclusion: it was a statement of fact. A year of lying to my father and concealing the children. She was proud of her handiwork. That secrecy is as striking as an annulment. As for my father, he was either dumb as a fire hydrant or had stars in his eyes, feeling lucky to be dating the dishy Polish dumpling. Or maybe he didn't care if she had a dozen kids. Maybe he was in what somebody might call love.

In January 1953, then, these were the particulars of the domestic situation: Catherine Palermo was a divorced, unwed mother of four boys, ages ten, nine, three, and two, all residing at 625 Humboldt Street, with a daughter living apart from her under the legal custodial care of her alimony-paying ex. 1950s Brooklyn, Catholic working-class Polish neighborhood, a first-generation American—her domestic arrangement was hardly a predictor of tranquility, bliss, material prosperity, and social success. She must have been steel-willed or at least exceptionally stubborn, must have been emboldened and self-assured, must have been more than a bit scared or embarrassed some of the time. What must have come in handy was that she possessed world-class skills of dissimulation, obfuscation, defiance, and manipulation. And she was tough. She would get in the face of anybody.

Her domestic situation significantly altered on February 21, 1953, when, four years after her divorce and three and half years after her annulment, Catherine finally married Joseph Di Prisco at St. Cecilia's Catholic Church in Greenpoint, and her name became Catherine Di Prisco. It is noteworthy that they chose to get married in another neighborhood church in Greenpoint, while St. Stan's was a two-minute walk from the apartment. Curious, too, how she used to speak fondly of one priest who, so she said, "looked out for me" and "felt sorry for me."

If the annulment was some attempt to rejoin the flock, to take her place as a solid Catholic citizen, then why get pregnant and give birth, not once but twice, out of wedlock, a social abomination and a grave series of sins? Once might be accidental, but twice seems purposeful, obstinate, or willful. Then again, maybe she had some vague Catholic re-entry plan in mind, but never followed through. Or maybe things happened, as they inevitably do. This was a woman whose motto of "We'll see" might have been justifiably emblazoned on her family crest, had there been a crest to emblazon.

Bobby and Eddie were different from Catherine's younger boys, in ways her son Joseph could sense but not elucidate. The four of us shared the same bedroom, but Bobby and Eddie would leave for stretches at a time, inexplicably. But I figured out everything on my own one day.

That was the day my parents were screaming at each other in the next room, their bedroom, which had no door, and my father was calling my mother a very bad name, and saying something nasty about another man. He used the word "whore," or as he explosively pronounced it, "hoor." These words meant nothing specific to the boy who was listening closely, but their impact shook me: Mom was dirty, Mom was bad, a hoor, and men were bad and dirty, too.

It dawned on me that Bobby and Eddie must have had a different father, that they were somehow not really quite my brothers. I can't explain how I put this together in the moment, but I did. I would learn the scope of the familial connection when I found out they could be called half-brothers. I must have been four or five, and this information rocked me. It constituted my version of a primal scene. It felt like some betrayal on the part of my mother, one that implicated my father, too, because he never told me the truth. This moment furnished the material for every first session I would ever have with the latest lucky psychotherapist.

The consequences of this new knowledge? Perhaps I was overcompensating, but I'd never thought of Bobby and Eddie as half-brothers, and I never would, though as a child I was dimly aware of the distinction. How they came into existence and came to be related to me was a story I did not understand. All I did understand was, though they were my brothers, they were not quite of me. Beyond that, I realized once and for all that I could not trust my parents to give me all the information I needed, and what they did parcel out would never prove reliable.

When my parents split from Brooklyn, Catherine took me and John, but she left behind Eddie and Bobby, then seventeen and sixteen years old. They were forced to live on their own, scrounging to make money and survive any way they could. Eddie didn't speak to his mother for many years because of what she did before she hightailed it to California. He had saved up $200 from his paper routes—all the money he had in the world—and before we took off, my mother stole it. She promised to reimburse him, but never did. When Eddie met his eventual mate, Gary, who would be by his side for the remaining twenty-five years of his life, Eddie told Gary his mother was dead. At Eddie's funeral, his friends wanted to know who this elderly woman was. They were shocked to discover it was his mother.

As for that annulment, Gary eventually told me that he and Eddie knew all about it, because she had boasted to them about how she pulled it off. She bragged she had that parish priest wrapped around her finger.

Did she actually seduce that priest? As Gary said, "I wouldn't be surprised if she slept with him. We never put anything past your mother."

There are no wedding photographs of my parents in all the boxes of pictures that have survived the years. I have no recollection of any wedding albums or portraits on my parents' shelves. They never, to my or anybody else's knowledge, celebrated their wedding anniversary. Still, the two of them lived unhappily ever after—or at least for the next fifty-six years.

ALL OF THESE PIECES began to fall into place when I went through the boxes of materials and papers sent to me after my father left Florida and I helped him return to California in March 2010, after my mother's funeral. I telephoned my aunt Susie, my mother's big sister and her last living sibling, who was living in New Jersey in her assisted-living residence. Aunt Susie always possessed more than enough intelligence and fortitude to run any complex organization, including perhaps the state of New Jersey, which some say could use better management.

"Aunt Susie, did you know my mother got an annulment?"

"I did not know that, Joseph."

"Not a divorce—I'm talking about an annulment, from the Church."

"Your mutha was something, Joseph."

"Seems like a big deal, getting an annulment. Strange that nobody knew about it."

Long pause. "Joseph, your mutha was such a flirt."

That did not seem responsive to my question. Then again, maybe that was the perfect answer.

On this score, I do have one crystalline memory that disturbs me. It is a recollection of a strange man in my parents' bedroom. My father was not present, and I must have been three, maybe younger. The man had a shaved head and he was looking out a window, taking something off the top of the dresser and putting it in his pocket. I almost remember his name, too. Something like Skolnick. My mother was laughing in the adjoining room. Aunt Susie had no recollection of any such person, any such name.

The image of a burly man taking personal effects off a dresser, a nattily dressed man in a white shirt, has periodically strayed into my mind. I remember he was handling his own jewelry, maybe a watch, maybe a ring. He didn't brush me off. He was very kind and somewhat shy. Perhaps I had woken from a nap in the next room? I can still see his bovine head and his physical ease with being in my apartment, in my parents' bedroom. Then he was gone. I heard the name Skolnick at some later point, when my mother was talking to a friend.

Skull, Skolnik—what am I remembering? The idea of jewelry connects here, and I gained the sense that Skolnick had something to do with jewelry, maybe being in the business of selling it. But there is another possibility, of course: that he had given her a piece of jewelry. She loved jewelry. When she uttered the name Skolnick to a friend, she did so in a knowing, playful way, and she brightened up and smiled, the way a girl might who was flattered by the generous attentions of a man.

Truth is, I think I have always wondered about my father. I have lost count of the instances over the years when people said how much I resembled my mother, but never my father. I'd never had a serious girlfriend who, upon making the acquaintance of my parents, didn't raise an eyebrow and gently inquire if I was adopted. This was, I suppose, a polite way to ask where I came from without really asking. When my girlfriends met my parents, the temperature in the room dropped several degrees. Indeed, my mother had a special way of welcoming women in her home.

"I don't know about your father," an old girlfriend would say years later, "but I know where your brains come from. Your mother."

Then there was the matter of that priest in shining armor, somebody who had in all likelihood driven the annulment process. The few times my mother spoke warmly about the Church, it was to praise this priest who "looked out for" her. She never named him, but she clearly had some intimate connection. He was assigned to the parish that was St. Cecilia's, the church where she would be married the second time.

After my mother's death, I installed my father in an excellent, sophisticated assisted-living residence in a beautiful suburban setting with trees and hills in the near distance. He was perennially unmanageable, and he needed professional care, and my house was on the side of a hill with lots of stairs, so there was no way to imagine his living with me and my wife. He had a comfortable apartment and he enjoyed continual attention from the staff. He had the pleasure of being served terrific food. I would have eaten dinner there any night. After a while, he mostly stopped saying what he was saying every day for the first few months: "I gotta get the fuck outta here."

My father's short-term memory was progressively less functional, but his long-term memory was still startlingly good. As I have learned, that's not unusual with dementia and memory loss. He routinely made connections about the past I never expect him to make, while his dementia insinuated itself into his mind. Increasingly, he asked about his wife, as in, where was she? What happened to her, how come nobody told me? He believed she lived on the other side of the residence.

I asked him if he remembered when he was married. He said he did. He remembered it was 1953, though he did not put together that I had been born earlier. I asked him if he recalled the priest my mother talked about. He did. He said the priest encouraged him to marry her. I asked him where he was living before they married. He remembered he lived on Graham Avenue with roommates in an apartment house owned by my grandparents, which was within walking distance of Humboldt Street. Did he remember when he moved to Humboldt Street? He didn't.

"I used to visit there," he said.

"You used to visit Mom at 625 Humboldt Street?"

"Yeah."

"You used to visit?"

"Yeah, I would take the kid to the park."

"The kid?"

"You know, the park." Meaning, presumably, Winthrop Park, two blocks away.

"The kid? What kid?"

"You."

"Me?"

"Yeah, musta been you."

Is that the way a father talks about his own son? Or is it the way *my* father talks about his son? That was all I required to spur my curiosity. I asked his doctor to assist with a paternity test. She half-heartedly tried to talk me out of it, but she acknowledged I had a right to know. We did the swabs under her supervision and sent them in. My father had no clue as to what we were doing, but this was a non-invasive procedure.

"Are you sure you're prepared to hear the results?" the doctor asked me.

I had always been prepared. I wanted the truth. It wouldn't make a difference in the care I would give him as his condition worsened and he got older and frailer. I would always see to him. He was the only father I ever knew, after all. If it ended up that he was not my biological father, I was sure I would have a complicated reaction, and there was a good chance of all sorts of ramifications that couldn't be anticipated, but it was time for truth and consequences. Deep down, did I really suspect he was not my father? My brother was his spitting image, and I looked much more like my mother than my father, and I suppose I have to admit that, deep down, I did have a doubt. Would I be angry, would I be relieved?

In about two weeks I received an email with an attached file, containing lots of numbers on an inscrutable—to me— spreadsheet pertaining to allele sizes and genotyping, along with this terse conclusion:

"The alleged father is not excluded as the biological father of the tested child."

The tested child had what he needed to know about his alleged father.

He was my dad after all. In any case, he could not be excluded.

Having solved for one variable, all I had left to figure out was this: Who was this tested child?

★

ABOUT A HUNDRED YARDS away from where I stand tonight on Humboldt Street in Greenpoint is the funeral home, Stobierski's of garden-view fame. My mother died on Saturday morning in You-Can't-Get-There-From-Here, Florida, one day after her eighty-sixth birthday. She should never have been taken to Florida by her husband eighteen months ago If her husband were capable of reflection, which he normally avoids the way he avoids the bookies he owes money on square-up Tuesdays, he might admit this. He should confess, he should concede he was an idiot to take her there—which is what I helpfully pointed out two years before, when I was told what my father was planning to do.

"This is the dumbest move of your life," I said at the time, not invoking the position I was further tempted to: *And this is saying something for you, considering your lifelong pattern of dumb moves.* This opening gambit inspired my father to invoke a few choice observations of his own, including a summary judgment: "Your son has been more of a son to me than you ever were." Both of my parents liked to draw blood, and they did so with surgical imprecision.

To be fair, it wasn't Florida that killed her, not really or not quite, though if any state ought to be fingerprinted and stuck in a police line-up, I am nominating the Sunshine State for shackles.

Strictly speaking, I *assume* my mother is at Stobierski's, but I have no visual evidence. When I arrived earlier at the funeral home in a cab, I needed to go for a walk, to prepare myself for what is called The Viewing. An innocuous-enough word, perhaps, though suitably incongruous for the purposes served by the grisly factuality of the moment. Catholics say they want to *view* the body, *have* a viewing. Some people find this viewing practice a tad barbaric. They could be right, but as the son of the deceased, I would not have it any other way. Death won't be reasoned with, at least not by somebody with my meager credentials. Death always puts me at a loss, as it finally will once and for all. I also remain of the firm opinion that death is a horrible and indefensible idea, but I have yet to conceive a sensible alternative.

Tomorrow morning my mother is going to be buried in the same plot as my two older brothers. First she is going to be remembered at Mass across the street from the funeral home, and tomorrow morning we will leave the funeral home whose non-garden view I know to the last inch. This is where I spoke the eulogies at wakes for two of my brothers, and where I will do the same tonight for my mother. And this is the last place I saw my younger brother alive, nine months before he died on the floor of his bathroom in San Francisco, according to the coroner and everybody who ever loved him, "of acute drug toxicity."

As I stare up at this tiny apartment building at 625 Humboldt Street, I imagine I will probably never stand here again. Always a risky proposition, predicting the future—almost as risky as hazarding an understanding of the past. I am not only interring my mother tomorrow. I am burying an idea of—what? Myself? Life? Death is not to be trifled with. You don't get in the face of the Grim Reaper unless you are a fool.

It was here in Greenpoint, in this triangulation of apartment, funeral home, and church, that I came into existence. My life doesn't pass before my eyes this time, either, but I do see myself telescoping and tumbling through time-lapsing decades, without any of those pleasing big-budget 3-D special effects or orchestral arrangements—

A boy leaning out the third-floor window, or sitting out on the fire escape, searching up and down the street, watching…

The snow coming down softly, bringing the quiet and the isolation he loved…

A man burying his mother…

I decide I'm ready to go inside now. As if I had a choice.

I did. I always had a choice. I go inside. I do not want to go inside, I go inside.

★

MY MOTHER IS ELEGANTLY turned out in white, and her top is trimmed with gold. To me, the whiteness of her clothing has a fog-like force. The Emily Dickinsonski of Greenpointherst? Not exactly, but she did always dress stylishly, and was tastefully accessorized, not that accessorizing and funerals are terms that should mix. The people are whispering that she looks beautiful, that she looks like herself. These are things people say on such occasions even when they are patently untrue, but in this case, they have a sort of point, if you look past what "herself" and "beautiful" normally connote. One high school buddy of mine, whom my mother always professed to like, had called me to offer condolences. She used to bake butter almond cookies for Tony because he loved them. Tony got caught up emotionally in the syntax of his condolatory sentences about her, and ended up saying, "Your mom was always so pretty."

She may indeed look beautiful, but as I look and look, I cannot quite see her. There must be some medical or technical term for such temporary non-hysterical meta-blindness. I can dimly register the presence of the flowers. My friends have come through. There are bountiful bouquets and sprays around the room, it seems, though it is hard to see them, too. At some point the background music goes silent and in that stillness I rise to speak.

"On behalf of my father, who was not well enough to travel here from Florida, and of my family, thank you for coming tonight for my mother."

It would take a while to count the prevarications, half-truths, and distortions in that opener.

My mother liked certain kinds of social gatherings, and if a funeral doesn't precisely qualify, she still would have loved seeing us all gathered here, a point I make that is met with knowing smiles. Long ago my mother legally determined she would finish her journey here in Greenpoint when she acquired the plot in the local Catholic cemetery.

Next her grandson Mario stands up to speak. He is an eloquent speaker with a style that is his own, funny and serious at the right time and in the right places. He loved his Nana. He speaks sweetly about how she smoked cigarettes until he was four, when he began to squirt her with a water pistol whenever she lit up until she swore off her cigarettes once and for all. He speaks about her intelligence. He speaks about her being Polish, about growing up in a family that did not speak English, and how she endured the Depression, the TB she had as a child. He speaks about her unmatchable cheesecake. He speaks about her skill with details. She worked as a bookkeeper for a long time, and she was a terrific one.

Once when she took a leave from her job—surgery, the details of which nobody can recall—I took over for her at the ironworks factory. I never had a gift for numbers and spreadsheets, and was certainly no bookkeeper, but my mother taught me about balancing a checkbook, paying bills, keeping records. Until three or four years ago, she would call the bank if the balance was off by a penny. A penny.

My mother's relationship with her grandson almost certainly represented her finest hour. Their connection brought out the best in her, and in him, too. Mario references a key point that his father sometimes tends to forget: that his grandmother, like his grandfather, was normally not much of a talker, or explainer. The two of them protested a lot. They lamented a lot. They complained a lot. But stories? They told no stories. His grandmother thought giving you the silent treatment was eloquent enough, or at least she wasn't going to lose that argument.

She hardly talked about the past, and she hardly discussed the present. I could say that silence was the predominant mode at home, but that makes it sound like a cloister. If it was, it was a bizarre monastery, because there was a lot of yelling, and if nobody was much for speaking in sentences, they were all for demonstrations of rage and sputtering expostulation. There were two set points on the volume dial in our home: silence and screaming.

I do not believe in ghosts, but if I did maybe I'd believe my brothers have taken up their spectral sentry posts around our mother's casket. This is the last place the four brothers—Eddie, Bobby, John, and I—were together, in Stobierski's without the garden view, gathered for Eddie's funeral.

★

EDDIE WAS THE KINDEST, most generous member of the family. He had the heartbreaking look of a lonesome cowboy. His face, his nose, his eyes reminded you of a sight hound, an elegant Saluki. His arms were full of ink—which is conceivably what killed him thirty years after he got his tattoos, when he developed hepatitis, because he never smoked, never drank, never used. My fondest memory of Eddie was one Christmas morning when I was maybe four, and Eddie had set up a chalkboard and demonstrated how to do arithmetic. For me, it was enthralling to have that much power at your mental disposal, to manipulate numbers into making logical sense. It was my first conscious experience of a teaching moment, and it stayed with me throughout my teaching career.

Invariably, Eddie otherwise communicated the self-effacing message that he did not need to be, or care to be, in the limelight. Sure, if you needed a few bucks, he could help you out and would never ask for it back, or if you needed a ride to the airport, he would do that though it was a pain in the ass. When I delivered his eulogy, I perversely asked for a show of hands: "Who here ever borrowed any money from Eddie?" Nearly everybody's hand shot up, including my own. At least I didn't ask the follow-up: "And who among you paid him back?" Everybody knew the answer to that one: hardly any, including the eulogizer. Even on his death bed, his head on the NYU Hospital pillow, his face sallow, his lips cracked and dry, Eddie conveyed self-consciousness and repentance over putting everybody through the ordeal of watching him die.

Then there is Bobby, talking out of the side of his mouth to some beautiful girl, because there was always a pretty girl around him. He is telling her a tale about some jerk with whom he had a beef in his cab. He was always talking. A lot of chatter—and smaller-than-small small talk, to tell the truth—but he meant well. As last utterances go, however, his final word is worth quoting. The night before he died in a Coney Island hospital bed, of lung cancer, as we were leaving him to get some rest, somebody asked, "Bobby, you need anything?"

He nodded slowly.

"Whaddaya need?" somebody asked again.

He took his time that last night, pretending to be searching for the answer, as if he needed more time to come up with the answer, and we waited and waited. Finally, his barely audible, perfectly timed reply:

"Pussy."

He said it so roundly and breathlessly, it was practically a single syllable. And a very important syllable it is in many a man's life, from the first syllable uttering coming out of the womb, the wailing *waaa,* to the last syllable on the way to the grave. To the very end, Bobby was consistent and honest, and that voice was his. Throughout his whole life, there was hardly any bullshit about him.

Afterward, Bobby's daughter Katherine paced the hospital corridors with me, struggling over what had happened. She was strong. At that time, she was seriously involved with somebody, and they were contemplating getting married.

"Uncle Joe, I want you to walk me down the aisle. I know my father would approve."

There was no conceivable replacement for her dad, but I said of course I would, of course. It was the most touching request anybody had ever made of me.

Then there's Johnny, out in the funeral home lobby. As for bullshit, when he was using, he was one hundred percent full of it. He was working everybody—for cash, for a car, for a place to stay, for a shower. Today, he won't come in because he is strung out on smack and there are dead people all over the place, and dead people terrify him. He is wearing a black pork pie hat and a black leather jacket and every stitch on his back is black. The morning after Eddie's funeral, Bobby put him on a plane back to San Francisco. He'd found him unconscious on his daughters' apartment floor the night before, his works still stuck in his arm.

Bobby took him to the airport without telling anybody. But the news leaked via Bobby's daughters, days later. Johnny had left town—that was all anybody was supposed to know. Bobby was like his mother in many regards, including this: don't say nothing to nobody. What lay behind the secrecy and the limits on information? It's hard to know how this covertness necessarily works to a person's advantage. The net effect for me was that I always assumed I didn't know everything and I wasn't going to be told. If there was a story that needed to be told, it wasn't going to be told by my mother, or my father, or my brothers.

Maybe that's a reason I became a writer: to fill in the blanks.

Sometimes it seems impossible to reconcile the brother who was shooting up with the vulnerable boy called Johnny Cake. There is no question that these days he would have gotten a diagnosis of attention deficit disorder. He could not sit still. He could not concentrate. But he was a terrific athlete. He was the star hitter on his baseball teams, first-string guard on the high school basketball team. But that was not his life. He would not strive for a conventional dream. He was thrown out of his public high school when he punched out the principal a few days before graduation. Johnny's chemistry was all screwed up—his brain and body had it all backward. He said more than once that when he snorted cocaine, he felt relaxed, and when he slammed heroin, he felt alert and focused.

My younger brother's death somehow stunned everyone, even though we had given him up for dead a dozen times. When I heard the news over the phone, I went about my business for a while. I read a book. I walked outside. I practiced Italian, did some written exercises from the textbook. I watched the sunset. It took two hours before I could admit to myself that this time it was for real. John was dead.

★

NOW MY MOTHER'S LAST living son takes the floor again. I speak about my mother to those who have come to her wake. That's the job of the last living son, isn't it? I refer to her as *Caza,* pronounced KAH-zjah, with the "z" like Zsa Zsa Gabor. Caza was her Polish nickname, short for Cashmera, her baptismal name.

For all I know and can observe, the people in the chairs may be listening. My voice keeps dropping lower and lower, softer and softer. It's like that pre-surgical moment as the anesthesia kicks in.

Count to ten.

Ten, n-.

Maybe I am whispering. My words come from a place that's an awful lot like silence. I experiment. How low can I make my voice before I am talking to myself? Truth is, I despise silence. Sure, I need silence, to live, to work. Only here's the thing. Silence reminds me of prayer, which I would also probably hate if I were still capable of it. If I am honest with myself, I would have to say I have hardly ever prayed, at least with anything more than words—with the possible exception of that time in the lake when I almost drowned. Sure, the Our Father, the Hail Mary—but prayer, real St. John of the Cross/Dark Night of the Soul kind of prayer when I wasn't facing death? Not so much.

I have failed once more tonight at my mother's wake.

But I go on nonetheless, whispering.

Of course, a lot has changed for me since I was eight or nine and drowning, begging God to welcome me into His embrace. Since then, I have figured that if there were a God, then God knows me more perfectly than I could ever communicate, so what would be the purpose of prayer? I cannot make the leap to understanding what the saints understand, that prayer is more about understanding yourself and your needs than it is about appealing to God, who, for all His supposed omniscience, evidently has a pathetic attention span. The smell of the flowers gathered around her casket, flowers whose names I will never know, makes me feel a bit nauseated. I go on, hoping that emetic wave will wash over me soon enough.

Now I understand prayer's purpose. Prayer's like feeling what death feels like—to be known by God, here tonight in Brooklyn, the place of the origin of death as far as I know.

Tonight at the wake I describe a picture, actually a rectangular, framed piece of embroidery, that my mother put up in every kitchen where she imposed her will. A Polish expression was stitched in red thread: *Boze blogoslaw nasze dom.* God bless this home. Too bad He didn't deliver. Or maybe He did, and worse didn't happen. So, yeah, sure, why not go for it—God bless this home. A rarity for her: a good plan she had for God and for her domicile.

Then her son wishes her goodnight in Polish. *Dobranoc, Matka.* And then goodbye. *Do widzenia.*

Who is the audience for a eulogy? The deceased? That seems fatuous, sentimental. Instead of articulating valedictory words, perhaps it makes more sense to lift the body into a canoe with deerskins and knives and beads and other keepsakes and set it adrift down the river. Or is the audience the surviving? To what purpose are these words shaped and then uttered? Is every other's death of necessity a sort of cautionary tale? Or is it a reminder? *Memento mori?* Death, be not proud. O, death, where is thy sting?

I myself, the two-bit eulogist, am not crying tonight. Couldn't do it. Here's something I have never admitted before, a fact unnecessary to belabor. The truth is, to this day I have yet to weep a single tear for my mother. Not one. This sounds, even to me, terrible and indefensible.

To put this in perspective, I cried every day for six weeks when my beloved dog, my constant companion, died, and I still cannot glance at a picture of Eddie the whippet without feeling bereft. All of this tells you what you have likely suspected all along—namely, that there might be something deeply, deeply wrong with me, something locked up and frozen inside, a buried treasure that is buried but not a treasure. At least one conclusion seems inescapable. I just might be one poor excuse for a son.

If it is only the dead who end up knowing Brooklyn, then tonight my mother finally knows Brooklyn through and through, something her son is thus far in no position to claim. She always knew better, as she told me so many times, and now she was in a place where no one is going to argue with her ever again.

★

AFTERWARD, IN THE LOBBY of Stobierski's, I overhear somebody asking Mario if he is worried that his dad is writing a memoir. Like most experienced teachers, I can hear several conversations at the same time, especially those in the back of the room, and most especially when I am the topic.

"Worried?" Mario says, deftly landing on the curious word choice. "I don't know, but it seems like there are two kinds of memoirs. One where you land a plane on the Hudson. And the other, which involves hookers and blow in Las Vegas. As far as I know, my dad never landed a plane on the Hudson."

"As long as there is death, there's hope," wrote Giuseppe *Tomasi di Lampedusa*. "*Finchè c'è morte c'è speranza*." He wrote that sentence in one of the greatest novels ever written that was almost never published: *Il Gattopardo,* or *The Leopard,* which is composed in stylish, elegant prose. It contains a great, great death scene. This was the author's one finished book, and at the time of his death at sixty, it remained unpublished, rejected by every single Italian publisher. That's the novel in which you can also read: "*Se vogliamo che tutto rimanga come è, bisogna che tutto cambi.*" "If we want things to stay the same, we're going to have to change."

If Caza's son has learned one thing in his life, it's that you can't learn everything you need to from books, important as they may be, and they are to me. Beyond that, what I have also learned is something I still find hard to believe, but which is confirmed every day: that there's a way in which you can always live your life all over again, *through* books. That may be among the most useful things that books teach, if they teach anything useful whatsoever, not that usefulness is automatically useful.

Wise men and women are going to tell us that living your life all over again is anathema. The notion runs counter to the Zen philosophy of life, in which people live in the moment and non-frantically notice stuff. To notice—as if everyone and everything is outside of oneself. You notice the clouds, you notice sexual yearning, you notice mortality, you notice suffering, you notice you notice you notice and you notice some more. Indeed, I notice that they are all noticing, and what I notice about myself is that the very contemplation of Buddhism makes me feel drowsy. At the same time, living in the moment is fodder for every self-help vision and every commercial happiness theoretician. I am all for self-help, if it really helps, and all for happiness as long as it is not theoretical and as long as hedonic adaptation is not the law of the species. Zen is everywhere these days—it is perfect for anyone who wants the uplift of a religion without a religion, the exhilaration, say, granted by a great bottle of Barolo without the messy complications of opening it, decanting it, pouring it, drinking it. This position says nothing admirable about me, I realize, and I am defenseless. And let's not absolutely undercut my credibility by pointing out that one of my heroes found Zen remarkably congenial to his own devout Catholicism—Thomas Merton, a Trappist monk, great writer, great poet. All that said, not that it's much, I will take instead some of Evelyn Waugh, from *Brideshead Revisited*: "These memories, which are my life— for we possess nothing certainly except the past—were always with me."

You see, where there's death, there's hope, and if we want things to stay the same, we're going to have to change.

This memoir of mine is also the Book of the Dead. As is the case with most lives, my life has been full of death and will be full of more death, including inevitably one particular demise I fully expect not to relish. If *The Leopard* is correct, however, I should feel full of hope. And if I have stayed the same person since Brooklyn, it is because I have continued to change, which is because I could conceive of no alternative.

When I was a teenager in the late 1960s, I had a mentor by the name of Reverend W. Hazaiah Williams, the late charismatic African American preacher, pastor, professor, sociologist, musician, and intellectual, who enjoyed considerable reputation in the East Bay and beyond. Reverend Williams (I never imagined calling him Hazaiah) went to divinity school with Martin Luther King Jr., and was himself a national player in the Civil Rights movement. He was a force. The reverend had his own church, owned a bookstore in Berkeley, started a classical music concert series that is still going, taught at a community college at night, and served as a member of the Berkeley school board.

Mostly, Reverend Williams and I talked ideas and politics as we drove around from one grassroots organizational meeting to the next, where the likes of a Jesse Jackson or a Ralph Abernathy would regularly show. As the reverend's driver, I was more than occasionally the one white person in the room in those heady Civil Rights and March on Washington days, as well as those horrible, horrible assassination days. As we traveled, the reverend debated with the thinkers whose books he had inhaled. He lectured about Bonhoeffer. He disputed Freud's ideas. He quoted the Bible effortlessly, chapter and verse. He laughed at the stupidity and frailty of the human race when necessary, and was kind and compassionate if he had to be. One elicited a great cackle, the other a beatific smile. The few times he spoke with Caza, he was courtly with her. She was clearly mystified as to what was going on between him and her son, but she resisted using the racist terminology that was otherwise commonplace in the household.

The reverend was the executive director of the East Bay Conference on Race, Religion, and Social Justice, and he lived according to every single notion implied in that name. His office was in downtown Oakland, and his young Latina secretary— this was before the age of administrative assistants—was named Lolita. Lolita was very smart and competent and funny and, to the reverend's teenage driver, who wasn't much younger than she, very likely the foxiest girl in Oakland.

Hazaiah Williams was a great man, and he once said something unforgettable. His driver cannot recall the context, or what he said to provoke such a response, but this is what Reverend Williams said: "What makes you think that the God who created you is done creating you?" Now, the reverend made vatic pronouncements from time to time, but honestly, nothing quite like that.

"I said, 'What makes you think that the God...'"

I'd heard the reverend the first time.

"'...who created you is done....'"

OK, maybe so, maybe so, but if so, how come for most of my life I had felt discouraged recreating and recreating and recreating myself?

What did Thomas Wolfe say? "It'd take a guy a lifetime to know Brooklyn t'roo an' t'roo. An' even den, yuh wouldn't know it all."

Now, I have a theory as to why death never fails to feel like such a bad idea. It was *always* a bad idea, nothing but a tediously logical Plan B. If you trust the story of the Garden of Eden—that is one heck of a story, and if you ever want to trust any story, that's a good place to start—death was never part of the plan. Human beings were intended to be immortal. Then things went sideways: ribs, fruit, trees, serpents, cover-ups. The wages of sin, and so on. That's why we feel keenly the pang of death's disappointment: immortality was once in our grasp, and we tossed it away. Even so, to this day, in story and in love, where and when we live our best lives, we remain immortal because we can somehow never forget we once were immortal. The truth of this position can be proven, too. Who doesn't feel immortal at times? In those moments when we fall in love or make something beautiful, who among us doesn't believe that we're going to live forever?

You can't learn everything you need from books. This was the very best lesson I ever learned in my life—and I learned it from books.

Dirty

MY FIRST ACT OF remembering was committed by my mother. Though it seems highly probable that this was *her* recollection, she referenced this particular moment so frequently over the years that I can almost, *almost* convince myself of having experienced it. It appears that once I was sitting on a beach blanket alongside her, probably at Rockaway, maybe Coney Island, back in the early fifties when people could ride the roller coaster or the Ferris wheel, when you could swim in the bracing saltwater or eat a sticky spool of cotton candy and afterward not head straight to the emergency room for a tetanus booster. So there I am, the roly-poly baby boy burbling on the beach blanket, and I am dusting sand off my hands and articulating my first word. My first memory is my mother's memory that my first utterance was "Dirty."

Dirty. And if it wasn't my first word, it was the first word I was told was my first word. If anything, this would be slightly more revealing.

So dirty on the beach became the substance of family narrative and mythology, along with another anecdote I repeatedly heard.

Here is an example of what the family found to be hilarious. When I was still barely able to hold my head up, I would be given a book. They apparently liked to hand me said book upside down, or sideways. Though none of them donned lab coats or clutched clipboards, this was their experimental method in action. Upon receipt of the book, it was said, I invariably, slowly, deliberately repositioned the book for proper apperception. I could not read the thing, of course.

Admittedly, nobody in my family ever boasted I was a budding John Stuart Mill, or had an inkling as to who John Stuart Mill might be. In terms of normal child development, this sort of behavior hardly portended genius. This is the predictable functioning of the baby who is a "scientist in the crib," according to the wonderful book so titled, and my rage for establishing order seems fairly ordinary. But the legend grew, nonetheless, and the image stuck, more than likely because I was fated to have some connection to the act known as reading—certainly more than anybody else in the family. To this day I remain an embarrassingly deliberate reader. What's more, my natural inclination remains to turn a book around and around, figuratively speaking, to get a better vantage.

The one fundamental question that baby boy might have had for his family about the book, had he possessed words in addition to dirty, was: A book? Where the heck did you get this thing? For aside from a single rogue Mother Goose volume and that well-thumbed dictionary, I do not recall any other such artifacts in the entire apartment.

★

WHEN I WAS OLDER, five or six perhaps, my mother dragged me to the pediatrician because she observed I was continually washing my hands. It wouldn't have been out of character for her to mention the part about my first word, dirty, when she made the appointment. The revered Dr. Gyves was a great doctor, or at least a kind and wonderful man with a moon face and avuncular tortoiseshell glasses and a swinging stethoscope, which he must have stored in a freezer. The application of his stethoscope gave me the chills, but even so, I trusted and liked him. I didn't even complain when the good doctor sneaked up and stabbed my ass with a hypodermic or administered a revolting enema during house calls.

The diagnosis is lost in the dunes of time, but not the prescription for treatment, because my mother recounted the news at least a hundred times over the years following. The doctor prescribed applying lotion to my hands to keep the skin from drying out. The hand-lotion wonder drug. To this day I give thanks for Dr. Gyves's brilliant common sense—although the doctor may have proved a bit too wishful or optimistic, ultimately, about the doomed little rabid hand-washer.

The way my mother recounted this event, and the number of times she faithfully recounted it, suggests that she was somewhat disappointed with the diagnosis and the treatment. There is also the chance that she was seeking validation of her mothering skills, or at least an indication she was not going to be blamed for further damaging her child.

That wasn't always her M.O. with members of the healing profession. The sicker she got as she aged, the more she butted heads with her doctors, and she changed them out the way some women rotate purses. Medical appointments were a principal feature of her life, but in general, she preferred to diagnose herself. One of her favorite games took place during visits to the doctor's office, and she would continually relate versions of this same anecdote. Her latest doctor would ask how she was feeling, and she would say fine. And he would say something like, "That's great, the medication is working," and she would say something like, "I didn't take the medication." Why didn't she? She didn't want to.

Over and over again, she disregarded doctors' orders and their prescriptions. When she was diagnosed with congestive heart failure, for instance, she decided against taking one of the main drugs of choice of the medical establishment. Her reasoning? "I don't like Coumadin," she said.

"You haven't taken any."

"Never mind."

Who knows how much creativity she might have exercised had she learned to surf the Web in search of pseudo-medical information or discovered how to purchase alternative pharmaceuticals from Canada? Among the family, when she bragged about her independence and contrariness, a question often asked was, "How is medical school going, Mom?" She dismissed that insolent inquiry with a chirp: "I am thriving!" Admittedly, if anybody else said that, it might sound like breezy cheerfulness. When she said it, she intended something like, "I'll show them motherfuckers."

★

ON THE HAND-WASHING POINT, I have wondered since if my mother and I would have been better pleased had we both been born a couple of decades later. Then maybe her boy could have been prescribed some obsessive-compulsive disorder psychoactive drug, Baby Prozac or Starter Paxil or Trainer Zoloft.

As I entered high school, I was still washing my dried-out hands all day long in many an unsuspecting sink. In addition, my obsessive disorder took the form, among other activities, of packing and repacking my book bag, of doing and re-doing homework, of consuming food in internally and mysteriously dictated sequence, and of ferreting out the magical number of repetitions for any action. I also entered a distinct phase of a particularly embarrassing form of obsessiveness that has a suitably grotesque and hideous name: *dermatillomania*, an impulse-control problem, commonly called skin picking. I didn't scar myself, at least not to the eye of a casual observer, but I continually picked at and around the ear, the top of my head, the left nasal vestibule. I did this when nobody was around, perched at my desk at home, because I understood this activity was so gross to behold. I could not stop. Psychologists suggest this condition functions as a type of self-soothing when somebody is anxious, or a kind of stimulation when bored. Sounds on the money for an anxious child susceptible to boredom.

Generally speaking, since stealing admission into the amusement park of adulthood, I have continued to be just this side of controllably OCD, or so I controllably imagine, controllably enough. The obsessive picking has not entirely subsided, though, to tell the truth. When stressed or fatigued, sooner or later I have been known to reach for my skin. Otherwise, in the not-so-distant past, I was OCD enough to alienate a potential girlfriend and permanently damage her psyche, if not my romantic prospects, when I re-parked the car, then re-parked it again, or checked and rechecked to see if the lights were off or if the iron had been left on. At the same time I was not quite compulsive enough to lose a day straightening out the imperfectly aligned books on the shelves or to bet the horses and lose every dollar. Yet it remains true that when I pack for a trip, for instance, I can have a *petite mal* nervous breakdown checking and rechecking my bags. It can take me a solid half-day to pack for an overnighter. By the time I arrive for check-in at the airport, I am worn out.

As for airports and airport security, forget about it. I turn into a neurotic bowl of quivering jelly, as my son has remarked. An airport is one place where it is not easy to manage for all the variables. So much is out of one's power, so many rules and strictures not of one's own obsessive making. I can visibly decompensate when I walk in my socks on the filthy airport floor and place my jacket in a common bin for the purposes of electronic scanning. Taking a seat on the airplane also poses a challenge. I arrange and rearrange the carry-on and the book and the headphones, the carry-on, the book, and the headphones. Carry-on, book, headphones. Carryonbookheadphones. People who have been unlucky enough to play the role of my doomed travel companions order cocktails early and often. For this reason alone, they should earn triple miles. Sometimes these fellow travelers go right for the salvation of a cool blue Valium 10. With any luck, they coax me into swallowing one or two and taking a nap already.

On other fronts, when I have a speaking engagement, for instance, I print out my written remarks even if I am going to speak extemporaneously. Actually, I print out one copy for the coat pocket, and one that I leave in the car. In case. Just in case. You never know, you simply never know. I also have text accessible on the smartphone nestled in my shirt pocket. And when I send out a business email, I read it over and over again. And then again. And that's after it's sent. How typos still get past me is anybody's guess.

There were other obsessional obsessions, too, more serious ones, that will figure prominently later on. I could go on and on and on with the humiliating examples, but that would be downright obsessive.

Maybe one more example. Here's something I often catch myself saying to my wife as we are about to leave the house:

"You didn't lock the back door."

"Why bother? I know you're going to check."

★

ANOTHER CHILDHOOD MOMENT BURNS brightly. This much more vivid early memory also involves my mother, but it is one hundred percent *mine*.

I am sitting at the kitchen table in the Greenpoint apartment, long before current neighborhood gentrification. Those were the days when I might have been positioned before the black-and-white with a goldfish bowl for a picture tube and avidly watched new programs like *The Honeymooners* starring Jackie Gleason, Audrey Meadows, and Art Carney. In reality, though, since that classic show didn't begin its thirty-nine-episode run till 1955, I could not have watched it before that night at the kitchen table, which means this recollection predates the heyday of the "Bang-zoom!" "To the Moon, Alice!" *Honeymooners.* Even so, today I can summon up the theme music and the star-bursting images at will. And whenever I watched it as a child, I studied with keen interest the Kramdens' Inverse Decorator Showcase of an apartment, and its familiarity unfailingly stunned me: *Hey, that's where I live!* I must have spent serious time with that great new novelty, television. I certainly spent a lot of time by myself, and television is a good companion for childhood solitude.

It is dusk, probably early autumn, and I am three years old, possibly four. An orange sky can be glimpsed far away through the window near the stove. The reason I feel confident about my age is that I am drawing a circle, and this high-concept work of art tests my limits. I want to get it right, this circle, which I am coloring, which leads me to believe it might have been a red balloon. Red crayon or colored pencil? If pressed I would have to go with crayon. I want to get the red circle right for one sole and crucial reason: to get the attention and approval of my beautiful mother.

Then she proceeds out of the bathroom, transformed into an incandescent vision, her pretty face framed by auburn-tinted hair. She rustles about in a red, poofy crinoline poodle skirt. Her dress is swish-swish-swishing like the summer shore. Her heels click like castanets on the linoleum, her carriage suggesting she might be gliding across a glitzy nightclub floor.

Here's the spatial layout of the apartment. The door opens from the hallway landing onto the kitchen and dining area, which is where I am tonight the artist in residence, and this room must be at most nine by twelve. The apartment extends for three additional, continuous, undoored rooms leading toward the Humboldt Street side of the building: from the kitchen with the bathroom, to a sort of TV room/parlor, to the parents' bedroom, to the bedroom where my mother's four boys slept.

They might have called this a railroad apartment (as in railroad cars coupled together), or a shotgun apartment (as in you could shoot a shotgun and the pellets would go from one end of the apartment to the other). I do not recall hearing either term at the time.

There are two windows near the stove, and on nice days you can look down on the back yard three floors below through the geometrically chaotic grid of multiplying, crisscrossing lines of laundry hanging out to dry. Across from the stove is the door to the bathroom, six feet away. The tub has stunted tortoise legs and a handheld showering device, which, because I can recall no plastic shower curtain, must have been employed by a bather seated in the tub. Perhaps as a consequence, for a very long time the notion of a stand-alone shower, or a mounted showerhead, struck me as exotic and luxurious. The chain for the toilet, when pulled, triggered a wave from the fascinating and dangerous water box located overhead. This is the sort of toilet behind which Clemenza hid the gun for Michael in *The Godfather*, when he needed to kill the crooked police captain and his father's betrayer during their secret meeting at a neighborhood Italian restaurant.

The bathroom itself loomed as a strange, strange place, where strange, strange things happened. I recall the fury and the panic that set in one summer night when some enormous insect was discovered there. There was a scream that must have been my mother's. Had my older brother rallied to help her confront the bug? That seems plausible. In any case, I didn't see it, which didn't help one bit, as the bug assumed greater and greater mass in my imagination, growing from the size of a fist to the size of a shoe, to the size of a sewer rat, to the size of a cat. I never did discover what happened with the poor creature—or was it the *terrifying* creature? Yes, yes, psychoanalysis would someday hold appeal.

I was always a chubby boy who was self-conscious about being chubby, and I must have spent a lot of time by myself at that plastic-top kitchen table. I sat in a metal chair with a yellowish daisy floral pattern on the plastic back, so that when I sat back in it, it produced a whooshing sound. That was the place where I must have consumed a lot of food—I do not recall a lack of provisions at home, not once. With regard to dinner, as in the assemblage of closely identified people gathered at the board to share sustenance and company, I have virtually no recollection. Food was cooked, food was prepared, food was consumed in audible isolation. Misophonia is the name of the condition when somebody, a person like me, feels fury and disgust in response to offending stimuli, like the sounds others make while masticating their victuals.

Nonetheless, the kitchen was the room where big moments took place. Like the time when a hurricane blew into New York and I sat at the table and felt secure and safe, knowing nothing bad could possibly happen in this Greenpoint haven, though we were going to be scared for a while by the battering wind and the torrential rain. Like the times when massive snowstorms hit, and I would hunker down in the apartment while my older brothers worked down in the cellar, shoveling coal into the furnace to heat the building—or more accurately, to *overheat* the building. The hulking, red-mawed, crackling furnace belched and roared like a dragon, and I gave the beast wide berth.

My mother is dressing to go out, though my father, as per normal, is nowhere in sight. It never crosses my mind that my mother is going to meet her husband somewhere, either. At some point I stopped asking where my father was because I never received useful information. ("Where's Dad?" "He is *out*.") My mom did not say he was at work, because my father did not appear to have what other dads had: a job. That is, an occupation involving coveralls, forklifts, a factory, and the vigorous application of sandy speckled soap on greasy hands at end of day. As near as I could tell, the man hung around with other men who also did not go to work in the morning. Whatever they did, they did full time, and nobody had keys on their belt or a lunch box in their hand when they went off to do it.

It never crosses my mind to wonder with whom my mother is going out, or where, or when she is returning. Somebody must be staying with me and my little brother, but I have no recollection of a babysitter that night—nor, for that matter, ever having one. What does that mean? At a minimum it means she needed a night off more than the Old Woman Who Lived in a Shoe.

Meanwhile, that dress. What a dress. It is an incredibly red dress. Red like something scary red. Like racing fire trucks. Also like lollipops. And she has on lots of make-up, and she looks stunning. This was the generation of crazy, dangerous women, women like Bette Davis and Joan Crawford, not that I knew it then. This was the age of fuzzy-sweater girls with brassieres like missile installations. An epoch of screamers and schemers, when grease monkeys in gas stations and gazillionaires in swanky penthouses alike fell victim to the cracking-wise wiles of the busty broad, the tomato, the pulp-fiction noirish hot tamale with gams up to here. At this point in my life, on all such subjects I would have been uninformed, and may still be, for all I know.

But here's the one thing I know for sure, and the ultimate point of this remembrance: My mother glances down at her son's drawing and says something that must have approached approbation. I know this because my heart fills up and overflows. I adore my mother, feeling so lucky to have her for my mom. I must have smiled, my whole body must have radiated. Then I make the imaginative leap, which is this: *I want her to be happy.* From early, early on I linked these two notions: *I love my mother* and *I want her to be happy.* I must have intuited that somebody needed to help her be that way, and it looked like there were no other candidates around.

I do not say anything in response to whatever it is she's said about the red balloon. I may not enjoy the use of many words at this point, but this constraint is a moot point. For even had I been born another Samuel Johnson, that evening I was rendered purely, joyously speechless. What need for words? My drawing had performed the astonishing trick of pleasing my mother, my pretty mother going out on the town. To this day, this remains the most romantic memory of my life.

★

SO MY MOTHER'S DOCTOR, Doctor Smith, would have committed suicide if she had been his mother? Really? Needless to say, this doctor did not grow up in Brooklyn. Not that that made him a bad guy.

My mother produced extreme reactions in many, and not only in her physicians. Nurses, teachers, nuns, clerks, bank tellers, waiters, her children, her husband, her siblings—all could feel her lash on their backs if they weren't fast on their feet. Colorful results were often obtained around her, including triage vodka consumption, ceramic-tossing competition, emergency therapy scrambling, and weapons production. I will never forget one handgun's magical appearance in the kitchen that one Christmas day, when she wanted to make a point about my father's gambling—the "degenerate fucking gambler's" losing. And then, like that, the gun's equally magical disappearance.

Dogs, on the other hand, loved her unambivalently—all dogs, absolutely every single one of them, stray or family, mutt or twenty-generation champion pedigree, from unexpectedly pliant Dobermans to suddenly obedient toy poodles. This undoubtedly speaks volumes to her credit and should make her the envy of any dog whisperer.

Contrary to her physician's prognosis, I never did commit suicide—or to make a fine distinction of far greater import to me than perhaps to others, so far I have not done so. I have, strictly speaking, never formed specific suicide ideation, either—

though admittedly the near-drowning incident complicates the argument. However, the plot gets more complicated still.

So what about the woman's son, her fourth child, first of her union with her second husband? And not only *career* suicide, which by all standards I have achieved rather spectacularly, but *suicide* suicide?

On the suicide question, I would chant the mantra of my former gambling friends and associates, which is this: smart money takes the points. Nothing new here. Smart money always looks first to the underdog. Amateurs and fans? They love the favorite, not that they quite know why they do, but they do. If favorites came in all the time, all gamblers would live on Easy Street. Truth is, the vast majority of gamblers can't find Easy Street with a guide dog who can read Google Maps.

As for committing suicide, unquestionably my mother's son used to regularly detect the Sirens' sweet song wafting in the air, though sometimes I was humming to myself and sometimes I thought those Sirens sounded reasonable enough. Their tune was catchy, too. And the truth is, while never technically suicidal, self-destructive and self-subverting and obsessive-compulsive behaviors indeed titillated and exhausted me, even as they simultaneously bored and emboldened me. And I came upon the perfect drug for this OCD. There was really nothing to compare with the daily, hourly, minute-by-minute freshets into the brain wowed by the ingestion of cocaine, which insinuated its way wherever I was, especially during those seventies *Night Fever* moments suitable for disco consumption. Beyond that, I would not say entering a Catholic religious order at age seventeen was a self-destructive gesture. There were lots of good things to be said for my brief vocation as novice Brother Joseph.

After leaving the Brothers, did my relationship with my mother make it difficult to sustain healthy relationships with sane women? To hear such a thing, my exes would stomp, hoot, or chortle, which may well be satisfying activities for an ex to indulge in. For now, let's leave aside the Bushmill months (and months and months), the Vegas blackjack team, graduate school at Berkeley, going into the restaurant business with the Strenuously Voweled Individuals, the parade of criminal attorneys, and the once-upon-a-time impending RICO indictments that pended for far too long. That was when I was advised by the FBI that I was the "prime suspect" in a "criminal conspiracy." I was also told in no uncertain terms: "Don't leave town."

★

IS THERE ANYTHING INTRINSICALLY wrong with an impressionable little boy's wanting his unhappy mother to be happy? Could that be the whole problem? How about part of the problem? From the first, misery moved me, which was why it was so wondrous to come upon manifestations of desolation wherever I came across it in later in life—at parties, in restaurants, during meetings, inside classrooms, around casinos, at 30,000 feet in the air. No wonder, perhaps, that throughout a good part of my adult life I cultivated falling for damaged women who could not comprehend that they needed me as much as I needed them— or maybe as much as I knew they needed me, or ought to need me. No wonder, too, that these relationships were often founded on pacts of mutually assured destruction.

Exciting times indeed, as if exciting meant being worth the candle. Big feelings abounded, as if big meant healthy. Those were the days, as if it was anything but midnight all the time. That was when furniture was known to plummet from windows, undies to flutter on bare branches. Cars squealed around corners at unpredictable times. Manic make-ups followed days or possibly hours later by twist-the-knife betrayals. Making out of spite a pitcher of Sangria from a bottle of a rare vintage of super Tuscan wine called Sassicaia, which singular incident sent my prospective wine-collecting career spinning into oblivion.

Could life be more perfect? The more it hurt, the more dejected I felt, the more I could trust I was in love.

★

MY MOTHER WAS END-STAGE Alzheimer's for seemingly years. In some sense it became easier to make my peace with her when she could not recognize me in person or my voice on the phone, when she spoke giddy gibberish and not, as before, like somebody in a Scorsese movie. And I would say that our relationship had never been better. But that is a cheap shot.

I retain a picture of that young woman going out for the evening, but the kind of social occasion she seemed most fond of was a Back from Prison party, though she also had a weakness for a Going to Prison party—my little brother provided the occasion for a couple of each. Sometimes, depending on the vicissitudes of the criminal justice system, and the very fluid social circle, these events took place back to back. Whatever the occasion, she would look for an opportunity. And she would appear with her *fuggetaboutit* New York-style cheesecake that would make her the rock star of the gathering.

When my mother did deign to attend a party, she waltzed regally into the room, her husband in tow, having been assigned the charge of transporting the sacred cheesecake, which she herself baked and upon which, as everyone was reminded, she'd "worked all day long." In all fairness, let us concede: her heliumized cheesecake was definitively world-class, tall and creamy with a toasty top. The cheesecake practically floated off the fork into your mouth. If you think you have had better cheesecake (and everybody in New York thinks they know the best cheesecake), you are wrong. That is, I would respectfully contest that opinion. Sometimes, my mother would change things up and also bring fabulously irresistible and delicate cream puffs. These tiny pastries were sweet and light and so subtle that they had a shelf life measured in milliseconds. Everybody loved these so much, and if I could imagine my mother being happy without qualification, that would have been the time. Those cream puffs were enough to make some people wish somebody would hurry up and get sentenced or paroled already.

"Great cream puffs, Caza," somebody would always say.

"Yeah, they come good," she would respond.

For her part, was there an edge to the delivery of these spectacular desserts? Yes. She was famous for finding out about dinner and what the hosts were making, including desserts, and she would make a point of bringing the cheesecake, which would surely subvert anybody else's effort. But you could never pin her down in advance. She wouldn't tell anybody she would be making dessert, so you could never plan. Thus, she could have it all ways. She could experience the irritation of a host who had made her own dessert, and she could experience the adulation of having made the star dessert. Win-win, for her. Lose-lose for somebody else.

There was one particular party, however, she chose *not* to attend. The social gathering she avoided was my one and only wedding.

★

No, SHE WASN'T ILL and she wasn't out of town and she didn't have a scheduling conflict. She simply indicated she was not going to show. Did she explain why she would not be coming? No. Was she wooed? Most certainly, and extravagantly, with enough swag to match Oscar nominees'. And when she refused to accept the invitation to her son's wedding, she was cultivated, catered to, targeted, and cajoled week after week, and when that failed, she was begged to attend by the marrying couple's friends. These friends embraced the role of emissaries to the Court of Catherine of Bonny Brook-Lynn. But she wasn't going, next subject.

Her track record was intact.

I guess the only way she liked viewing a bridge was with torch in hand.

No one knows for sure why she took a pass, and even after many years elapsed, no explanation was ever forthcoming. This leaves open the distinct probability that perhaps the obvious is true—that is, it may have had something to do with her son's choice of a wife, if not her son's very choosing of a wife.

My mother was famously competitive, or maybe combative, with any other woman getting attention in her vicinity. Every room was potentially the scene of a cage fight. But she seemed to have extra in her reserve tank of venom to use with my significant others, as well as those doctors and waiters. I myself never did see the percentage in antagonizing people who are in a position to palpate me or my dinner.

My prospective union was not with a doctor or a waitress, so that augured well perhaps. But it was a union with a woman. Another woman. And my mother despised every woman I dated. For the record, she had little difficulty dealing with Eddie and his male partner—at least as long as Eddie was alive. Still, my proposed union with a woman was not founded on détente. The two of us did not make each other miserable. And for somebody like my mother, somebody for whom the appellation Drama Queen seems tame, that may have been precisely the sort of prospect she could not stomach. Looking back, I wonder if her not showing up for that wedding was confirmation that I was doing the right thing—a blessing she was bestowing in her signature style, unconsciously.

Also for that record, she regularly extended her claws in the vicinity of my son's mother, whom I never did marry for reasons to be explained later.

★

I MET PATTI IN 1989, through her goddaughter, a cherished student of mine, after I made the commencement address at that student's graduation. It might have been a pretty good speech, because a couple of years later Patti and I decided to marry. We wanted a small event. Father Shane, my longtime friend and former colleague, conducted the service. Mario, then in high school, was the only other witness in the church. The next day we threw the big party that my parents did not attend.

Patti was different from any of my potential mates of the past, a more serious rival to my mother. Maybe it was as plain as that. Or maybe the proposed daughter-in-law was too much of a Californian for the Brooklyn mother-in-law's taste.

Nobody could be more purely Californian than Patti. She was born in Hollywood and grew up in Beverly Hills. She and her family lived next door to Peter Lawford, the suave leading man of Frank Sinatra Rat Pack fame. It so happened that Lawford's home was the setting of some not-furtive-enough get-togethers that entered the national lore. From time to time, a cortege of black limousines would majestically descend on the estate. That signaled the arrival of the president of the United States. A while later, Patti would watch from her upstairs window while JFK and Marilyn Monroe sipped cocktails by the pool.

Patti's dad was one of the legendary California surfers. There is a famous picture of him striding along the beach, a picture that not very many years ago was still pasted up in Nikon ads. He is holding a lobster in each hand. The lobsters are bigger than Thanksgiving turkeys. The man was an Adonis. He was there on State Beach and Malibu in the 1930s and 1940s when surfers changed pop culture forever and contributed toward the transformation of California, when the state caught the wave that made it *California*. He learned from the likes of surfing pioneers like Doc Ball and Duke Kahanamoku. He was also a justly celebrated photographer, the first surfing photographer, in fact. His gorgeous books of surfing shots were praised in the pages of national periodicals, and once his pictures were used for a spread in *The New Yorker.*

It will come as no surprise that a supermarket tabloid sniffed out the trail of the president playing footsy next door. The fishwrap wanted revealing pictures of the handsome married president and the bombshell much-married movie star. They asked Patti's father to do the dirty paparazzi work. But her dad had principles. A good man, he believed in being a good neighbor. He turned down, by 1960s standards, a fortune: $100,000. That's what Willie Mays, the best baseball player in the land and maybe the greatest of all time, and JFK himself were being paid for the whole year.

When I met Patti I was thirty-eight and I wasn't looking. Decades into my relationship wars, I was flying the white flag.

Patti's Southern California roots were unlike my Brooklyn pedigree. She detected the accent during that commencement speech—but for her that was a plus. Difference may be a turn-on, but she was no typical L.A. child of privilege. She had been shuttled off to a Swiss boarding school—and been expelled. At eighteen she impetuously wed a forty-year-old French painter and lived in Paris. She was arrested for drug possession in Texas—charges eventually dropped. She had been raped by an international celebrity, and I shed no tear over the front-page obit in *The New York Times.* She had even gone down a fundamentalist religious path for a while.

We'd both been through the wars, on different continents and coasts, but paid a similar, high price. More important, she was sane, kind, smart, strong, and loving—which precisely described few women I had ever fallen for. Then again, maybe I could learn from her. Maybe we could bring out the best in each other. Maybe we could even love each other.

★

ONE WEDDING MY MOTHER did attend was my brother John's wedding, which took place a few years after he was released from San Quentin. As it happened, I was in the wedding party with three of Johnny's friends, two of whom seemed to have been affiliated with the Hells Angels, or at least affiliated enough to wear the jacket (and John himself vaguely claimed to have some associate status). We were at the church the day before the ceremony for rehearsal. The priest positioned us off to the side, and we were awaiting instructions while he reviewed procedures with the other members of the party. I overheard one of those gentlemen addressing the other:

"You remember when you got married?"

"Like it was yesterday."

"Yeah?"

"Yeah, I was going to the joint next day."

"Why'd you get married, going to prison next day?"

He throws up his hands at the guy's rank dumbness.

"On account the congenial visits!"

The Hells Angels behaved. The one notable misbehaver in attendance was the one whose words you are reading here. I didn't want to wear the tuxedo my brother rented for me. I wanted to wear my own tux. Why? I don't like wearing rented tuxes, I guess. Mostly, though, because I am vain and shallow and because in a flush moment I had bought my own tux. John was probably hurt, but he had the graciousness to go along with my boorish insistence. I very much regret putting him through it, and that I can't make it up to him.

My brother's oldest and best and most loyal friend in the world was serving as best man, which was a good call. It so happened that his name was on the front page of the *San Francisco Chronicle* the day before. He was being sought by authorities— evidently not all that energetically, because here he was at the wedding, in plain view, a big guy impossible to miss. The police wanted to discuss with him the much-publicized murder of a very well-known figure in the exciting and spirited world of horse racing.

"You OK?" I asked him, as he was standing there without handcuffs.

"Sure," said the best man, who resembled John Belushi and didn't seem broken up.

"How come they're looking for you?"

"I didn't kill the guy."

That was a relief. Not that I'd ever had the slightest suspicion, honest.

"Though I was sleeping with his wife."

At least somebody around here was capable of taking the high road.

What a motley crew was assembled that day in San Rafael, a fifteen-minute drive from where John spent a few years in San Quentin. I refused to visit him in that prison. I had visited him in other prisons, but this time I resolved to do some version of tough love, I suppose. He had let it be known that he was now a member of the Aryan Brotherhood, but I didn't quite believe it. He was no skinhead racist, but he needed affiliation to survive in prison, he said, and who could argue with that who hasn't lived inside?

I guess my hard-ass tough-love approach was arguably the right one, but if it was, why do I still feel so bad about that decision? And maybe *tough love* was not the right term, because all I sometimes felt was tough and not too much of the love. Like the time he stole a few boxes of my graduate student books—my collected Shakespeare, my Montaigne, my Chaucer, la de fucking da—and sold them to a secondhand bookstore on Telegraph Avenue. I had let him have my $125 a month apartment when I moved out. His then-girlfriend, who was living with him, was turning tricks on San Pablo Avenue in Emeryville. I didn't take the theft in stride, and I did something worse to him. I destroyed his stuff in response, and I didn't have the excuse that I was a junkie. I ripped up a sentimentally valuable photo of his old friend, Kip, who was killed before John's eyes in a motorcycle accident. I couldn't use drugs as an excuse. I was just mean.

In the past I had gone to see him where he was sentenced, including maximum security somewhere in the Nevada desert, where he did three years. I remember once when we sat outside at a picnic bench in the brutal sun. He said it was crazy inside, crazier than I could imagine. He wasn't trying to impress me. He was scared. He saw things happen to people in fights that made him throw up. He said there were guys inside they called "chicks with dicks." I didn't press for details, because I could imagine them and I didn't want to hear him lie to my face.

He had asked me to bring him some money, to put on his books for smokes and sundries. As we sat there, he asked me to slip him the cash. I was a little bit stupid, or a lot naïve, as I had expected to handle this through prison channels. But okay, I decided, and I secretively passed him a hundred-dollar bill. It took me a second to understand what was going on. His eyelids fluttered and his breathing turned halted as he evidently inserted the rolled-up bill, to judge by the painful blinking look on his face, into his ass.

He did most of his prison time for violating parole for various and relentless drug-related offenses, like boosting, or shoplifting, credit card forgery, and possession of a controlled substance for sale. A rap sheet of his that I unearthed, dated March 13, 1986, goes on for pages, with arrests noted in El Cerrito, San Leandro, Martinez, San Pablo, Redwood City, Albany, Oakland, Richmond, Concord, Berkeley, Daly City, and San Francisco.

On July 6, 1986, he was arrested once again in El Cerrito at one o'clock in the morning. El Cerrito is a town not far from Berkeley, in Contra Costa County. Coco County, as the felons called it, is a bad place to be arrested. It was supposedly the harshest jurisdiction, reputedly much harsher than Alameda County, where Berkeley and Oakland are located. According to police testimony recorded in the Reporter's Transcript of Preliminary Examination, on November 20, 1986, he was pulled over for a broken light on his license plate. What comes out in the course of vigorous cross-examination of the police officers on the part of John's dogged defense attorney is disturbing. The police got him out of the car without establishing—according to his attorney—probable cause (the broken light was dubious), and they patted him down without his consent, and at some point he took off running. They said they thought he was carrying a gun. As he ran, police said, he discarded dime balloons filled with heroin, twenty-two of them. When the other police cars on duty that night in El Cerrito converged on the scene, they gave chase. And when a cop caught and tackled him, my brother allegedly punched him. They took him to the station. They had found the dime balloons on the street, but they never found any gun. They took no picture of him, which was their usual practice, and they did not explain why they did not follow protocol. In fact, they technically released him, and sent him in an ambulance to the hospital. They said they sent him there because he was having trouble breathing, and that he told them that he was a drug addict with a heart condition. Did he leave the police station, the defense attorney asked, with cuts and bruises all over his face? No, the cop said, he did not. But the real reason, insinuated John's defense attorney, they didn't take his picture before sending him to the hospital is that they beat the living shit out of him.

In the end, he was sentenced to San Quentin Prison. I wrote him off.

The most serious crime he committed that I knew about was one he got away with. He and somebody else (I never found out who) knocked over his old restaurant in Berkeley one night, after closing time. He had a ski mask on his face and a gun in his hand, which he waved around, and he may have hit one of the busboys when he pushed them into the walk-in refrigerator and tied them up. He took the money from the cash register but couldn't break into the safe underneath, where drops were periodically made throughout the night. Evidently, he kept trying a combination on the safe, but without luck. As the restaurant owner himself told me, it so happened he had changed the combination on the safe that week. All indications were, then, that it was an inside job, my brother working with somebody on the inside. The busboys said they knew it was John, and they were mad he hit one of them. In any case, the police made no arrests, assuming correctly, I suppose, that it was a family problem. John took some money, not a whole lot, and he got out without being shot. He also told me that his gun was not loaded.

Then, years later, that restaurant owner was pleased to be a guest at John's happy wedding. John had a way with people. People wanted to forgive him. I could understand the inclination.

Years after Nevada, before the wedding, I got a call at the school where I was teaching telling me that I should get down to the ER at Highland Hospital in a hurry. John was bad off. When I arrived, some of his posse were there. But they weren't family, so I needed to assert myself, which I did. I was let into the ER and briskly met by a doc in green bloodied scrubs.

The ER physician had the look you never want to see in a hospital, a look you recognize even if you have never seen it before. The Highland Hospital stare. I had seen that grave look before, when people wanted you to hold your breath and not move till they finished what they had to say because you were about to hear something you were not going to like.

"You're family of John Di Prisco?"

"Brother."

She pulled me to the side. She was giving me the no-time-for-bullshit, the-emergency-room-is-packed-so-just-listen-the-fuck-up attitude. "This is the worst case of dehydration we have ever seen, and that's from somebody who did two tours in Nam."

I was not completely understanding where this was going, but if what she said constituted an unusual circumstance at Highland Hospital, which was smack in the middle of the warzone of Oakland, then this was serious.

"Okay." That was half a question and half a statement of resolve. She answered the question and discounted the fake resolve.

"Because you need to get yourself ready."

"Okay."

"Because he's probably not going to make it."

"Okay," I said again, which was my way of saying I knew that, I had been knowing that for years. I knew that when he was sleeping downstairs in the lobby of my apartment house. When he was crashing in the VW Bug I gave him. When his fingernails were caked with dirt, when his face was picked over with scabs. When he was shooting into a vein in his leg because his arms resembled moonscape. I knew it, I knew it, I knew it.

But she was telling me with her eyes, *No, you don't, you have no idea what awaits you.* She led me behind the curtain.

There was John, skinnier than ever, loaded onto the gurney like some wounded animal, naked except for a sort of half-sheet functioning as a loincloth. His entire body, head to toe, was a dull, dusky purple, the color of a plum. He acknowledged me with his eyes but could not talk. Drips were flowing into him. He looked lost and sad and helpless, and I was the big brother who could not help him. It was like that time on the penny bridge in Brooklyn when Bobby held him out over the edge, only worse.

"I'm here," I said anyway, and stood by his side for a few minutes. We locked eyes. We were kids again in Greenpoint, frightened by the big guys who were roughing us up, pushing us around that time, but we knew when our brother came home from reform school he would kick their asses, all of them. I wanted to cry, I didn't want to cry. I knew I shouldn't, I knew I couldn't.

I stood there till I was told to go wait in the ER lobby, that more information would be available later. I had watched the TV hospital shows. I obeyed. I waited. Who needed information? I needed a miracle.

After a while, I was called back into the ER.

"He's touch-and-go. We're putting him in ICU." They would find out that he also had endocarditis and pericarditis and phlebitis—infections and all manner of maladies of the heart and the arterial system, all of which were practically inevitable for a junkie's life, and all speedways to mortality.

The next time I saw him, several hours later, he had been transferred upstairs, and he was glassy-eyed and zoned out as well as intubated.

"He can have ice chips if he asks, but no water. The morphine drip is easing him along, so he is going to rest, if he can."

"Morphine?" It was a dumb question, and I knew it. I would be summarily slapped:

"One battle at a time. He's in restraints. The last thing we need is him tweaking, being forced to kick. This is about saving his life."

That was the first of many nights I spent at his bedside.

After a month with a tube down his throat, he was released. Within one week, he was shooting up again. You see, he was addicted to heroin, and nobody understands who isn't addicted to heroin. Life is a dream when you are on heroin. Why would you want to be anywhere else if you could live all day and all night long in a lovely dream? I did it exactly two times, and that was enough to know it was too good to toy with.

★

SO HE SURVIVED HIGHLAND and the aftermath, though I don't know how, and he got married, and was elated that day.

Until one day, when he would never be happy, and never be, ever again.

We had a memorial service and afterward he was cremated. My father wept. My son comforted everybody. My mother was stoic.

In adjacent aisles sat five, maybe six women I knew who had slept with my brother. Two of them sparked, I was told later, one of them saying that Johnny loved her best of all, while the other begged to differ, concluding her rationally presented argument with a friendly "bitch." I sided with the other in this argument. She was tougher, and she was also right. This was the one who once pulled a gun on me, but that is another story. I looked around the room, and there were maybe two hundred people. In his paid-for newspaper obituary, I wrote that if all the people who loved Johnny showed up at his memorial service, we'd have to rent the Oakland Coliseum. He moved people. He was charismatic. He made people feel good to be around him, despite everything. That was a gift he could not ultimately use to his advantage.

In any case, Johnny would have been happy to see the turnout, if such an absurd statement stands the test of meaning anything. But that is the crazy thing about death—everything I say about it makes me feel stupid.

★

DESPITE THE FACT THAT my wife did her utmost to be a good daughter-in-law, my mother was mostly having nothing to do with the marriage. A few years after the maternally ignored nuptials, mother and son had a bitter exchange on the phone when she complained that I was working against her on the resolution of my older brother's estate. As far as I was concerned, my mother was inappropriately taking money (*stealing* is not the word, not technically), at least some of which belonged to somebody else—namely Gary, Eddie's lover and mate of twenty-five years.

"Eddie and Gary lived together, Mom. They were a couple. Eddie was gay." Though, true, Eddie was of a different generation, and kept his orientation private. Not that my mother could have missed that Eddie and his mate shared the same bed.

"Why do people think I don't know he was the word what you said?"

"Because you don't use the word is why."

"What word is everybody so hung up on?"

"*Gay*, Mom. *Gay* would be the word."

"This word has nothing to do with me, this word. People can do what they want."

"He and Eddie were together."

"All I know is that his so-called friend had free rent for twenty-five years."

"Free rent? They were partners, Mom. He wasn't a college roommate."

"Free rent, college roommate, Mister Professore, twenty-five years."

The uncomfortable truth was, Eddie did leave the estate in untidy shape, despite my last-minute attempt to get him organized. When Eddie was lying in his deathbed at NYU Hospital, I brought him and Gary the papers and a local lawyer reference (a college friend, now an attorney in Manhattan, had offered her help) to get matters in order. But nothing was done. And this left open—at least legally—what Eddie's true intention was.

"And another thing," my mother said. "About your wife."

I was dreading when the other shoe would drop.

"I don't appreciate what she is doing, talking to Eddie's roommate."

"She is trying to help."

"Help, my ass."

"What do you think she is doing?"

"Help, my ass."

"You said that already, Mom."

"I think she is a…" And then she went off using crude street-level descriptors I never relayed to my wife, nor hinted at to this day.

"You should stop now, Mom."

She also made some wild charge about Patti's stealing jewelry.

"My wife stole whose jewelry?"

"Don't you worry."

"You losing your mind, Mom? Jewelry? You're talking about stealing jewelry?"

"Jewelry, yes, jewelry," she explained.

"Jewelry?"

"Jewelry is very important in this family," she declared, dispositive as a judge.

That statement was accurate—as accurate as anything else ever said with regard to the Di Priscos. Jewelry was very important indeed in the idea she had of her family. And looking back, I think that this was around the time—2005 or 2006— when the Alzheimer's was beginning to kick in. But she could compensate like mad, and it would be years before she couldn't keep up her guard.

"Stop, Mom. You have to stop."

That didn't work. More *Taxi Driver*. *"You talkin' to me?"*

"You really should stop now, Mom."

More *Raging Bull*. *"Go on, hit me, you little faggot."*

"You have crossed the line."

More *Goodfellas*. *"Funny, how? Do I amuse you? What am I, a clown?"*

I give my mother this much credit. She knew who was writing her material. But she was only getting warmed up. Then she delivered her coup de grâce:

"I had sons who died who loved me. And you? You have never done anything for me."

Click. She hung up the phone. Nest of bees, in the service of their queen.

She had sons who died who loved her and I had never done anything for her.

How does a mother talk like that to a son of hers? I wondered for years afterward. Where and when did she achieve the notion that saying such stuff was her prerogative? Did she care what effect she had? Or did she imagine she had no effect, so she could say whatever she wanted? Maybe that aggressiveness was born of a conviction that her powerlessness gave her the sort of permission disgruntled postal workers take for themselves to deploy automatic weaponry—spread the suffering around, the way it has been spread around her, and in the process achieve the status that she cannot otherwise attain.

She had sons who died who loved her? John, the most sensitive of my brothers, hated both his parents. He said so many, many times, straight and high. Bobby and Eddie, perennially resentful over having been abandoned in Brooklyn, had somewhat different takes. By all accounts, they were both heartbroken when she left them to fend for themselves as teenagers. Nonetheless, Bobby cultivated a sentimental attachment to her, though he was angry that she never fixed his mangled teeth, about which he was always self-conscious. And Eddie, who didn't speak to her for years, regularly said she made him crazed. Even so, on his deathbed, he wishfully assured his partner that his mother would take care of him after he was gone.

Eighteen blissful months of maternal silence followed that phone call, till something like an uneasy peace was brokered by my father, who talked me into coming over to see my mother again by adopting this meager reasoning:

"Joe, lissenname. She don't mean what she says. She's a junkyard dog. A junkyard dog."

As Gary would one day tell me, however: "In some way, your mother killed all three of her sons."

★

FOR DISCUSSION. LET'S BREAK into one group and discuss:
1. I was a bad son.
2. She was a bad mother.
3. She was a bad mother and I was a good son.
4. I was a bad son and she was a good mother.
5. I was a bad son and she was a bad mother.
6. She was a good mother and I was a good son.

Which of those statements is true, if any? Is there a mathematical possibility they could all be true? Or possibly none?

If I could make discriminations among the statements, my calendar would be opened up. I would be done with therapy once and for all—or maybe writing, which would be another problem. Mostly what I felt around her was this: I had disappointed her by being born and staying alive.

★

SHE WOULD LIKELY NOT concur with any of my reasoning.

"I disagree, Mister Professore": that was something she liked to say while squinting her eyes, hitting the extra Italianate syllable with a sarcastic hammer. It is difficult to understand how she missed the fact that I never attained any such professorial status. Or maybe she assumed that high school graduation automatically made you a professor. I could say that I ultimately forgave her for that, but that seems pathetic if not beside the point, and besides, she never asked for forgiveness, never apologized once for anything she did or did not do. Maybe she was no Medea, no Blanche DuBois, no Clytemnestra, no Mama Gertrude, not even a Courtney Love. And maybe she was neither of the Madonnas. But she had plenty in common with each of them.

No, she wasn't some crazed, depressed baby killer who strapped her children in their carseats and drove into a lake or threw them calmly off a bridge. Her damaging designs were subtler. She merely drove her children a little bit insane every single day. And she was my mother. My impossible mother.

"I get along with everybody," she observed about herself—often. Did she believe this, really?

★

SHE KEPT HER SORROWS in a jewelry box. When I came over to visit as she became more ill, I would sometimes catch her by surprise, sitting in her easy chair grasping a pendant, or a necklace, or a ring, cleaning it and polishing it and holding it up to the admiring light. It was transparent that each apparition of a diamond momentarily vanquished her sadness. As she would be the first to tell you, jewelry was very important in the family— and more important in her *idea* of a family.

After she died and her stuff was packed up, some of the boxes made their way to the home of her last living son, the one who had not died yet and who had not done anything for her. Now that she was deceased, her business needed a lot of attention, as did my surviving father, who was soon going to need assisted living and management of all his affairs. That was clearly a matter of time. In the aftermath of her death, and with the disposal of all her effects, there had been concern expressed about that jewelry, of which she was so proud. I was frankly concerned it had been stolen by the usual candidates in that *Zorba the Greek* kind of opportunistic moment—maybe by the help or the hangers-on at the Florida assisted living residence, or perhaps by my half-sister, still nursing grudges over her supposed mistreatment, greedily seeking reparations.

"No jewelry, Dad?" Yes, I savored the irony of the inquiry, but I was managing the estate, so I had a fiduciary duty, didn't I?

"Nothing."

"Come on, Dad. Caza loved her baubles."

"No joolery, I'm saying."

Was my father totally demented now, too? Maybe, but the more he asserted there was no jewelry anywhere to be found, the surer I was that he had pawned it all off. There is practically no place you can go and not be able to play the ponies. I would bet anything he was losing his money on the horses in Florida.

There were many boxes shipped my way, including many containers of junk. Whose idea was a box of nothing but empty picture frames? And yet, what a perfect image. All this along with various legal documents, bills, certificates, memorabilia. The caregiver in Florida looked and looked, but found no jewelry, and everybody was resigned to the loss. Still, boxes were packed and shipped to California, since they had to go somewhere.

Day after day, new packages arrived, boxes inside boxes. Toiletries, clothes, ceramics, CDs, etc. There was a box of ceramic statues, called Hummels, supposedly very valuable, clearly the former property of her favorite child, Eddie. Piles of unorganized photos. Unexpectedly, too, there were torn-out newspaper book reviews written by me, along with a couple of cut-out articles about me.

Then there arrived, inside a big box, a smaller, heavily wrapped shoebox. In large, bold, red-felt-tip-pen letters, it was labeled *Ammunition*. This was curious. Yes, my father liked his Smith & Wessons, so ammunition of all types was also very important in this family. But weren't all his handguns disposed of when they moved into the assisted-living residence, which was the law in Florida, as it should be everywhere, including places dedicated to non-assisted living? Well, maybe the ammunition was being retained for a future application.

I opened the box, and there it was: in place of ammunition was a trove of jewelry, some of my mother's missing things. There were rings and gold chains and earrings and a few strings of pearls. Some of it was very beautiful indeed. There was also Eddie's purple amethyst ring, which he used to wear all the time. Maybe this find did not constitute the entirety of her jewels, but it was enough to remember her by. More importantly, the small cache of jewelry would be symbolically sufficient to dispense over time to her grandchildren and great-grandchildren, because, like it or not, as I kept learning and re-learning, jewelry *was* very important in this family.

Fortunately, nobody had stolen the box mislabeled *Ammunition*, yet it did raise a conceivably impossible-to-answer question. It made me wonder if there had been another box, that one labeled *Joolery*, which somebody light-fingered away. It was possible. Then later, when the thief ripped it open, hoping to find the Elgin Marbles, or at least a Cartier watch, he might have discovered inside some unused ordnance. In which case, maybe my father's ammunition came to good use, after all. *You lookin' for the jools? I gotcha jools right here.*

What are the odds that was the scheme? That my father had created this diversion, this false lead? When it came to my family, the odds were never easy to calculate. But whatever the plans might have been, the sparkling results were satisfying to contemplate. Fingering the baubles, I got a hint of the pleasure my mother might have felt polishing those jewels by herself. And as for Caza's son, I found myself moved by the sight of Eddie's amethyst ring. I wear it to this day and think of my brother. Evidently, jewelry was important to me as well.

★

ALL MY MOTHER'S PLEASURES were fleeting. Maybe they are that way for everybody. She unfailingly conveyed the sense that whatever was happening around her was insufficient. You could have done better, she communicated, if you tried harder. How you could have done better was not articulated, but it was clear. If she was at a gathering, she made you feel that there was a better party happening elsewhere, to which she was not invited—and you were to blame. No matter what you did for Christmas, there was a better Christmas not happening for her. I understand this point of view. Truth is, to my mortification, I catch myself sometimes thinking along the same lines.

Nonetheless, I wish she had been happier for the rest of her life—not that I could have made that happen, and not that I would know what happiness would look like for her, exactly. And not that *she* didn't think I ought to at least *try* a lot harder to make that happen. Maybe that's why it's called a wish.

With her Brooklyn heart steeped in Greenpoint and her Polish soul shipped from Warsaw, she was not called to a life of joy. Well, how many of us are? Still, nobody ever accused my mother of being a Pollyanna. Though the downside to that disposition is obvious (you miss out on a lot), there's a slight upside, too. The appeal of sentimentality, for one thing, is limited, and that can be healthy. I myself would never prove to be a Mister Positron or a weekend corporate retreat leader, either, and I never pretended otherwise. She liked to think she fooled people, that people thought she was a happy-go-lucky girl, and though hers may have been a convincing performance for some, I was not deceived for one second.

In her son's precious memory, however, it is still and always a rare, beautiful Brooklyn night and my mother is still lovely, still going out to paint the town the color of my balloon and her dress. The world is very sweet but also very sad, because a broken heart is contagious for a little boy. Nonetheless, I will never forget that evening, when I created a work of art at the kitchen table for her and she was fleetingly pleased. If you think that is maudlin, you are wrong.

I hope my mother had a wonderful time that autumn night when she was twenty-eight or twenty-nine and wearing a red dress and I desired nothing more than that the big, bright world be nice to her. That was when I showed her the picture I was making for her, and she said she loved it, or something to that effect, and *my* heart was healed, if not hers, and life would be wonderful from now on, at least for one night.

Snow in the Mountains

IF MY MOTHER DID my first remembering for me, my father did my first forgetting.

Forgetting can be a professional skill, and selective amnesia—under oath or not, as the occasion required—was indispensable in the lines of business my father pursued. Without a doubt, for somebody in my dad's position, remembering details can amount to a risky proposition, depending on the identity of the interrogator. Not to mention that, with regard to the horses, you needed to forget as soon as possible the rough days, the bad beats at the track, otherwise you would go nuts. Which is not to say the man did not periodically go nuts. He did.

As for a boy like me, there was a lot to learn before I would have to forget, so I kept asking questions, sensing I didn't have all the knowledge I needed. I was sure of one thing, and it was painful to acknowledge: that there were things I needed to know that others determined I didn't need to know. My indiscriminate, relentless questionings were the equivalent of carpet-bombing everybody within reach, the ignorant and not-so-ignorant alike, from the high two- to the low three-digit IQ'd pilots who wandered into my airspace.

Other boys in the neighborhood had cowlicks, or crooked teeth, or a stutter. I was another sort of boy: I had a bad case of the curiosities. Popey's son always wanted to know. I always wanted to know the whats, the whos, and the wherefores. My never-ending questions were predictably met with a look of fatigue and why-you-gotta-keep-bustin'-my-balls dismay. I was the sort of boy who made others wish fairy tales and clouds had never been invented, along with birds and baby Jesus and so on. Thankfully, there were "cyclone-opedias," which was how my father referred to fat reference books, intellectual resources I ought to consult for answers, preferably right the fuck now.

"Where you goin?" "What's that word mean?" "How does that work?" "Can I try that?" I didn't care if nobody wanted a piece of me. I was an insufferable child.

Hey, go ax the liberrian.

Who wansta know?

Who you, a cop?

You gonna get a smack, canchoo see I'm tryin' ah watch TV?

Whaddayou, writin' a frickin' book?

That last one stuck for me, because that was a stand my father particularly liked to take. Apparently, my father didn't want to know too much, and he wasn't keen on anything going inside the covers of a book. And it was funny later to contemplate that he was indeed interested in a whole other sort of book, as in *making book,* taking bets. He worked a long time for and around the local books. Much later in life, briefly, I managed to get him to talk about his work.

"Did you answer the phones?"

"No."

"You were the bagman?"

"Tough guys collect."

"Ever get arrested?"

"No."

"Never?"

"Never. One time. I was sixteen. They paid me for taking the pinch for a book. Judge took one look at me, threw the case out, he knew I wasn't the brains ah the operation. I was a sixteen-year-old kid."

"You were prepared to go to jail for this guy?"

No response.

"So what did you do for the book?"

"We shook down other bookmakers stepping onto our turf."

"How did you do that?"

"Geez, that was a long time ago."

Not long after that judge threw out the case against him, he enlisted in the Coast Guard and joined the war effort. The beautiful black-and-white 8x10 photos of him in his dashing dress whites still exist to prove it, along with a jitter-bugging turn with some spicy Brazilian girl in Rio.

"What was the war like for you?"

"I was a fireman in the engine room."

That sounded dangerous.

"We ran the dice games on the ship, stole what we could."

"Anything else?"

"In Italy, these Italians tried to get us to pay to sleep with their sister."

"And?"

"That wasn't right. We didn't do it."

Facts were normally too few to go by. Even so, the incontrovertible fact of my dad's profession hardly explains why I wondered a lot about books, and where they came from. That search for books, for reading, was simple enough. Books came from the liberry where all the liberrians hung out supposedly waiting for your freakin' questions, and the liberrians were unrelated to the barbarians running amok in Brooklyn and on the Italian side of my family. But first of all, I wondered why people wouldn't share the immense wealth of information they presumably had at their disposal about clouds and birds and Jesus and baseball, and all the other subjects of my inquiries.

A sad day dawned. Maybe these people didn't actually *know* the answers to the questions posed. Maybe they weren't holding back out of a lack of generosity, but out of a knowledge deficiency, which condition they had to brush off with the back of their hand: *Whaddayou, writin' a frickin' book?* That was their way to plead for mercy, by punching out—oldest play in the world. And then it occurred that maybe—could it possibly be that I was smarter than all these people? That was one truly terrifying proposition. If so, there were dire consequences. Nobody under ten wants to be the smartest person in the room, or wants to believe he's the smartest person in the room. If that were so, that meant there was one person I could count on for the answers to my questions. That's about the time my questions came to an abrupt halt—when I discovered that nobody else could satisfy my curiosity. I had to learn for myself.

★

MY FATHER TOOK MY mother, both of them in their eighties, to Florida because that was where her daughter lived. Her Alzheimer's was now in full bloom, not that my father acknowledged the condition as such.

The day it first clicked for me that she was losing it, my parents were sitting at their kitchen table, about five years before. "Are you growing a beard?" she asked me.

Except for a short stint working in a restaurant that was fussy about facial hair, I have had a beard for several decades. It had been a grizzly-bearish beard in college, gradually tapering over time, shading from Miami Vice in the eighties to metrosexually clean for the nineties to the current it's-good-enough-to-go-out-in-public. So her question was weird, but it turned odder when her husband stepped in to help: "Joe grows a beard when he's not teaching in the summer." I had stopped teaching long ago, so my father's explanation was absurd.

The psychological term for my parents' relationship might be "enmeshment," a word that is no fun to say and not much more fun to see in action. My parents had always been enmeshed. Entangled. Entrapped. Ensnared. Caught up in each other, consciously as well as unconsciously, compensating for each other and decompensating for each other, too.

Florida was their latest, and possibly saddest, great escape. According to the plot my father never articulated but implied, *the daughter* could take care of her mother. If this was his grand scheme, and whether or not it was conscious or unconscious, this was another big idea that had no legs. Alice had come into possession of the house next door to hers when the man who used to live there died and bequeathed her the title—or so she told me. This story of magical property transfer always sounded suspicious to me. In any case, her mother was welcome to move into this house, but the daughter had ground rules. She did not cook. She did not clean. She would visit when she could, and would certainly look out for her mother, but her days were reserved for bingo. Alice also offered to rent them that house, at what turned out to be way above-market rates. At first it must have sounded perfect for somebody like my father, always looking for a slice of disappointment—especially because the part about above-market rent didn't become clear till later. This plan was destined to end disastrously.

When my parents eventually needed to be moved to assisted living across town, I made arrangements. Relations between daughter and mother had spectacularly deteriorated, and my parents insisted I not tell my half-sister where they were going. When I informed Alice that they had moved out, she was incredulous. Though she claimed she was keeping an eye on their welfare, as she'd said she would, she had completely missed this development—and the moving truck next door. Then she complained about the lost rent.

After hanging up with me, she called the local Florida police, who contacted me in California. Suddenly *I* was being investigated for perpetrating senior abuse, and they put out a national alert for the two missing senior adults with dementia. They wanted to know if my father possessed firearms and if he was dangerous, as Alice had advised them. (In Florida, they were questioning gun possession? *Florida?*) They demanded to know my parents' whereabouts. They said my half-sister was concerned for my mother's safety after she abruptly left the house—the house, she told the cops, supposedly provided rent-free to her mother and stepfather. They threatened to have me arrested in California. I had doubts as to their competence. Actually, I had doubts they had ever watched a single episode of *Law & Order*. If they had performed even elementary police work, they might have called my parents' phone. Had they done so, the phone company robot recording would have given them the new number, at their new residence.

★

MY PARENTS FIRST ARRIVED in Florida, eighteen months before that inevitable debacle, on the March day that Bobby died in his hospital bed in Coney Island.

I know the date because Aunt Susie called me on my cell phone. I was in my room in a Gramercy Park hotel. This hotel was so ultra-hip you needed a flashlight to navigate the corridors and locate the elevator. The menus might as well have been printed in Braille. When she called I was looking for more lights to switch on while making arrangements for my brother's funeral.

"Poor Bootsy," Aunt Susie lamented, referring to Bobby by his boyhood nickname.

Bobby had seemed to let go of his life the instant Patti and I arrived at the hospital from California and did what we could to help our nieces cope with the inevitable. Jennifer and Katherine— those two soulful, beautiful, smart, industrious young women— helped me more than I could ever help them, however.

My aunt and I had some connection. She reminded me that when she herself was once sick, I, age eight or nine, had asked the priest to pray for her. The two of us also went for a walk around

Winthrop Park that cold day we buried Eddie. We talked about how good Eddie always was to her, how he visited her every Sunday.

"Joseph, what is wrong with your father?"

I didn't ask if she was writing a book. I didn't have the energy to cover that ground.

"I called your mother in Florida, and he wouldn't put Caza on the phone. Why is your father such a barbarian?"

The sisters evidently shared the same weakness for the word "barbarian," though my father did not need to wield a double-blade ax or sport long Conan locks to earn the moniker. The answer to my aunt's barbarian question is that my father did stuff like that. Protective instinct? Maybe. Controlling instinct? Possibly, but what a vague catch-all so-nineties concept. Come on, who *isn't* controlling? Name one person anywhere who, all things considered, didn't want it his or her own way?

The truth is that my father was, for lack of a better word, thwarted. His development was stunted. You didn't need to be a psychiatrist to diagnose this. Maybe it had to do with the childhood cellar beatings, maybe he was a borderline personality. And sure, my father systematically denied my mother access to the world, to others, out of fear and out of deep-seated insecurity. And Mom and Dad—the two of them were a pair, enmeshed. She liked to paint the picture of herself as the victim of her husband's "antisocial tendencies," another pet phrase of hers. This idea was supposed to explain why people did not come over to their house, as in pretty much ever. But she was complicit, of course. Representative exchange:

"Caza, you going anywhere this weekend?"

"Going *where*?" Fresh out of Brooklyn, as in a mere forty years ago, her "where" contained a solid two, sometimes three syllables, the final one of which was "ya."

"Where are we going?" she continued without a smile. "We don't *socialize*." *Socialize* dripped with mock affectation. You could practically see her pinky lift up.

Aunt Susie wouldn't let it go. "Then your father said to me, 'Don't believe anything Joseph says.' Why would he say that about you—'Don't believe anything Joseph says'?"

I could see why he would tell Aunt Susie that. In the interest of full disclosure, my father does not stand alone in that regard.

"Your father put Caza on the phone for two seconds, then he grabbed the phone."

I talked with Aunt Susie about Bobby for a while, and Bobby's girls, and how I felt surprised to feel alone now, now that all my brothers were gone.

"Joseph, what are you saying?"

Bobby was dead, Eddie was dead, Johnny was dead.

"What do you mean, Joseph?"

Then I realized that she did not know about John.

"Johnny Cake?"

"Yes."

"Cake is dead?"

"Aunt Susie—you didn't know. Sorry to tell you like that."

"When?"

"Four years ago."

"All the times I talked to Caza, she never told me, never. What is wrong with these people?"

★

WHEN IT CAME TO smooth moves of any sort, my father was no Fred Astaire. On at least three occasions, against doctor's orders the man removed from the hospital his elderly wife, suffering from progressive dementia and congestive heart failure. The last time, he took her home and lodged her in her bed. The post-hospital equivalent of "We'll see." His wife required round-the-clock care, and he wasn't going to provide it. He didn't want to be in the hospital, and he didn't want anybody else in the house. Whenever I hired help for my mother, he fired them within days, if not hours.

One time my father stood in the hall with two of her pills on a tissue in one hand, a glass of water in the other. He was trying to demonstrate that he was being responsible, caring. He looked pathetic. It was an unconvincing demonstration of his solicitude, and the situation was dire.

"Are you trying to kill my mother?" I asked. And she looked like death, with her skin gray, her eyes dim as pewter, her lips dry and thin as rice paper, her body lifeless as a bag of bird bones under the covers.

By way of reply, my father strung along the usual curses and denunciations.

"If you're not trying to kill her, then you're the stupidest man on Earth."

Having no other choice, I got others involved, hired a care manager, and embarrassed my father into transporting his wife in an ambulance to the rehabilitation center—a quasi-hospital that provided constant care, which is what she needed. That's where she got the attention that kept her, for a while, alive.

★

DO YOU THINK YOU'RE dying, sir?

Sometime before that Gramercy Park hotel stay and Bobby's death, I had to make a medical appointment of my own in California. I couldn't recall ever feeling so sick before. A wheezing man on blood-pressure meds, I described my symptoms to the advice nurse, and I detected concern ratcheting up exponentially on her side of the phone, and simultaneously ratcheting up on mine. That's what the nurse asked:

"Do you think you're dying, sir?"

What desperation she must have detected in my drama-queen voice. I had practiced the role before. In my early-forties I was diagnosed with trigeminal neuralgia, which is paroxysmal, shooting facial pain. Think out-of-the-blue ice cream headaches to the nth power. The heavy duty epilepsy-drugs knocked me out but didn't help as much as acupuncture and Chinese herbs, which was fortunate because the next option was brain surgery. Here's a curiosity. Turns out that trigeminal neuralgia enjoys literary cachet. It's not on par with "consumption," but a close reading of Melville and Nabokov, my go-to authors, reveals that both Captain Ahab and Humbert Humbert were afflicted by this lightning-bolt-to-the-brain condition—then called *tic douloureux*. The pairing of the White Whale- and the Lo-obsessed seems less surprising the more one thinks about it.

Years after that I was leveled for six months by debilitating pain caused by spinal bone spurs, but from the MRIs, which are fascinating to me, I will spare you. When the conventional medical protocols failed, I consulted with a specialist in alternative, New-Agey therapies. Popping Percodan, Soma, and Valium all day gets old. You try anything. On the massage table, after a couple of hours' treatment, I felt her kind, knowing hands on my back as she compassionately remarked: "You remind me of another patient."

Maybe that was a good omen.

"Yes, he was a fireman… He had been electrocuted…"

But back to that advice nurse's question. Did I think I was dying? I did not hear the quiz show music in the background, so I knew I could take all the time I needed.

The inquiry must have been indicated by the nurse's handy manual, but I had never before been asked as much in quite that way. And I speak as someone who has been asked lots of very direct questions in my life, including some thrillingly direct questions I recall with a physiologically frissonish fondness for which there must be a perfect French expression. Nonetheless, where to begin with "Do you think you're dying?" In Theology class, had I been asked, I would have generated a Theology class answer.

On this occasion, all I could utter was: "What else do men like me think about?" I might have added: "Besides Penelope Cruz?"

I could have said much, much more, such as, "Are you implying there are people my age who don't think about dying?" As I had already learned from my father, and from all the other Brooklyn boys of summer, whenever possible, and sometimes when not, answer a question with another. On this occasion, I did not go on to amplify thus:

"And I ask, kind and competent and caring advice nurse, because I don't think I would want any of those people to take my vitals or drive next to me on the freeway or give the homily at Mass. And my regret is that I didn't start thinking about dying before tonight—though that's not true, because thoughts of mortality have never been very far from my mind, certainly not since as long as I can remember remembering. I had lots of excellent practice in this regard as a very good Catholic boy praying every night while kneeling beside my bed: And if I die before I wake, I pray the Lord my soul to take."

The advice nurse told me to hang up the phone, she would call back in a minute. She was going to consult with the attending.

So, do I think I am dying?

No, I know so.

See? We Catholics invented the subject—though Jews can make a case, too, I suppose. No wonder we're experts. We're very good on the dying question. It's with the living we Catholics can have a tough time. But to quote Saint Thomas More, nobody on his deathbed regrets being Catholic. Something tells me, however, that the same might not be said with regard to other times spent in bed.

To finish this anecdote, the advice nurse called back and asked to speak with my wife, for a reality check I suppose, and afterward the nurse decided I should come in tomorrow morning first thing.

When I went in, they did an EKG.

Here's one word you don't want to hear on a first date or when somebody is describing your heart rhythm: abnormality.

Even when it is meekly qualified—as in *slight* abnormality. Slight heart attack? Not helping very much. Next thing I knew I was surrounded by grave-countenanced people in scrubs and whisked down to the ER in a wheelchair.

Once there, I immediately chomped on the bitter aspirin pill the way you're supposed to. Swiftly I was stripped and gowned, my belongings tossed into a plastic bag. I was PICC-lined and tested and tested and poked and poked and scanned and scanned some more by good and competent people. Hours and hours and hours later, it was determined I was not really having a heart attack, and I could go home right after making an appointment to see a cardiologist ASAP.

Here's your heart, what's your hurry? But folks, we're not going to let him leave the show empty-handed. There was a consolation prize.

"Congratulations, you are part of the great pandemic now," the nice ER doctor said. I had the swine flu. Oh, well, considering the alternative, that was, as my MBA friends like to say, a good value proposition.

Let's back up. What's the first question a genuine philosopher must ask himself: Why haven't you committed suicide? Which is related to another proposition: Call no man happy till he is dead, as the Greek philosopher once said. Always count on a Greek philosopher to stop a party in its tracks. Not being naturally inclined to philosophy, I have read nonetheless a few of the books.

My mother's famous internist had a certain implicit formula pertaining to what the experience of a writer was or should be. Have enough pain and acquire a crazy parent, commit suicide. That's what makes a writer a writer? Torture? Misery? There must be happy writers. There must be, no?

Would I trade in my experiences for a placid life in the suburbs? Who says the suburbs are placid—not that I would know, but never mind. We are given what we are given. Some of us translate this experience into writing. If we are lucky, we are read by others. If we are really fortunate, we make art, we make something beautiful, once or twice in the course of a lifetime.

Stories happen to people who can tell them. I guess the question becomes: What is the connection between experience and writing, or between what happened and what is imagined? This is a dangerous question to be posing inside a memoir. Another way to ask the question is, what would be the ideal experience for a writer? There is no template, and I throw up my hands. I have no idea. The barest familiarity with the history of literature (and by that I mean writers) reveals that great writers have been rich, poor, middle income, and every other variation. Gay, straight, bi, transgender, experimenting, confused, uncertain, unwilling to declare, bondaged, celibate, and everything else. Black, white, brown, yellow. They cross political lines and inclinations. All religions and all manner of non- and un-believers. This catalogue can continue into infinity, but the point is a trite one. Great writers come in all packages. Some of them kill themselves. Some of them we have never read, never heard of.

I have been talking about great writers. But what about somebody like me: minor poet, novelist famous for his obscurity?

I wish I were in a position to know.

All a writer has is all he's got. A good deal of which he has appropriated from somebody else. Or even from himself, if that makes any sense, which it does and doesn't. He's a cat burglar and a bank robber, a hired assassin and a drive-by shooter, a carjacker and a credit-default-swap immanager. All the while, he lies to himself that he is invincible.

John Ciardi once wrote that going to high school provided enough experience for a lifetime of poems. He ought to know. And Henry James contended that a young lady passing the open window of a military barracks had all the experience necessary to write a novel. That sounds right to me, and who would argue with that proposition, particularly as applied to the work of Henry James, which is largely unreadable, for me anyway, with the exception of *Portrait of a Lady*, which is not as good as most of Edith Wharton. Still, I can see what that imaginary young lady might have seen through that stolen glimpse of the barracks. We all have stolen glimpses. In the glimpse derby, stolen is always the best horse in the race. And all experience is enough. More than enough. Any experience is a potential opening into the infinite. For we all learn the same lesson from life: that life and suffering are conjoined. We grasp early on that life is about loss, and the lesson is confirmed and reconfirmed continually through each heartbreak. Perhaps life is nothing but loss. With each passing day that ends up not being the last day, this notion ceases to sound mysterious. It sounds like common sense. And that recognition makes joy—as fleeting, momentary, elusive, unwarranted, undeserved, as surprising as it is—possible and possible all over again.

Which is what I get for trying to answer an advice nurse's good question.

★

TELEPHONE CONVERSATION, DAY AFTER Thanksgiving 2008:
"Dad, I called you ten times yesterday." I was not exaggerating the number of attempts I made to reach him in Florida. "You hear me? Ten times I called you. How was Thanksgiving?"
"Who's this?"
"Your son." He has one alive at this point.
"Who?"
"Your son!"
"Who!"
"Your son!"
"Why you yelling?"
You can never tell when the man cannot hear you, or when he does not want to hear you, or when he does not know what is going on, or when he is stalling for time to gather his wits enough to

misdirect you. At that point he was eighty-two, but this type of evasive conversation has been going on for as long as anybody remembers.

"It's Joe."

"Who?"

I repeat my name for my father to hear.

"Joseph?"

"Yes."

"*Yeah*," he says, with a tone of vague recognition, as if he were coming out of a deep sleep, which he probably wasn't, though admittedly this can be difficult to determine. This *yeah* is his warmest sort of greeting, his subtlest conversation marker.

I tell him again that I called ten times yesterday. Was I attempting to alleviate filial guilt? If I possessed any of that rare commodity, it was kept in a hidden, unconscious place. Those days I was more irritated than guilty. Was I trying to impress with dutiful-son behavior? If so, that would also be unconscious. Maybe I was filling up the air being on the telephone, calling because calling is better than not calling, though I am not sure why.

"You called?"

"Yes, I did." News flash.

"Maybe I wasn't in the apartment."

"*Maybe* you weren't in the apartment, *maybe*?"

"Maybe I didn't feel like picking up the phone," my father says. Ah, the truth slips out.

"How come you didn't feel like picking up? I phoned you ten times."

"I was fuckin' down in the dumps."

"Why were you down in the dumps, Dad?"

"Nobody fuckin' calls."

★

THAT WAS NOT MY father's idea of making a joke. Though true, he could remind somebody of Harry the Horse or Big Jule from *Guys and Dolls*, or any number of Elmore Leonard mouthy walk-ons. For instance, from another telephone conversation:

"Whadda youse guys doin' today?"

"Patti is out doing some volunteer gardening for the Shakespeare theater."

"Volunteer garden, huh? How much she get paid?"

Then one thankfully uneventful Thanksgiving, everybody was sitting around the table at the end of dinner feeling full from the *turkey à la tryptophan* and the stuffing and the wine. My father was getting visibly antsy, and he was sending obvious hand signals to his wife it was fast approaching time to go. But somebody began to hold forth expectantly and exuberantly and drunkenly about how nice the dinner had been to start the holiday season. You know. Oh, the holidays! How Thanksgiving was the *first* holiday, and then Christmas was the *second* holiday, and then New Year's was the *third* holiday...

My father, as if on cue, rose up from the table. He stood there for a moment before he tossed his napkin onto the seat of his chair and, in lieu of sharing social niceties or expressing thanks, he declared:

"One down! Two to go!"

My parents fled.

My father was always adept at evasions. He mastered a signature type of rhetorical dodge.

His grandson Mario once asked him an innocent question as Super Bowl weekend was approaching: "Gramps, you going to watch the game?"

"There's snow in the mountains."

Thus spake Mario's grandfather, shaman from the remotest elevations of mystic Park Slope.

"Uh-huh, but are you going to watch the game?"

"Snow, in the mountains."

And his grandson said, "There's fish in the sea, too, Gramps."

"*Who?*"

"What do you mean, there's snow in the mountains?" But the grandson understood the terms of their rhetorical byplay. He knew his grandfather was no transcendental master. But with this unofficial weather report he thereby implied much, namely that he was thinking about going to Tahoe to watch (and bet) the game, but that he had to think through the complications because he might get stuck in the Sierra drifts.

As opposed to his entire life's non-embrace of strategic planning, when it came to gambling jaunts, my father employed a literal exit strategy. When he drove the family up to Tahoe to gamble for a weekend, a customary jaunt, he made certain he would be able to leave if the wheels came off his junket and he tapped out. So before we checked into a motel (if, that is, we checked into a motel), he drove straight to a gas station and filled up his tank. He wanted to make sure if he busted out, he'd at least be able to eat the steering wheel the whole way home.

I have another, very different early childhood recollection connected to my father's driving. The man was by all measures a pretty decent driver, but the memory in question is the time when we were getting on the expressway, on the entrance ramp, probably on Long Island, and we were rear-ended. It didn't seem all that violent a collision and apparently none of us were hurt— except for my father. The man went limp in the front seat. He wouldn't budge and he started moaning. His tears were flowing. An ambulance arrived and he claimed to be in excruciating pain. They transported him to the hospital, which is where his wife and sons later met up with him. He uttered the word "whiplash" a couple of times, and this was before seatbelts, so maybe that was a proper diagnosis. Maybe he was indeed hurt. Or maybe he was laying the groundwork for an insurance settlement bonanza— not that this moneymaker was explained and not that any child would have understood the stratagem. I didn't know for sure what was going on, or if my father was in extremis, but that in itself constituted the real news, and it was the same old news. I could never know for sure if my father was hurt or not, lying or not. Later on that day, on the hospital gurney, the man didn't appear any worse for wear.

My father's teary speechlessness in the car by the side of the road that time is strangely reminiscent of a far different occasion. That was the night he was being feted at his Teamster retirement dinner. By all accounts, he had done a terrific job, first as a union business agent, and then as secretary-treasurer (effectively the chief executive officer) of his union local of milk drivers. He had handily won nine consecutive elections, no small feat, and he had clearly found a calling later in life. He was widely respected, loved by what the union organizers like to term "the rank-and-file." In fact, his personal cause was the drug-and-alcohol rehabilitation programs that the Teamsters had created. He steered many a strung-out man and woman into a program, some of whom managed to save their jobs and their families. He also used his juice to get his son John a dairy job at least twice, with excellent pay and benefits that had been negotiated by him. Both times, John was soon-enough fired, caught using or being wrecked on the job. It is plausible to make the connection between the rehab programs my father invested himself in and the hopes he had for that son, hopes never realized.

On the night of the grand retirement dinner, more than a hundred Teamsters showed up, everyone spruced up in coat and tie, along with the Teamster brass, in the banquet room of a spaghetti-and-meatball joint on the Oakland waterfront illuminated by fluorescent tubes of light. My father had made sure his family was in attendance, too. He was feeling proud of what he had accomplished.

The big moment, the moment we were all waiting for, arrived. He was introduced effusively by the master of ceremonies, the most powerful Teamster boss in town. My dad stepped up to the mic to enthusiastic applause. He stood there at the podium and gathered himself. He rustled the pages he had worked on with his grandson, and with me.

He cleared his throat. He stood there. He stared down at the podium.

He rustled the pages some more.

He stood there.

He cleared his throat.

He stared down at the podium.

He rustled the pages.

Tick tock, tick tock.

A minute of silence at the podium feels longer than dairy products' shelf life.

He stood there and looked down and rustled the papers some more. He had spoken publicly often during his election campaigns, and he had won the votes and hearts of the electorate. Tonight was different.

From the Teamster throng rose up heartfelt cries of support: "It's okay, Joe. You can do it." Then there was warm spontaneous applause, intended to encourage him to relax. Mario called out to his grandfather, "It's okay, Gramps."

He stood there.

He was never going to be able to speak. He was too choked up. The master of ceremonies rose up and gently grasped him by the shoulder and said something like "That's okay, Joe." He physically led him back to his seat on the dais. Up there was the man from Brooklyn whom they used to call Popey, because, according to my mother, he never shut the fuck up. Where had Popey gone tonight?

The emcee spoke for a few minutes about this union leader and good man, and he did so with kindness, as if nothing had happened. There was thunderous applause.

Now, Popey's son has trouble throwing stuff out. I am not a hoarder—check that. I am *something* of a hoarder. That's sound reason in itself to move periodically. During a recent relocation, the long-lost word-processed hard-copy text of the speech was rescued. The pages surfaced at the bottom of the hoarder's rummaged file cabinet.

These were the words composed for delivery at that retirement ceremony. Clearly, the speech had been edited, to judge by the few extant examples of the union leader's prose, his composition skills were limited. He certainly didn't type it out. He never learned.

According to the three hundred and forty-two words on the page, he planned to begin by introducing his family. Among other members of his family, his son John was in attendance, surprisingly, along with his fiancée. "I'm not one for making speeches, so bear with me," he pleads, the toastmaster's stock setup.

"I first won election for union office in 1979. This is a very long time ago. In 1979 I had long sideburns. I remember men were wearing leisure suits, though I personally never owned one." Then he makes a couple of timely, witty wisecracks about the current pathetic state of the local pro football teams. "In 1979, my grandson, who helped me with this speech and who is graduating from Georgetown this year, was four years old. So a lot has changed. I have changed." He speaks about his evolving conceptions of the workplace and workforce. "The employer has needs and the members have needs, and it's hard to make everyone happy. So all we can do is try, which is what I did in my years. No negotiation is ever perfect. But in my years of negotiating I have tried to do some good, for I believe there is a dignity in compromise, and it is honorable to work together." Then he rhetorically hands off the baton to his successor, praising him in the process. He assures one and all that the members will be well served by their new leader. "They better be," he says, "because he has their money."

"Finally," he concludes, "I want to say that my life has been full of wonderful surprises and challenges. As a seventeen-year-old sailor on a troop transport in the Atlantic I would never have imagined that I would be standing here before you tonight. So thank you for coming to share this moment with me and my family."

Those three concluding sentences cry out for a hundred footnotes, one of which might be this book. It was a memorable speech, three hundred forty-two words long, even if not one of them was ever articulated.

★

THAT SPRING OR EARLY summer afternoon of 1961, when the FBI would descend on my grandparents' farm, my father was behind the wheel of his 1951 snubnose black Ford, the hood reminiscent of a black sheep's head. We were driving out on the Long Island Expressway to East Islip.

My brother and I were in the backseat, and my mother was in the front, riding shotgun. With its woolen seats, the car never failed to smell like it had rained chicken soup on the dog. That gamey aroma was slightly undercut today, however. By local statute and family convention, we were required to stop at the local Italian bakery to pick up the obligatory box of cannoli and assorted other pastries, including Sfogliatelle, the filled shell-shaped pastry constructed of thinly layered dough—a crispy, custardy delight. That explains why there was also a kind of mouth-watering almondy, powdered-sugary bouquet in the air, along with the heady nutmegginess of the whipped, sweet ricotta pastry filling.

One thing I liked about the trip was that my parents would let me buy some comic books to read. The stories were usually about superheroes or wartime battles. They were pleasurable to read, and they made the time pass so that I didn't have to continually punch my annoying younger brother. Problem was, a half-hour into the ride, I was mostly done with, and bored by, these comic books.

I was always stunned when my parents managed to organize any sort of excursion. If there were ever any arrangements afoot, I never heard in advance. There was never any evidence of planning or anticipation, as in, for instance, conversation on the subject. Every journey appeared to be a burden and a chore for them, or maybe it was the result of a last-minute decision. Almost everything they did seemed to be last-minute, and information was doled out on a need-not-to-know basis. As a result, everything was perennially up in the air, intentions ready to unravel. "We'll see" ruled the day.

Day trips or big moves, everything seemed a challenge. Once my mother took a terminal dislike to an apartment where she and her husband were living. She packed dozens of boxes and stacked them against the walls of the living room. In her signature manner, she was signaling that she wanted to move. The boxes stayed in place for two or three years. So she got the best of both worlds: She was free to complain while at the same time she could be on the slow, slow, slow way out the door.

For an obsessive-compulsive boy like me, my parents' mantra of "We'll see" was maddening. I yearned for some measure of control over my environment, not that I really understood I had such a thing as an environment, because if I knew from environments, I would have said it was my mother's. I badly needed things to have a place. I desperately wanted to know when things would happen, in what order. Given my "We'll see" sort of family, I was destined to feel frustrated. This was different from the Church, where everything was ordered and clear. All right, maybe a touch too ordered and clear. Still, there were rituals that started at certain times. There were beliefs that were universal and true. Jesus never would have said, during his Sermon on the Mount, something like, "Blessed are the peacemakers, for we shall see." Jesus had a plan.

Then there was the vexed matter of the clothes my parents made me wear, a complicated issue for the obsessive-compulsive boy. For one thing, I hated to wear shorts. I didn't care if it was a hundred degrees, I hated shorts. There was an obvious reason. They made me look fatter. I was not merely vain about clothes. I was crazed on the subject. I was miserable. I would weep with helpless rage when my mother made me wear short pants. This did nothing to stop her from putting me in short pants. So that warm day out on the Island, it was a good bet I was in short pants.

A large number of childhood photos of me do not exist, but there is one picture taken on the streets of Greenpoint with me mounted on a pony. The photographer was a type of professional, or at least an entrepreneur with a horse and a flashbulb, and my mother must have paid for the privilege of her son's playing the part of a momentary, hatless cowboy on this stationary, beleaguered beast of burden. I recall that the horse was outside my favorite diner, where we bought "franks." I am in shorts, and the chubby legs resemble dumplings. Meanwhile, the pony looks as if it would rather be anywhere, including a glue factory, than here on the streets of Greenpoint with a chubby boy in the saddle. In the photo, the boy is not smiling. A dead man walking would look more lighthearted. What's there to smile about, the boy seems to be conveying. He looks so glum and beleaguered it is almost possible to imagine his saying, "And the horse you rode in on!" It is a genuine question as to which creature—boy or horse—was the more miserable.

But the non-ride on the horse was not half as interesting as those frankfurters nearby, hot dogs that were delectable. I preferred the frankfurter plain, without condiments like messy mustard or ketchup, which were hard not to get on your hands, face, or shirt, and which were therefore avoided like the occasions of mortal sin. And the frank should be accompanied by a cream soda, maybe a root beer if they didn't serve cream soda. Perhaps I had a milkshake or a malted milk, one made with chocolate ice cream, if life was particularly sweet that day. Maybe a second frank. Maybe that one with kraut, for a change, nestled in a soft, doughy pocket of a bun. You bit into the skin of the juicy, bursting frank and you could almost hear a pop, and the steam rose off and what a feast. A perfect prelude to a knish, which, fortunately for everybody, was being sold down the street in a cart by a man in a paper hat, and maybe my mother would let me have one, or at least a bite of hers when it cooled off enough not to singe the roof of my mouth.

★

DEPENDING ON TRAFFIC, IT took about an hour and a half to get out to the country, otherwise known as East Islip. No population figures exist for the town in 1961.

As for such country roads upon which my father led his two sons for their passeggiata that fateful day the cops showed up, there was a distinct shortage of such thoroughfares in the borough of Brooklyn. This experience dates from a time when country roads still existed on Long Island. This was back in the day when there was lots of open space and woods and tract homes were few and far between—though doubtless soon looming large in the wet dreams of scamming real estate developers.

On this summer day, I am a month or two away from being eleven years old. Johnny would turn ten in mid-September. We were born fifteen months apart. Did I feel like Johnny and I were twins? I heard people make presumptuous remarks along those lines, about which I was mystified. I never felt like anybody was my twin, and not only when the two of us were raining down punches upon each other's heads.

We could not visit the grandparents' farm often enough as far as I was concerned. For one thing, it was my grandparents' *farm*. That meant pigs and rabbits and chickens. That meant a docile or bored-enough donkey whose rough nose the animal allowed me to scratch, which was very amusing, and educational. In summer, the farm also meant achingly chilled watermelon and buttery sweet corn, water pumps being primed and water coming out so cold and fresh, swinging in the hammocks between the trees and afterward sipping iced tea. Walking down the rows of peas and zucchini and bitter curly lettuce, feeling drunk and sick on the DDT in the air, watching the relatives play cards and drink Canadian Club with Coke under the pergola. It meant tomatoes and tomatoes and tomatoes and somehow more tomatoes.

Sometimes I helped my Nonna make tomato sauce, extruding these tomatoes through some medieval torture device, getting high on the fumes and taking horrible delight in all this tomato matter on my hands—not easy for a compulsive being to cope with, but it was all right because Nonna could by definition do no wrong.

I "helped"? More like got in the way. And tomato "sauce"?

Here comes one subject that gets complicated quickly. For contemporary Italian Americans of a certain sophistication, there's *sauce* and there's *salsa,* there's *sugo* and there's *ragu.* Gastronomes and chefs and food culture historians have spent careers delineating the fine distinctions. And these distinctions are significant culinarily—and significant pragmatically when making discriminations in certain restaurants in America and in Italia. For the Di Prisco family, these potentially vexatious distinctions were absolutely, completely, totally irrelevant. If it was red and made with tomato and cooked and poured over pasta, or anything else, it was not sauce, or salsa, or sugo, or ragu. It was *gravy.* And thus it was that the gravy v. sauce battles began between the generations. Back then, however, it was all much simpler.

"More?"

"More?"

"Eat."

"Mang'."

As for Italian food controversies, my extended family also appeared divided on the spoon-twirling question. Some twirled the pasta with the fork against the spoon held in the other hand, while others took their chances freestyling, brazenly and spoonlessly. Southern Italians have traditionally been the leading practitioners of the spoonerish practice. I myself never saw the great advantage of the spoon, and I cannot recall anybody correcting me. Apparently, Emily Post herself once upon a time used to hold forth that using such a spoon constituted proper table manners. Neither I nor my grandfather knew the etiquette books, however, and the Nonno, who reigned over his table like the capo, was a spoon twirler par excellence. You could almost hear the plucked strings of the chitarra or the mandolino as he did.

At the same time, nobody looked down on a boy who ate one-handedly. For beyond all such petty considerations, my Italian grandparents made plain how much they prized their oldest grandson, namely me. I may have been a middle child in my own Greenpoint apartment, but here on the island my half-brothers' existence went unacknowledged, and they never came out to the farm. Here, my playing field was bigger and better, and I was in charge.

Now, being Italian, or Italian American, has its well-documented risks and pitfalls. (See: Cinema, American: History of; also see: Criminal Justice, Organized Crime Division of the Excessively Voweled, History of.) But in real life, being the eldest grandson in an extended Italian family was the next-best thing to royalty. And being a spoiled boy like me, a good student and an altar boy who might wind up a priest someday, I had license to do whatever I wanted whenever I wanted.

"Dad," I asked my father many years later, "did everybody really expect me to become a priest?"

"I heard there was talk." Downtown Popey. He persistently and effortlessly phrased assertions in deniable formulations, even when he wasn't in handcuffs.

I can tell myself the tale that I did not take unfair advantage of this princely status, that I was kind and respectful to aunts, uncles, and all my cousins, unworthy as they indeed were, and I tolerated them despite their social standing inferior to mine, which they were helpless to change. Admittedly, here is one place where I cannot trust my memory a hundred percent.

★

SUNDAY SUPPER WAS A big production. Sausages, chicken, pillowy ravioli, spaghetti, crusty bread, chilled red wine taken out of the refrigerator in pitchers. Nonna was a great cook, and she infused her personality and liberal spirit into the usual menu. As for my grandfather, he would chew loudly and bark out a word from time to time, usually a *No!* to some misbehaver, but he also had an impish side to him, especially as the pitcher of wine got closer to the bottom, and he would smile proudly at his brood gathered around, twelve to eighteen adults and children, eating and gabbing. But the Nonno never really talked much while food was in front of him.

For all his life, my father continued his own father's tradition: he ate without saying a word. In his eighties, he was more monkish at the board than a tonsured monk observing the Great Silence. Was he always self-conscious about speaking at a table? Seems so. But it is a remarkable lifetime's worth of performances. Never saying a word while consuming food. Never never never. Was my father unconsciously repeating the pattern of his own father? Perhaps. It's not that he has terrible table manners, either. In this regard, he is almost courtly.

His grandson once asked him why he never spoke during supper.

"'Cause you could choke."

At the dinner table, my father ate silently, slowly, intently, and gravely. There is likely no connection, but the truth is that for a long time I myself was uncomfortable to the point of apoplexy when in restaurants, at other people's homes, anxious and unsure as to what to say or do near the perilously situated place-settings of glasses and goblets, china and linen, knives and forks.

★

I HAD COUSINS WHO were beautiful. To put this another way: I had some raven-haired, olive-skinned, tiger-eyed, lithe-limbed, rockingly gorgeous cousins. One particular *cugina* lingers in my memory.

When did it occur to me that first cousins were discouraged from marrying? And "marrying" was the term—not the other term, for the time being anyway. This seemed like more than an academic question for a boy possessed of such an overactive fantasy life and such excruciatingly appealing cousins. Maybe I was jumping the gun, but was that really encoded in legal statutes? Or solely in social convention? My older brother probably explained what prohibited the union of first cousins. Not that those minatory and frightening words can be remembered, though the recollection of the images can be swiftly summoned up. Contemplating the progeny of coupling first cousins, gargoylish images would bloom in my mind. These monstrous creations would have three eyes on a head small as a baseball and no available arms to throw one.

Years and years later, when I was in college and visiting my aunt and uncle's house, there was one complicated, exhilarating moment on this score. It was evening, long after dinner, and I was in the guest room, reading on top of the bed, shoes off, of course, but dressed. My cousin…let's call her Olivia, because O is the most alluring, open letter in the alphabet. Olivia nonchalantly hip-swayed in for a bedtime chat. She sat there on the bed in her short-shorts and tank top, and the first cousins talked.

Olivia was in high school, and she was very smart. Maybe she was merely high school smart, but I doubted it. And funny. Maybe not merely high school funny. And intense. No manner of intense is more intense than high school intense. And maybe sixteen or so. Solid fifteen. A very mature fifteen, or possibly with any luck whatsoever sixteen. Probably a good sixteen. Sixteen, almost assuredly, fifteen, long shot. And I was nineteen or so. Nineteen, probably almost assuredly nineteen. And there on the side of the bed—well, she reclined across the bed silkily, stretchily, sketchily.

Can you spell "odalisque," and for God's sake I sure hoped not.

On the side of the bed, with her dark, glimmering, feline eyes—where could she be concealing the poison-licked dagger? Her outfit that evening did not offer one obvious centimeter of sanctuary for a weapon, but she was every bit as dangerous as a Sicilian assassin. Her dad, my uncle, had to be skulking not very far away.

Come on, Olivia, are you fucking crazy?

Her father was right down the hall, and he wasn't going to be the least bit avuncular if he walked in on us. And her perfect cheekbones were delicately sculpted, and her perfect white teeth sparkled, and her perfect lips were like rose petals, and she was like a coruscating diamond, like a cubist painting I had studied in arts survey class. Nobody had given me a glass of wine or two or seven at dinner, either. Cousin Olivia was darkly, deeply beautiful—and then some invisible switch was flipped and she smiled like a rascally angel and a moment of certified madness took place as all the oxygen was instantly sucked out of the guest room, and that was more than okay, because breathing in somebody like her was better than oxygen any day. Then there was a very exploratory kiss, packaged with maximum deniability, and that is when somebody gently, self-consciously laughed, and it may even have been me, and the moment passed, a bit painfully, but sweetly, too.

The music that swelled so tremendously was not exactly *Appalachian Spring*, and that was not exactly a divining rod popping up to make an appearance. Thump thump thump went my pounding heart. Thumpety thumpety thumpety did *not* go the bedboard.

There it was. One of my favorite kisses of all time. It was an illicit, ill-advised, evolutionarily bankrupt, morally suspect, possibly statutorily forbidden kiss I sometimes contemplate with a sort of feral, shamed delight and horror. It was such an amazing kiss, but it never really truthfully happened because it almost never quite technically happened, though it did, and when I remember, it happens sweetly still.

★

So THERE MY LITTLE brother and I were, curiously and suddenly alone on the road in East Islip as our dad scampered into the woods. Where was he going? Why was he running away from something—or someone? Fathers aren't supposed to do that. They are supposed to run *into* battle.

But okay, the father is running away. Into the woods. Which was very bizarre, except for how it also wasn't. On the surface, this logistical maneuver was not consistent with the universal message he had hand-delivered about standing up for yourself. This was his all-purpose admonition and counsel, surely applied to every available circumstance, and it went like this: "Don't take no shit from nobody."

As words of advice go, "Don't take no shit from nobody" doesn't superficially rival doomed Polonius' words of advice to his equally doomed issue, Laertes: "This above all, to thine own self be true blah blah blah." Though maybe they have more in common than it may seem. Then again, Polonius is purely an idiot and a dolt, for all his high-flown, orotund, quotable verbiage. His main flaw, his psychological and theatrical flaw, is that boneheaded Polonius has no grasp whatsoever on his audience (as in this case, his own son), which is a talent Hamlet has in spades. Hamlet's genius lies in seducing everybody from Ophelia to the audience at the theater, which in turn loves him madly and saves him over and over again until it finally kills him in the end. Polonius, on the other hand, is always talking to and for himself. He is not listening, he is pontificating. And as is the case with *Don't-take-no-shit*-etc., Polonius's counsel lacks much in the way of subtlety, or strategy. But it is clear, and it is direct, there is no whiff of pontificating.

As for pontificating, there was the matter of my father's street name: Popey. So let us concede that my dad's *Don't take no shit* was intended to get his sons out of trouble when we were kids. It didn't work all that well, honestly. It is a sort of either/ or proposition, an absolutist stand. Sometimes, it would have been smarter not to have heard something, or to have made a joke of it, or to have walked away. And later on, when I tried to apply the maxim to the challenges of adulthood, it didn't work all that well to get me out of trouble, the sort of trouble that could be avoided by a more supple approach. People don't like either/or. What's more, people give shit to other people all the time. Sometimes whole careers are built around such a shit-giving. So if you have to kick ass every time somebody gives you shit, you would be fighting all the time. You would be subjected to every asshole in the car in the next lane, which I confess is something that's happened to me a few times. Okay, maybe more than a few times. Because yes, that's me getting out of the car to take up a problem somebody seemed to be having with me. "Every puny whipster gets my sword," says Othello, that son of a bitch, and he's right, and that's not the half of it. I endured my share of anger-management issues as a young man, but really, and obviously, it was my fearfulness that made me quick to lose my temper.

Sometimes it seems like it's taken my whole life to unlearn the lessons learned from my father, or to revise them, or to put the finishing touches on his designs, such as they were, to keep his son relatively safe in an absolutely risky world, every dad's foremost desire.

But to return: It was a Sunday afternoon, and the brothers were walking down a country road with their dad before he split. It's not something that happened very often, walking down country roads, or anywhere else with our dad. Or being much of anywhere with him. I do recall going to one movie with my father and mother. I am very young. It is probably a Western starring John Wayne, my father's idol, and the theater seems crowded, so it is probably a hit movie. At one point I pick up my dad's fedora, which is on the seat next to mine, and place it on my head. So it's probably winter. But this rash act causes widespread chaos in the row. It's not my dad's hat, after all. It's another man's. I am mortified, though the other fellow laughs it off. I was easily mortified back then. I am easily mortified now. The pattern began early, and since then I have never been at a loss for something to be mortified about.

Where did my dad go every day? No idea. Recently, when my father is asked a question or two about the past, sometimes he gives up a grudging answer quickly followed up by a plea for mercy—"That was a long time ago"—implying that this sort of interrogation is crossing the line and he's going to lawyer up.

In the 1950s, my father did work for a while as a stonecutter, alongside his own father, who transported the skill with him from Southern Italy. That was grueling, dirty work, and soon his life took another path toward a different sort of grueling, dirty work. He tended bar at the Made Guy's local bar and grill on Engert Avenue, where a lot of action was taking place. As near as I can determine, my dad was a sort of soldier in somebody's crew. And he gambled. And he probably risked his life more often than he'd admit. It's what certain guys did in the neighborhood. That was the way.

One Christmas I realized there was no Santa. So I asked my father if we were rich, because it was Christmas Eve, and he may have flashed a roll of cash, and maybe he was going down the street to buy presents. Hearing the question, he laughed, so that solved that mystery. We maybe were rich.

I can summon up images of his hopping into a car and speeding off down the street with other men. I also have a vivid, humiliating memory of trying to stop him from driving off one time. I must have been very young, and I was crying, and he was taking off as I was begging him to stay. I learned in that instant a lesson. I saw it in the eyes of the other guys in the car, who were looking at the boy with withering scorn. They were all wearing those Banlon shirts, guys who had places to go, along with my father. They were on their way to tracks and to bars, to gambling on cards and dice, and horses, and games. It was never too early to learn the following: don't embarrass yourself. Never make a fool of yourself. Don't act like a girl and cry. I learned the lesson that day and never again pulled a stunt like that. Almost all the lingering images of childhood with my father were pictures of flight, departure, haste, secrecy, inarticulation—all variations on the theme of absence.

Now I can see the appeal of his life, as I could almost glimpse it then. No slaving away in some factory or in some store, no driving a truck or a cab, nothing like being everybody else. His job was making money the sweeter way—gambling, stealing, conning somebody. And if somebody was dumb enough to be conned, that was his problem, not yours. That was the life. It was not answering to anybody you didn't respect or didn't fear. His was the life of the small-timer, the hustler, the gambler, looking for a big score one time, hoping this was finally the time when your number comes up right, and afterward calling attention to yourself in the right sorts of ways—with your Cadillac convertible, your Banlon shirt, your shiny loafers. Not exactly the stuff of *The Godfather*, but the stuff of my father.

My father never was convicted of anything, never went to prison, was arrested only once. What does it mean that his son, the altar boy who got a PhD, may have committed more crimes than his father? Law enforcement would one day hold over my head the possibility of serious jail time. I was never arrested, but the FBI threatened me with heavy accusations, and if I had been convicted of those alleged crimes, I would have been in prison a lot longer than my father ever would have.

★

PERHAPS THE MOST AMAZING development that day in Long Island when law enforcement descended in force was this: my father saw it coming, and in fact he watched the search unfold with his own eyes. It turns out he doubled back through the woods and perched himself on the garage roof, a close but safe distance from the house. Earlier he had concealed his car, so he must have had a clue something was about to come down. Paranoia pays off, when it does, anyway. And when the cops left, he climbed down from the roof, got in his car, and drove off to the sort of place where the surveilled go for the night, wherever that is. Were those cops and FBI agents the laziest in history, or were they outfoxed?

My mother and my brother and I were tailed by law enforcement when we drove off the next morning, and when we stopped at a diner for breakfast, everybody looked over to the table where the cops were eating, too. I do not recall who was driving that Monday morning, so it must have been one of my uncles, because our car was not available, being the vehicle of my dad's escape. I also remember for sure that I did not attend school that Monday. After we got home to Greenpoint, for a while we were followed sporadically, and men in suits and fedoras sat in cars across the street and watched the front door. Then the surveillance ceased. Maybe my dad was small potatoes, after all.

The next time I saw my father, it was later that summer and it was only for a minute. He ran up the stairs into the apartment, grabbed some things, threw them into a valise. They called a suitcase a valise. He hadn't stopped by for a family meeting or to confer any last-second wisdom. Then he ran downstairs, jumped into a car, and sped off all by himself. He later said he traveled for weeks across the land, coast to coast. He took odd jobs in factories in places like Revere, Massachusetts, to make some cash to pay his motel bills.

A few months later, my mother told us we would be going on a vacation. I don't remember packing, but I sometimes lost track of time. I did that. I would go off into a dreamlike stupor, or maybe that's a trance. I did notice that there sure was a lot of luggage for a vacation. And it was more than a bit shocking that morning when we headed to Idlewild, not yet JFK, Airport and boarded an airplane. I had never been on a plane before. I drank a Coke in the economy section, and I somehow understood I would never see my pals or Brooklyn again.

When we landed, the stewardess said over the intercom, "Welcome to San Francisco." My mom had assured us we were going to Long Beach, Long Island.

After picking up our baggage—those valises—we took a cab to a gas station inside the San Francisco Airport. Back then, there was a gas station improbably smack in the middle of the airport. That's where my father was, scrunched down in the front seat. He did not get out of the car. He looked anxious. Why was he hiding here?

We drove to Santa Rosa, sixty some miles away, where we rented a motel room and stayed for a long time.

1961: the Berlin Wall. JFK, a Catholic and a president, though not for long. Robert Frost, poet at inauguration. Astronauts. Civil Rights. Martin Luther King. The Bay of Pigs. Cuba. U.S.S.R. and sleeper-cell Commies in our midst. South Vietnam, North Vietnam, Ho Chi Minh. Pope John XXIII, who called into session the historic Second General Council of the Vatican. I'm going to stop before this turns into a Billy Joel song.

How much information did I take in? Did I read a newspaper? I did. That was the year enigmatic and tragically unlikeable Roger Maris was going for sixty home runs, Babe Ruth's record, maybe sixty-one. Meanwhile, country boy nice guy Mickey Mantle was banging them out of the park at almost the same pace, including sometimes when hung over. What an amazing year 1961 was. That was the year my family left Brooklyn, and never went back.

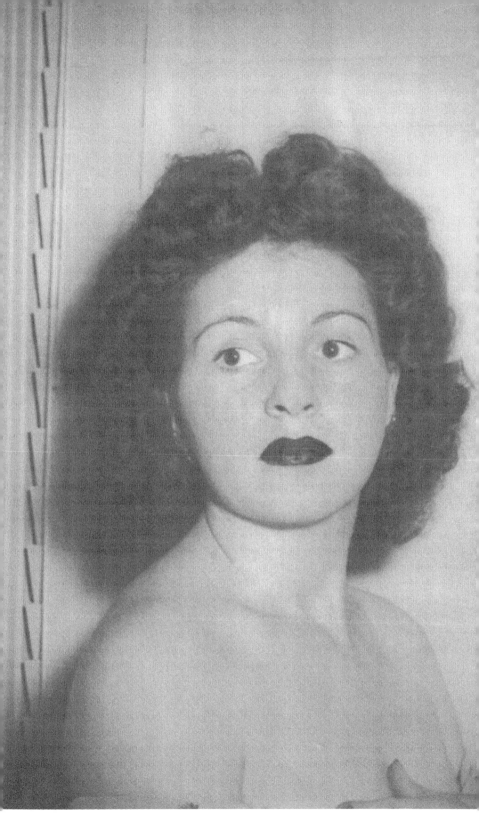

PART TWO

Telling the truth is, to be sure, no simple thing. Sometimes it is uncalled for; often it is hard. But telling it is by no means always the most difficult aspect of truth. That may be knowing it.

—Leslie H. Farber

Brother Joseph

I PLOTTED THE CLANDESTINE rendezvous with Ella with the precision of a pincer movement. She was sort of my girlfriend and I was living in a Catholic monastery.

My maneuver was logistically unrelated to the pincer. That classic military tactic involves double encirclement and the strategic cutting off of escape routes. Then again, maybe this rendezvous *was* related to a pincer, after all.

I drew her a map, provided detailed driving instructions, alerted her to possible complications. When she saw the road that diverged toward the chapel at the top of the hill, she was to take the other way. That was the key: don't drive up the hill on the private road. She was a girl. There were no justifiable reasons for a girl to be in the vicinity of the novitiate. Roger that, Ella? She did.

I was seventeen, living in a secluded place far removed from the world, in the beautiful, remote hills of Napa Valley. And I was a novice brother—that is, I was aspiring to become one day a full-fledged member of a Roman Catholic religious order, in this case an order whose mission was teaching. After going through a moving, lovely ritual in the overflowing chapel one Sunday afternoon, where I swore with meekness and emotion sacred promises to live a life dedicated to poverty and chastity and obedience, I took on the simple garb of an unadorned black robe with a white collar. I also took on a new name. I became *Brother* Joseph.

Via letters and phone calls over many weeks, the plan with Ella took form. It was excruciating. I might have assumed I was capable of delaying gratification. Now the evidence to the contrary was gathering like electric storms over the rocky landscape of my adolescence. That is where I was figuratively standing in the open with an umbrella over my head. I may have been Brother Joseph, crossing his fingers behind his back as he promised chastity and whatever the other two things were, but I was also a teenager.

Once I had kissed Ella. That was before I graduated from high school and packed my bags to move to the novitiate and embrace this vocation. As far as I could determine, she had kissed me back. I knew next to nothing about the protocol of kissing and being kissed, but I had seen some racy movies and read a few trashy books and magazines, so I was working on the equivalent of a high wire without a net. This kissing transpired in the White House. Not *the* White House, but the so-called White House of my high school. During the summer before my senior year, I had drywalled and refurbished and painted white the tiny infirmary abandoned at the far edge of the campus. It became a sort of boy cave. I would drive there at night supposedly to study chemistry or some other academic subject. I used the school phone lines to call any girls thought to be willing to be romanced by a big man on campus such as myself. The list was shorter than my attention span in chemistry. Nonetheless, that's where Ella had shown up one Saturday afternoon, the place where I would make, though not Ella herself, some personal history.

Her letters arrived in my novice's exposed mailbox in small pink envelopes with red wax to seal them, and I secreted the missives up to my cell. That is where I gathered myself to read and reread her words, seeking intimations, information. Seeking. I did not understand the part about the wax. Was this what girls normally did? But why? Did it signify? Where did they get the wax? I knew about words. I felt comfortable with words. With words, you could look them up, you could roll them around in your mouth.

Gradually I had picked up the fundaments of the California non-accent, though it was practiced with trepidation. My parents were hopeless. They still talked like they were sitting on their Brooklyn stoop on a humid summer night. My own Brooklyn accent could sneak up on me, too, like a hiccough, when I got emotional.

You from New York?

You gotta problem wit dat?

As for my parents and the novitiate, I observed something unexpected the Sunday afternoon when they dropped me off to live in the novitiate. They looked miserable. As I watched their blue 1962 Ford Galaxy drive down the hill, I saw my mother put a handkerchief to her eyes. I had no idea they cared about my joining the Brothers. It was then about seven years since I had been shanghaied from Brooklyn to California.

I kept rereading those letters from Ella. Looking for hints. Clues. Clues to what? It would take time to understand what the mystery was. Or if there was one. Then again, owing to my attendance at an all-boys Catholic high school, I had dated rarely, never took a class with girls, and was currently living in a monastery. Technically, they called it the novitiate, but considering my age and experience that was a distinction not worth making.

In my letters to Ella, I told her about the days on the hill, about my friends, my fellow novices. She told me about the days in the city, her job, her friends at work. I likely did not tell her how conflicted I was, how I was struggling over this vocation, wondering if I were called. I explained where there was a very nice creek, which would serve as an excellent isolated spot to converge. We determined a day and a time. She would be driving from Oakland, ninety minutes away. She was still living at home, getting ready to go to college, someday become a nurse.

That morning had been the usual mix of prayer, class, and work, then the noon praying of the Daily Office, then lunch. Afterward, I went up to my cell, got dressed in jeans and a short-sleeve shirt, because it was in the valley, where it was very hot and dry. Outside my cell window I spied spectacular multimillion-dollar vistas extending far into the distance, beyond miles and miles of vine rows. A few times I picked those grapes under a brutal sun. This was tough work, but satisfying, too.

No shepherds were keeping watch as I exited through the back door. It was a good walk past the winery, down to the road, and when the private road met the country road, I turned left and headed down to the lower elevations. Clean getaway.

I took up position on a big boulder. I practiced a casual look, the kind movie stars like Steve McQueen affected on the brink of the dramatic or the tumultuous, such as a bank robbery or a shootout. If I was expecting fireworks, they were not of that order of magnitude. Perched where I was, I did strive to radiate absolute masculine confidence, to allow my body language to indicate that I was cool, meeting a girl under these circumstances.

The sunlight filtering through the canopy of eucalyptus dappled the bubbling stream. The trees furnished some shade from the midday heat. The leaves rustled gently, expectantly, in the warm valley breeze. I loved the massive eucalyptus, their wistful and misunderstood monstrousness, their minty scent and their acorns, the way the breeze kneaded the branches, their poignant strips of shedding bark. My high school used to have lots of eucalyptus trees.

I missed high school less than expected, maybe because in a way I had never left. On some level, the novitiate was an aggravated extension of high school. It was early fall and the rains had yet to begin to run off the mountain tops, so the water was relatively calm, and the sound it made flowing over the rocks was soothing and beautiful…

Much like the puttering of Ella's bubbly Volkswagen Bug motoring down the hill to our rendezvous. Her brakes squeaked and she lurched to a stop and the door creaked open and she popped out. She wasn't in her Catholic girls' high school uniform, because she had graduated, but she was still the cutest girl in California. This wasn't the Garden of Eden and nobody was being tempted by Satan, but she was a sight to behold and I was tempted, in a vague, vague way without sexual teleology. It was pure fantasy. But not a pornographic one, not at all. It was so romantic it hurt in the bottom of my stomach—or not far from there.

If the monastery knew about this meeting, I would have been in deep trouble, if not drummed out. My hormones were probably working overtime to insulate me from such fears. Girls dig risks, don't they? But that was not the turn-on, breaking the rules (well, maybe a little). No, the real turn-on was seeing Ella again, very possibly, as previously noted, the cutest girl in California.

We hugged and proceeded to settle down to talk, which we were good at. I cannot recall what was talked about, but without a doubt I never touched on the true subject. I was looking for a reason to stay in the monastery, or a reason to leave. Maybe I was looking for a reason to live. She had auburn hair and a faint scar on her lip, which absolutely maddened me with all I knew of desire. We talked and we talked some more.

After a while, she made plain—possibly without using words—that she wasn't sure why she was there in the first place. It wasn't that we were boyfriend/girlfriend anymore. That hurt, but she was right. It's hard to date a monk, she implied. Little did she know—little did we both know. I was no monk, but the point was taken. We hardly knew each other, though there was that kiss. She was smart and droll but that's not a lot to build a lifetime upon. Or is it?

Yes, yes, yes, indeed, I was jumping multiple guns at the same time.

We talked. There was nothing to discuss that required the use of words.

I gotta get back, she might have said, much too soon, much too soon.

She didn't go. Maybe there was a kiss. She liked me and I liked her. Wouldn't there have to have been a kiss? Even as we were talking too much, I realized there was no future for me. No future with Ella, I meant, but did that recognition open up or foreclose a future in the religious order? Clearly, as any witness of the proceedings would have observed, logic was not holding sway. It mostly never did for me. I was seventeen, and it looked to me, based upon all the current evidence, like I would never have sex. But that sounds crass. I called it love. Once upon a time, a life of celibacy seemed like a tolerable bargain to make for the purpose of achieving eternal salvation. But now? Hard to say.

The famous sexual revolution was famously going on a very few miles away in the Bay Area, but I was clueless, infamously clueless. Oh, I had a sense of the biology. Well, the bio *textbook* was accessible. My wishes and desires were blurry, non-corporeal. Was I too young? Did the hormones not yet kick in with all their hairy force and fury? Where was my inner Zorba when I needed him?

For there she was, the cutest girl in California, and she was giving me a sort of ultimatum, as in *Tell me what the fuck I'm doing here, last chance, Joe.* And I could not answer her. What was I looking for? I was looking for everything—for meaning, for love, for salvation, for truth, for *her.* How could I manage all these contradictions?

I couldn't.

Ella was adorable. If she had said the word, I would have…

Who knows what I would have done?

I have never before told anybody about what happened that day at the creek, because nothing, and almost everything, happened. Besides, nobody would understand, for which I could not fault them, because I didn't understand, either. What was also clear, if unstated, was that, if she and I had never quite been a couple, sometime during our visit by the creek we had most definitely broken up.

How had I found myself up that particular creek? The usual way. Silence, exile, a lack of cunning. Considering the history of my family, my piety, my penchant for solitude, and my ability to compartmentalize the clashing pieces of my life, Brother Joseph, had he possessed a few years of therapy under his belt, might have regarded that scene with Ella at the creek as virtually inevitable, if not foreordained. Yet another mad effort to middle my life had come to naught.

She drove off too soon. Any time that day, that week, that month, that year, would have been too soon. And Brother Joseph walked slowly back to the place where he came from, which may or may not have been the place where I belonged: the novitiate.

★

As for Berkeley, where my family landed years before Ella's visit to the novitiate, that college town was as wildly improbable a destination for us Brooklyn exiles as any on the planet. Borneo, Brazil, Bermuda, Beirut, Burma, even the Bastille and Babylonia would have made as much if not more sense. Did my parents select Berkeley because nobody would have thought to look for people like us there? A shrewd strategy or an accident? With my family, you could not tell, but smart money was on accident.

Newly arrived in California, I played on organized baseball teams, as long as "organized" is loosely defined. I loved baseball, but I was, sad to say, not gifted. That puts too dull a point on it. I was terrible. Standing at the plate, I was clearly no Ted Williams, who could count the feathers on a hawk in flight. The eyeglasses were relatively new, and they should have helped, but maybe they were part of the problem. I was nearsighted and my lazy eyes crossed, and the corrective lenses did only so much. For my part, I could only hear the ball hurtling toward me. Not having the sonar aptitude of the nocturnal mammal called a bat, and with another sort of bat in my anxious grasp, I was flummoxed at the plate. This incapacity made it challenging to make contact. I was an okay second baseman, a position worthy of scorn, a position that limited the damage I could wreak on my team.

Instead, dreamy boy that I was, I did compensatory reading of every possible book about baseball. I also wiled away hours sketching on big pads the cool, beautiful baseball parks of my imagination. I envisioned crowds filling the stands. This park would have a short left field, that one a challenging power alley to right center. I would fill in the dimensions meticulously, ingeniously. This one had a big wall like the Fenway Park Green Monster. This one looked like Ebbets Field. Another was like the Polo Grounds, with those short porches down the lines. I calculated where I would hit imaginary home runs. I made out lineup cards and put myself third in the batting order. Hitting third and muscling up for a home run? According to Church law, you need three certified miracles to qualify for sainthood. Hitting a home run would have been my first and, to this day, only one.

★

WE WERE IN THE kitchen in Berkeley when I told my mother I wanted to be president of the United States.

"That will never happen, Joseph." She didn't miss a beat.

I believed her and I was depressed. I refused to believe her and I was angry.

Those two sentences neatly summarize my lifelong response to her view of me.

Maybe she knew something about my situation that I did not know, something that would constitutionally disqualify me from holding high elected office. Like being from Greenpoint, perhaps. Or like being the son of my father, who had run off into the woods and was still on the lam.

At this juncture, we are staying with my mother's sister and her husband. My loopy, henna-haired alcoholic Aunt Helen had an unfortunate voice that sounded like a cockatiel on Red Bull. Cha Cha Helen, as she was called, scared me when she high-heeled around the house with a slippery highball glass in one hand and a smoldering cigarette dangling in the other. One day she and my mom had a big fight—so I was informed. It would have been a fair contest. When the dust cleared, we were kicked out into the street. Sooner or later, my mother would have a fight with everyone. As with the wars that took place between and among New York's mob families, every now and then she needed to spill some blood to rebalance and reinvigorate relationships. On one occasion, the wedding day of one of Alice's children, Aunt Helen stepped outside the church for a cigarette, and my mother was offended. She stepped up to Helen, slapped her hard in the face, and said, "This is my day, don't ruin it."

Many years later, the sisters reconciled. I would come to enjoy my aunt more over time, as her drinking at the nearby Hotsy Totsy Club eased up and she slowed down. Every Christmas she knitted scarves and made cookies, all of which reeked of cigarettes. Her presents were diabolically brilliant. She had a genius for acquiring objects of fantastic awfulness. We came to look forward to opening her packages to see what the heck she had come up with. One memorable plaid shirt she gave my brother Eddie set a new standard for horridness. "A blind man wouldn't wear that shirt," he said, laughing to keep from crying. Italian has the perfect expression for such awfulness: *un pugno a l'occhio*—a punch in the eye. Cha Cha also had a go-to motif for my mother: owls. You have no idea how many sweatshirts, sweaters, ashtrays, cups, and towels are monogrammed with the face of an owl. "If she gives me one more fucking owl," my mother would say, "I'll kill her." Those owls probably still hoot on some Salvation Army shelf.

Cha Cha did have a different sort of gift for connecting with people. Her nephew realized this all over again one day while occupied at a urinal at Cal. My professor stepped alongside me. As we noisily voided bladders, my professor said to the wall in front of his face, "I met your aunt Helen at AA the other night. She is a pistol, and she is very proud of you." Good to know, even in this vulnerable social context.

Helen became a fixture in the family after her husband died. She was there at my house one Christmas Eve when we were serving prime rib with Yorkshire pudding, the traditional non-Italian feast. My brother John was in the kitchen carving, being an expert in culinary respects, and we were jumping trying to serve twelve people. I asked my father to find out how everybody wanted the prime rib: rare, medium, or well. In a while he returned, troubled. My aunt Helen had baffled him. I looked at my father struggling to communicate, not a look of his that ever surprised me.

"I asked Cha Cha how she wanted her prime rib."

"And?"

"She said she wanted ham."

I reminded him that the prime rib menu concept was in force.

"OK," he said, expectantly, as if he were looking for an opening. "So can you?"

"Can I what?"

"Make ham for her?"

Jesus might have multiplied his loaves and his fishes, but nobody in that kitchen was capable of a miracle like that on Christmas Eve.

As for my aunt, the woman mellowed as she aged, and she was always sweet and kind to her grandnephew, my son, and the owls and the plaid shirts never ceased coming as long as she lived. I felt close to her at her hospital bedside when Cha Cha blinked and died.

That dinner was also memorable for an exchange between my brother John and my father. Momentarily clean, John was big into group therapy, which involved lots of directness and honesty. At one point, my brother abruptly addressed his father who was seated across the table:

"Dad, I love you."

To which my father replied: "Yeah, well, keep it to yourself."

★

FRESH TO CALIFORNIA, I tell my mom I miss my friends in New York, and that I don't have any friends in California—which is not quite true—and that I want to go home. "When can we go home?" She doesn't say, "We'll see." She doesn't say anything.

I kept myself busy, my presidential aspirations dashed. I listened to the local professional baseball games on the radio, and fantasized playing one day. Automatically I rooted for the Los Angeles Dodgers when they played the San Francisco Giants. It look a long time—first, to root for the Giants, and second, to root against the Dodgers. As for the suddenly evil Dodgers, I learned anew what love was. I had been hurt before.

My father took me to two Giants games at Candlestick Park, which on a midsummer night can be colder than a November World Series game at Yankee Stadium. I was elated. There was the incredible Willie Mays patrolling center, and Orlando Cepeda and Willie McCovey in the field, too. My father also took me to a Warriors game at the Cow Palace, the name of which auditorium perfectly captures the ambience and the smell. It was the Warriors vs. the Celtics, Wilt Chamberlain vs. Bill Russell, two giant gazelles spectacularly sporting on the court.

I spent a lot of time by myself, and on the bus. The bus was a magic carpet that dispensed transfers. I studied the AC Transit schedules, learned all the exotic routes, and was comfortable taking hour-long trips costing a quarter across town. On

Saturdays I hung around the Berkeley Public Library for hours and hours. I loved how books felt in my grasp, how they smelled. Like toast. In a library, you could learn amazing things, about bugs and birds, about countries and cannons, about maps and magic, and about people, the strangest species, and what they did to and for each other.

From the Berkeley Public Library I checked out the collected stories of William Carlos Williams and the collected poems of Stephen Crane, and I read them with fascination. I did get it wrong, of course. As any snarky English graduate student would have snarkily advised me, I should have opted for Williams' *poems* and Crane's *stories*. Still, I acquired the arrogant sense that I could write poems if Crane could.

Two bestselling mass-market paperbacks I recall reading were *East of Eden* by John Steinbeck and *Another Country* by James Baldwin. Why I selected these adult narratives, I could not reconstruct. Maybe they were literary crimes of opportunity— that is, they could have been eminently shopliftable. Now I can appreciate that one was the author's take on Cain and Abel as reimagined in California, with lots of sordidness and violence. The other was a New York author's view of Greenwich Village, a depiction of the bohemian life, dramatizing then-taboos like interracial sex and homosexuality. Things happened in those books that were over my head, so I had to reread some passages several times (Is what I think is happening in the bathtub really happening?), but I hung on every inscrutable word. I doubt I exploited these novels for the purpose of fulfilling grade-school assignments called Book Reports.

As for books, once my mother did a particularly considerate thing. She knew I loved dogs. And maybe she noticed the name of the author on the cover of my *East of Eden*. In any case, she came home one time with a gift for me: *Travels with Charlie*, by Steinbeck. I cannot remember her giving me a book before. The book itself? It was okay. Charlie was a very good dog, but the narrative didn't deliver the same forbidden thrill as *East of Eden*. And that's a big part of what reading was for me: forbidden thrills. Along with *Travels with Charlie*, she also gave me *The Incredible Journey*, a saccharine tale about the heroic trek of a couple of dogs and a cat. I couldn't get interested. It was made into a Disney movie I did not see, though I was a sucker for books with dogs, like *Old Yeller*. She had missed the mark so completely that I was sympathetic, and I was sincere when I thanked her.

You can call me ungrateful. She did, with regularity and often with cause. I almost wished I were the sort of boy she imagined me to be, the boy who would relish those sorts of books.

I say these are the only books she gave me that I recall, but that is not accurate. There must have been a crackerjack door-to-door book salesman working the neighborhood, sticking his foot in the door, sweet-talking the little lady of the house, because suddenly one day an encyclopedia—a cyclone-opedia, as my dad would say—took up residence in the house, along with the green, gold-embossed, look-of-real-leather-bound Harvard Classics. I loved possessing these classics, having them in my room. I should add that I couldn't read them, because I was intimidated and the typeface was so forbidding, but I loved them. I did learn a lot merely by looking at the titles. *The Voyage of the Beagle* always made me laugh—what could that be about? There were volumes of Dante, Plato, Aristotle, Cervantes, and so on, the whole madcap Western Civ gang. To this day, twenty-two volumes remain on a shelf upstairs in my house. I have lugged them around in boxes in the course of who knows how many moves. I still have not read them.

My mother signed me up for a speed-reading course, then the pedagogical rage. I absorbed in a flash the speed-read gist, and "in a flash" was all there was to absorb. Speed-reading consisted of mentally latching on to clusters of words and concepts, moving down the page with determination, like a goat through fields dusted with crystal meth. Of course, this program had nothing to do with the pleasure one would take from actual reading. I rebelled. In a weird way, I am thankful for having been subjected to that silly course: I am proud to say that today I am about the slowest reader I know.

My mother also brought home a reel-to-reel tape recorder, then a hot new gadget. It was industrial gray, heavy as a stack of bricks, and it resembled a bloated double hot plate. She and I would make recordings, sometimes of the music that played in the background on the stereo. Into the microphone, I would practice making speeches—reading into the tape recorder Clarence Darrow, Cicero, Abraham Lincoln, Mark Twain, the usual suspects. I also recorded passages from the Bible. I recall, in especial, the Sermon on the Mount. *Blessed are the peacemakers,* etc. And also William Faulkner's speech when he accepted the Nobel Prize: the "man will prevail" speech. I must have been moved by those grandiloquent words—either that or I was preparing for a speech competition. It was likely both.

I also used this technology for other educational purposes. My mother heard a rumor that the brain was capable of acquiring knowledge while asleep. Given that my brain was not unfailingly reliable during waking hours, it was worth a shot. Some goofy ideas have staying power. In fact, this strategy of learning while asleep was later adopted from time to time by students of mine in classes that were scheduled after lunch.

So my mom and I experimented with this subliminal technique, and the tape recorder played by my bed while I slept—formulas, readings, Latin verb conjugations, that sort of thing. The results were unconvincing, if not disappointing. Maybe I was a very sound sleeper. The once-promising delivery-of-knowledge device was abandoned, and it mutely gathered dust in the corner. Nonetheless, that machine gave mother and odd child the chance to do something fun together.

We would alternate reading, my mom and I. She would read a passage into the tape recorder, then I would read a passage. I can still hear her voice when she read the entire Faulkner address. This is where he declines "to accept the end of man. It is easy enough to say that man is immortal because he will endure: that when the last ding-dong of doom has clanged and faded from the last worthless rock hanging tideless in the last red and dying evening, that even then there will still be one more sound: that of his puny inexhaustible voice, still talking. I refuse to accept this. I believe that man will not merely endure: he will prevail. He is immortal, not because he alone among creatures has an inexhaustible voice, but because he has a soul, a spirit capable of compassion and sacrifice and endurance. The poet's, the writer's, duty is to write about these things. It is his privilege to help man endure by lifting his heart, by reminding him of the courage and honor and hope and pride and compassion and pity and sacrifice which have been the glory of his past. The poet's voice need not merely be the record of man, it can be one of the props, the pillars to help him endure and prevail."

I loved that speech. I can still hear my mother's clarion voice articulating those words—especially "endure" and "prevail." These words spoke for her, and perhaps she unconsciously wanted to be on the record. I told her that I liked her voice, liked the way she sang. She sniffed. She said she did not have a nice voice. What did she know?

★

CAREER DAYS AT SCHOOL mystified me. I should have played hookie. As a young boy, I was never one to fantasize being a fireman, cop, or doctor. As for baseball player, I gradually came to appreciate that was impossible, so that did not count. And basketball? At five feet two inches tall in the ninth grade, that was a long shot. I had nothing against any of these futures, except that they did not apply.

As I grew older nothing changed much in this department. I knew plenty of people who said they wanted to be lawyers and doctors and so on, but I never seriously considered these to be options. I would look out across the Bay at the big buildings looming in the distance downtown in San Francisco and wonder, who were the people inside those buildings, and what did they do? The macaws and the monkeys at the Bronx Zoo were more comprehensible. My own son would one day enjoy professional success in a Wall Street–like firm. Mario had no trouble visualizing opportunity in those high-rises. The sins of one father were not visited, at least in this respect, on his son.

Along the way I deservedly earned the reputation for being a pious boy—different from actually *being* a pious boy, which I was—a reputation that was not an unqualified asset. Such a reputation left me open to character assassination, to being called a pussy. I wrote sanctimonious religious poems that I showed around, afflicting the unfortunate if not the innocent. I can summon the blank stares that greeted the performance of these poems, which I volunteered to read at the slightest instigation. My listeners' dumbfounded responses are reminiscent of the awkward moment that takes place, for instance at a dinner party, when somebody announces she is a surrealist painter or a sex therapist or a fundraiser, and everybody puts his nose down into the soup bowl and waits for time to quickly, politely pass.

As for those Berkeley weekends when I was in the eighth or ninth grade, I would leave the library and head for the dicier parts of Oakland. I would finagle my way into X-rated movie houses. Soon I would be anticipating the fantastic uncoupling of bras and the cascading unleashment of gorgeous breasts. I have no idea what I did to gain admission, but for the record, I did not employ the hat and moustache disguise that consistently proved a sensation on Halloween.

Once I found myself at the transcendently seedy Moulin Rouge, its name seared into my memory. I must have tracked its rich, varied program offerings in the newspaper listings. The atmosphere was soggy as the old GG cross-town to Queens Plaza in summertime. Men with coats on their laps surrounded me. I did not understand what accounted for such a fashion choice. Panic overtook me. I needed to get out, immediately. I hurried to the ticket booth, asked the man on the other side of the glass for my money back. For some reason the cashier complied. It was an expensive movie: five bucks, serious money, the going price for such fare. My ears burned. I boarded the bus back home and hoped I would never be caught in such a place again.

Did I confess these sins? I have no recollection of doing so, but if I did, I might have generalized such transgressions along the lines of "bad thoughts"—a good catchall fishnet stocking for the confessional box. The priests who heard my confessions didn't press for color. Thank God. I might have lied and invalidated the just-completed confession.

Running out of the spongy-sounding, sticky-floored Moulin Rouge that awful Saturday, I used some magic words that reeled back in the five bucks. I said my mother was ill. Why I thought this implausible excuse would fly, I have no idea, but it did the trick. It must have been a soft-headed, kind fellow working the booth. But what does it reveal about the boy, that I invoked my mother and tried to make some connection with her, even if that was based upon a pathetic fabrication in a squalid joint? It reminds me of the time I was beat up by two big kids in a park. They made me kneel down and called me names, including motherfucker. And I bristled and fought back and said they should not say that because my mother was dead. And they backed off. What does this mean? Humiliation and sexualization and more humiliation were perennially connected with my mother. But also rescue, as well.

I also liked other sorts of movies, especially foreign cinema and art movies—not that I knew what those terms delineated besides the extravagant appearance of ample breasts. I used to go the

University Movie House when I was eleven or twelve or thirteen. I watched every Fellini movie I heard about. This was before the age of Child Protective Services dominion. As a child, should I have been shielded by such mandates? I suppose so. Though I would not trade those experiences for any others. I can still call upon splintered, fragmented images from *8½* and *La Dolce Vita*. I could always count on fabulous fountain scenes and beautiful speeding cars and the copious shedding of dresses. I loved these movies because they were excessive, mysterious, and made no sense. They were also in Italian, which was music to my ears. They also featured bountiful, plentiful breasts and doe-eyed girls who pouted or punched with passionate intensity. *Mille Grazie*, Signor Fellini.

When I returned home, the check-in could possibly have gone like this:

Where did you go today, Joseph?

But you know what? I do not recall anybody ever asking.

★

IN 1962, WE MOVED to Dwight Way in West Berkeley. My most unsavory Berkeley memories are connected to this address, including being jumped and beaten up by those thugs in the park and having my cherished baseball bat, which I had shoplifted, stolen from me. When I got home, my father realized something was amiss and I grudgingly told him what happened. I didn't tell him about the kneeling down, because that was emasculating and I had taken shit from somebody. My father immediately took off for the park, with me behind, to seek out not only the stolen and re-stolen bat, but justice. We couldn't find those guys, thankfully.

We resided in a courtyard of cottage-like structures strung together like the dullest, grimmest tree ornaments. The ambience was mobile-home park. Across the way lived two bruisers, sister and brother. They spoke in boisterous backcountry tones, were four or five years older, thirty or forty pounds bigger, a head taller. Each had a total of two looks: full-on scowl and squinty, spiteful smirk. They were pissed off all the time. Who knew what would not set them off?

After school I would shoot basketball in the back of the courtyard, where the corroded cars and the pungent garbage cans were lodged. Sometimes I could shoot hoops unaccompanied. But then one of the bullies would show up and demand to play. The bruiser boy had the natural animal grace of a pickup truck in low gear. He would barge in, elbows flailing, shoulders lowered, to the hoop. He didn't wear tennis shoes, he wore work boots. The bully in clodhoppers had no basketball skills whatsoever, and the shoes didn't help. He could not shoot, and when he dribbled the ball, it was like he was driving nails. These limitations frustrated him, because he would lose to the short, chubby New Yorker across the alley—who unaccountably taught himself how to shoot the ball, and who may have enjoyed too much scoring baskets over the Neanderthal.

Then the bruiser girl would show up, hair tied back, and she would play the game with a comparable *joie de vivre*. Her face was sweet as a rusty pitchfork. But she wore T-shirts and had breasts that were invariably unholstered by a bra. And when she ran toward me on her way to the hoop, her breasts would flop around, side to side, up and down, sometimes side to down, and up to side. It was not an attractive sight, but it still qualified as fascinating, which even then I knew was disgusting. When I guarded her, she would say, "Don't you grab my titties." But touch them I did from time to time—accidentally. "What'd I tell you? Knock off touching my titties." Then she would drive around or through me, and throw up a crazy shot, screaming foul. To tell the truth, she had more skill than her sledgehammer brother, but it was hard to say whom I despised more. It was easy to imagine these siblings moving to the mountains and spending the rest of their lives together distilling moonshine, starting a family of slope-shouldered, pumpkin-headed, knuckle-scraping morons.

I came back to the apartment with a bloody nose one day, and my mother dragged me over to the boy's apartment because she was going to give that family a piece of her mind. The two mothers went at it. In one corner, from Brooklyn, Killer Kay Di Prisco. In the other, from West Virginny, Menstruating Mama Bear. But it became clear after a while that the bully's mother was willing to back off. She was not going to defend her son. Perhaps he would grow accustomed to that before being incarcerated someday. She herself was enormous, and yet she turned surprisingly deft and diplomatic. She Solomonically decreed that the two boys should not "play" anymore.

Then, for some reason, emotion ratcheted up all over again. The bully leaped over a couch like an elk and pounced on me, sending me sprawling across the room into a chair and a table, knocking over and smashing a lamp. The bully's mother pulled back her boy from the fray and that was the end of that.

★

I WAS HOME FROM school with my parents on Dwight Way, so probably it was the weekend. Living space was limited in the furnished apartment, smaller even than 625 Humboldt Street in Greenpoint. My parents slept in the front room, on a Murphy bed that pulled out from the wall nearest the front door. My brother and I slept in the only bedroom. We went to a Catholic elementary school, so my parents must have been sacrificing financially. My dad found employment in a dairy, moving crates in refrigerated walk-ins, breaking his back in the process. He would come home with all the milk and Rocky Road ice cream we could eat, on which we splurged nightly in front of a black-and-white television set with rabbit ears.

The grade school, Saint Joseph the Workman, was a ten-block pleasant walk in the morning. John and I would meander in uniform green cardigans and salt-and-pepper corduroy pants, pausing along the way to buy candy or baseball cards with fabulous gum. On this particular day, no walking to school was on the agenda. The Murphy bed was still down, so it must have been early, and a piece of luggage waited at the door. Unusual for him, my father was dressed in a coat and tie. The sun shone—maybe early spring, maybe late winter.

An authoritative knock on the glass-paned door. Two grave-countenanced men in hats and flared-open tan trench coats stood on the landing, shoulder to shoulder. They did not come inside. My father departed with them. If he said anything, any sort of farewell, it is lost to memory. Nobody explained where he went or when he planned to return. My mother sat in the kitchen and smoked and sipped coffee.

Years later, information leaked. It was the FBI that had arrived at the front door. The whole thing had been prearranged. They had caught up with my father, and his days of being on the run were over. They took him back to New York City on an airplane, his first flight, where my father would testify as a material witness in a trial of corrupt cops. So the story went. The age of Frank Serpico had dawned, when police corruption became big national news. Somebody shot Serpico about a mile from Humboldt Street, on Driggs Avenue, a street I walked every day of my Greenpoint life.

"They put me up in a hotel, took good care of me," my father explained long afterward. "They were squeezing me. I had a lot of information." When pressed by me as to what he knew, he didn't offer up any details.

Afterward, in the now-defunct *Berkeley Gazette*, a tiny news article appeared in the Siberia inside under the fold: "Berkeley Man Apprehended by FBI." Something like that. My father clipped it out, stuck it in his wallet, and showed it off until it disintegrated. From then on, after he returned from testifying, my father avoided Brooklyn—actually, he avoided New York City and the East Coast for the next thirty years.

"I don't wanna bump into nobody."

★

IN THE LATE SIXTIES, religious vocations exploded in America, a movement proceeding incongruously parallel to the sexual revolution. Pope John XXIII had called into session the Second Vatican Council, and wrote the famous encyclical *Pacem in Terris*. Nobody appreciated in advance the genius of the poor Italian boy who became pope. The better students in Catholic high schools were being targeted, assiduously recruited to a reinvigorated religious life. Nuns took off their wimples. Priests sported leather bombers. It was a rare month when some religious order—the Paulists, the Dominicans, the Franciscans, and so on—did not show up at school to pitch their case to sign on the dotted line. I loved my high school, which was run by the Christian Brothers, now called Lasallian Brothers. The Brothers and the Jesuits were, and are, the two most prominent teaching orders in the world. The Brothers were blue collar, working class, as opposed to the Jesuits, who were reputedly more intellectual and narcissistically full of themselves.

I was not much challenged academically, except by one or two teachers such as Mr. Niles, a terrific math and English instructor who may have secretly aspired to being a poet. One Sunday afternoon, Mr. Niles took me and a few other seniors to San Francisco, where we visited with a one-name beatnik poet— something like Celeste—in her Haight-Ashbury apartment. She brewed tea. She read poems. The jazzy rhythms and incantations were confusing, but okay. She was outfitted in a gingham dress and had big searchlight eyes that cast an encompassing gaze into your soul—or so it felt. Mostly I kept thinking, how did Mr. Niles know a real, live poet?

I watched *all* my teachers closely. I wanted to understand what they did and who they were. At the same time, I wanted to impress them—all of them, including the less-than-sterling teachers. I continually recalculated my GPA the way baseball players update a batting average. I typed A papers on crackly erasable bond paper using a portable Royal typewriter my mother gave me, a machine I continued to use through college and most of graduate school till sometime in the seventies when I—being an early adopter—bought a Kaypro computer and a dot-matrix printer for a staggering sum of money, around $5,000. That computer brought to mind a small, unreliable Eastern European automobile and whirred like an eggbeater, but it ultimately cooperated enough to spit out my dissertation after hour upon agonizing hour of pointillist dot-matrix printing.

Robertson Davies's *Fifth Business* is a terrific novel centered in a sense on teaching and learning. It is also eminently teachable. This is a rarer occurrence than is commonly thought. *The Great Gatsby* is another great novel that seems to teach itself. *Hamlet* is a play that works similarly, as does a fair amount of Shakespeare. Charles Dickens, Flannery O'Connor, Vladimir Nabokov, Joseph Heller—these are authors of great and highly teachable works. If you get out of the way of such books, you will be rewarded by the pleasure students take in them. It is tempting to call it ironic that there are more terrifically teachable books that are *not* such terrific books. This is one reason why curriculum meetings in English departments can be dreary affairs, and why discussions in the 1980s about canon formation were terminally tedious. Of course, I speak as a not-yet-dead, off-white male. And maybe I can sneak off this train of thought without getting my ticket punched for *To Kill a Mockingbird,* which I was obliged to teach a few times and whose appeal has largely eluded me.

Davies's protagonist muses perceptively about teachers: "I liked the company of most of my colleagues, who were about equally divided among good men who were good teachers, awful men who were awful teachers, and the grotesques and misfits who drift into teaching and are so often the most educative influences a boy meets in school. If a boy can't have a great teacher, give him a psychological cripple or an exotic failure to cope with; don't just give him a bad, dull teacher. This is where the private schools score over state-run schools; they can accommodate a few cultured madmen on the staff without having to offer explanations."

As for eccentric teachers and cultured madmen in my acquaintance, there was Mr. Franco, an Italian American who was the Civics teacher. His syllabus covered the predictable Civics topics like the bicameral legislature, the branches of government, jury duty, and the rights of citizenship, all of which were at best semi-interesting. But Mr. Franco himself was the hook. He had slicked-back black hair and dressed flashily, in fancy shiny shoes and shimmery sharkskin suits, which looked like they might slice up your fingers if you grazed a sleeve. This was one of many things that set him apart from the Brothers in their black robes and the other lay faculty in their mopey tie and chino garb.

Mr. Franco owned on the side a thriving bail bonds business, which we all knew about from the omnipresent billboards: *When You Land in Jail, Let Franco Go Your Bail.* Practical Civics in action? Maybe. And the man must have been suffering from an ulcer or cirrhosis of the liver, because he continually swigged from a milky bottle and hocked into a handkerchief big as a tablecloth, which he folded up elegantly after making a visual assessment. It was a bedazzlingly disgusting sight to behold, but despite the gross-out factor, the man proved entertaining and intelligent. The question that kept recurring was, how did this guy talk his way into this job?

Mr. Franco did orchestrate a memorably bizarre moment when he passed around a newspaper photo of the Berkeley protestors who were currently in the national limelight. He went off. He pointed to the adoring faces looking up at Mario Savio, the brilliant and ferociously articulate leader of the Free Speech Movement. He stressed that these students were mesmerized by the charisma of Savio, and that they had handed over their rational faculties to this Savanarola. He said they were all brainwashed. Even when Mr. Franco jumped into the shallow end he was captivating.

Remarkable how far away those student protests seemed. Although the Cal campus was only a long walk from the high school, these protests had nothing to do with us. As in *nothing*. Vietnam was a million miles away, even if it wasn't, and though the Selective Service was beckoning for our legally required registration. We were blissfully oblivious. That was all destined to change before long.

Mr. Franco was fired. So it goes in Catholic schools.

★

THE SCHOOL CULTURE WAS typical sixties Catholic boys' institution: jockish, conforming, violent, bullying, homophobic. *The Lord of the Flies* was required ninth-grade reading, which qualified as a colossal redundancy. What boy wouldn't feel at home at a school like that—or more precisely, pretend to feel at home? I myself could not compete athletically, and I was cut from every team for which I absurdly tried out. I was among the smallest and least talented, and by far the youngest in my class. One weekend the football team went en masse to Mustang Ranch, the infamous brothel across the Nevada border. They came back regaling everybody with boastful graphic tales. They were suspended, and the team lost the big game as a consequence. Afterward, they swaggered about sporting an imaginary badge of injured merit.

Nobody came out back then, but there was one boy who absorbed the standard, stupid taunts without arguing or defending himself. He steamed silently. He was one of the editors of the literary magazine. He published a particularly great poem under his name in the one issue ever printed. The few readers of the publication and its illiterate faculty advisor were shocked to discover that it was Emily Dickinson who had written this poem a hundred years earlier, whoever she was. Soon after graduation, the closeted plagiarist would commit suicide.

Corporal punishment was common practice. From time to time, some Brother would play Typewriter with a recalcitrant student. How do you play Typewriter? "Fold your arms in front of you," a student was instructed. Then Brother would "type" on the guy's arms before hitting the "return carriage," which was, you see, a heavy slap.

One time, a wise guy said the wrong thing—whatever it was—to the football coach who was posing as the American history teacher. This was during the course of a lecture that contained the following unforgettable military observation: "The British and the Americans were tied on the border." That was the day the teacher punched out that kid. Perhaps no one will ever again witness somebody, outside *Harry Potter*, fly across a room stuck in a desk.

I myself was paddled once, during detention. It hurt a lot more than expected. I had gotten in trouble because of an after-school fight with a creepy guy who wore a green military fatigues jacket every single day, rain or shine, hot or cold. He called me out. The two of us fought up on the field till Brother Psycho, the dean of discipline, broke up the fight. He suspended us both. When my opponent came back to school, he had a cast on his arm. The two of us sat in the same room for a week of detention.

Brother Psycho, designated paddler, was the overlord of detention dungeon. He had a close-cropped head of grey hair. His very haircut looked to have caused him pain and suffering that he was of a mood to pass around. He was threateningly lean and he smiled without cause, sarcastically, menacingly. His thin lips wrinkled as he instructed his latest victim to bend over while he delivered sinus-clearing smacks on the ass. I thought Brother Psycho was a sad guy, and, like everybody else at school, never wanted to be in his vicinity, especially if he was armed with his paddle. I didn't feel sorry for him. One thing I learned early on was that, if you ever feel sorry for somebody, he will try to kill you.

Brother Psycho left the order and the school. A couple of years later, the former dean of discipline appeared on campus during lunch hour behind the wheel of a red convertible. He drove by slowly in a single-car cortege, past the boys who lounged on the grass and stared in disbelief. As he passed, he mirthlessly grinned and flipped them the bird.

★

ONE DEEPLY INFLUENTIAL BOOK in high school was *The Myth of Sisyphus* by Albert Camus. The book begins, in translation, of course, this way: "There is but one truly serious philosophical problem, and that is suicide. Judging whether life is or is not worth living amounts to answering the fundamental question of philosophy." That's the kind of idea that gets your attention when you are a restless, questing teenager. Camus was the real deal, a debonair connoisseur of the absurd: "All great deeds and all great thoughts have a ridiculous beginning. Great works are often born on a street corner or in a restaurant's revolving door. So it is with absurdity." Camus's friends believed he was embracing Catholicism shortly before he died in a car accident at forty-seven.

Not for one fleeting instant did this high school student ever conclude life was absurd. Never did I consider seriously the prospect of suicide, unlike the beleaguered lit-mag editor whose image disturbingly flickers to this day in my memory. In the interests of full disclosure, there was that heavy Nietzsche spell in college, when occasionally life was stupid-seeming, and LSD and mescaline were as available as beer. By the way, I never much liked pot, which only made me want to eat ice cream and listen to Led Zeppelin on the roommate's headphones. Friday nights on psychedelics, however, seemed to provide the reliably magical occasion to hallucinate and have non-conversations with people who with any luck turned out to be gorgeous

redheaded philosophy majors in white turtleneck sweaters—
well, that did happen once. As any Nobel Prize or Lotto winner
would probably concur, once is way better than never.

My thoughts on suicide constitute fundamentally a glib
position. I have never had cancer, never lost a child, never...fill in
the blank. Yes, there were rotten times. I had a son whose mother
didn't allow me to see said son as much as I needed to, which
broke my heart. I fell in love with the wrong women from time
to time, by which I mean continually, until I found somebody
who would not qualify—at which point I married her. I also fell
in love with a lousy drug for a few years, the dependence upon
which controlled substance made me feel humiliated, angry, and
weak. All that said, I never truly believed life was absurd. Then
again, I have never been a French guy in a beret driving along
the Seine in freezing, dark January.

Camus was heady stuff for high school, or so it might seem,
but such was the nature of the intellectual life as advocated by
Brother Paulus. I would never have a better, more inspiring
teacher in my life, and I have been lucky in this department, having
known a number of good and great teachers. The genius of his
teaching consisted of this: As a student you cultivated the illusion
that Brother Paulus said *nothing* in class, that he mysteriously led
discussion without direction and you put together everything on
your own. It was a fabulous trick on the part of Brother Paulus,
and it is one his former student mimicked when one day he
taught his own classes. My unachievable holy grail was to teach
an hour in which I seemed to say absolutely nothing, which I
almost *almost* achieved a few times. What I loved about Brother
Paulus's class is we talked about things I normally kept in the
back of my head: love, death, and the meaning of life, which
other classes and ordinary teachers avoided or never conceived.

During a discussion of love one day, Brother Paulus's student
made an urgent point in class, which went roughly something like
this: "I think there is only one person we can fall in love with."

"One person in the whole wide world, Joe?"

"Yes, one person in the world."

Brother Paulus smiled slyly and stifled a chuckle, so I intuited I had said something my revered teacher regarded as ridiculous. But I didn't know why the teacher found the remark risible. In fact, I felt pretty sure I was correct and that Brother Paulus had it wrong. These days, I might still think so.

Brother Paulus was fallible in other regards as well. He was an Anglophile, for one thing, and his snobbishness skewed his aesthetic judgment. I can recall remarks Brother made on subjects like Chaucer and the bawdy, amusing "Miller's Tale" that were on the money. But they were not always. For instance, the teacher adamantly ventured views about the poets Shelley and T. S. Eliot that I believed were off the mark. I possessed fully formed, however uninformed, critical positions. Once I presented my teacher a packet of my poetry, and after reading them the teacher's response was, "What makes you think these are poems?" I took that as sobering criticism—not of me or my poetry, but of the teacher. Poor Brother Paulus didn't get it.

Our paths would cross again later in life. As a doctoral student I applied for a teaching job at a Catholic college where Brother Paulus was on the faculty. I was invited for an on-campus interview. I taught a so-called demonstration class. Afterward, the department chair said that mine was the best class ever taught by a job prospect. It is obvious where this one is going, isn't it? I did not get the job. Based on my later, long experience with hiring committees, I believe it more than possible that Brother Paulus did not advocate for my candidacy. Perhaps he never did have as high an opinion of his former student as the student had of himself. Brother Paulus may have considered this student a striver, not a good thing for an Anglophile. Deep down, I have come to terms: I was not a favorite of Brother Paulus, at least not the way a few others were. Brother Paulus was a man of principle, and he may have had sound cause to determine this student undeserving of cultivation. Fair enough. Nevertheless, at the most impressionable time of my life, I placed Brother on a pedestal, and there he will remain forevermore.

There was one other unnerving aspect of Brother Paulus's class junior year. At some point we began thinking about next year, when we were looking forward to the charismatic Brother Angelo, whose classroom was next door. He was by reputation as good a teacher as Brother Paulus. Alas, that Brother was reassigned to another Brothers' school, to everybody's keen disappointment. Many years later, news spread about the man who used to be Brother Angelo. The Brothers settled claims made against him for $6.3 million. He had been molesting boys for years. There the monster had been in Berkeley all along, hiding in plain sight inside his Brother's robes, teaching the boys next door to read and write and suck him off.

★

I BEGAN TO SHAVE—EVERY few days at least. I had a growth spurt, all the way to a towering five foot six, maybe. At the end of eleventh grade I was fifteen years old, thanks to skipping the second grade in elementary school. Other big changes were in the offing. I decided I wanted to be student body president. Admittedly, this was a step down from president of the United States. Yet the decision was momentous, for me if not for the free world. It was a different era. High school politics were big. Everybody voted. Voting may have been mandatory. Feelings ran high. True, it would have been difficult to conceive a more conventional aspiration. Yet that aspiration was mine. Being student body president was a means of validating one half of the cherished twinned concept of myself: good boy with a high GPA and social status, and somebody who wrote poetry and languished in isolation and OCD depression. Win-win situation.

Standing in the way of my political holy grail was the handsome, dashing star quarterback of the football team on his eventual passage to Stanford, somebody whose inauguration was a foregone conclusion, and in this jock culture I was the essence of underdog. I never liked him, but I envied him and his access to that part of conventional school life from which I was excluded. Me? School plays and musicals, first tenor in the Glee Club, speech competitions. That meant I was a two-touchdown underdog, if not more.

As we entered the gym for the final, formal campaign speeches, the day before voting, the school packed into the bleachers, my opponent's buddies passed out a mean-spirited hit sheet, denigrating my so-called qualifications. That was nothing. My best friend and campaign manager had quit days earlier, telling me I wasn't the right man for the job. He was supporting my opponent.

As for why my opponent made that preemptive move, I could not understand. He didn't need to take a shot unless he was worried, which made no sense. Maybe it was simpler. Maybe he assumed he enjoyed an insurmountable advantage and he would take me out at the knees for the pure sport. Maybe he was telling me my ambitions were ridiculous, that I was not to be taken seriously. Maybe he was kicking sand in my face. Technically, this move went against campaign rules. I was pissed. I was disrespected. A man's gotta do what a man's gotta do, and so did I. I was introduced first (alphabetical order) and stepped up to the podium:

"I had a prepared speech." My voice did not crack, the way it sometimes did at most inopportune times. The pages I dramatically lifted from the podium testified to the assembled that I was telling the truth. "But I am not going to read it. Instead, I need to respond to this scurrilous attack…" Those speech contests came in handy. I extemporaneously answered every one of the accusations with the passion only adolescent grievance can generate. I was fighting for something more than a mere election. I was defending my very existence. I reveled in the power wielded by mere words. Underdogs are dangerous. "Don't take no shit from nobody," somebody once said. When I was done, thunderous applause echoed off the gym rafters. My little brother and his pals stood and cheered like mad. I hope he didn't shake down all his classmates to vote for me.

My opponent stepped up. He launched his leaky vessel christened I-too-had-a-prepared-speech, but he could not bail himself out. His candidacy sank. Next day, the vote wasn't close.

★

SUMMER VACATION BEGAN AND my brother was expelled. John didn't want to be at the school, or any school. I got it, and John got it. I worried about him, I did, but he was elated to be out of the place.

My mother could have been prescient about my never being president of the country, but in the interim I set out to be the best student body president in the history of the school, if not the United States of America. I worked energetically all that summer to prepare for my upcoming reign. Doing what? You have no idea, and neither do I. But stuff, lots of student body president stuff. The job was intoxicating. When student body cards were issued that fall, I arranged for my picture to appear on the reverse of every card. What was I thinking? I wasn't. I was feeling my oats, but the funny thing was, I did a good job. It took my friend who had resigned as campaign manager into his college years to apologize, to admit he had made a mistake. We stayed friends for a long time afterward.

That post-election summer, a buddy drove up on his new motorcycle. I asked him if I could take a spin, and he reluctantly agreed. It proved to be a short, fateful jaunt. In a minute, not wearing a helmet, I crashed into a fence. I was soon on the ER table getting stitches. They cut away my pants and plucked pebbles embedded in my bleeding limbs. At some point my mother charged in, glaring. "Look what you did to your new chinos!"

★

NOW, A VOCATION IS different from a profession, or from a career choice, a different metaphor, a different concept. When you're sixteen, it might be hard to hear the calling, what with the hormonal din and social cacophony and brain tempests. I thought I could hear, somewhere in the distance, the calling to be a Brother. What does one do with a calling? You obey, you respond, you give thanks. You wonder if you have the strength and conviction to live up to its terrifying demands.

I was concerned as ever about my parents. I wanted, well, to save their souls. I am not proud to admit as much, but it was true. The Brothers' vocational director thought that was a poor excuse for a plan, and, to his credit, said so adamantly. Still, I wanted to be a Brother, and maybe my parents' salvation would be a nice holy byproduct. To that end, I endured personal interviews with bearded, kindly psychologists the Brothers retained. They wore tweed elbow-patched sports coats and blue jeans. I took psychological profiling tests, having brought along my two No. 2 lead pencils. I was candid in every response, and because I did not have any idea what they were looking for, I probably said the acceptable things. They deemed me worthy to step up to the Brothers' bar.

A novitiate is where you learn to live the life of the Brother, to pray, to exist in harmony with what is called the Daily Office, the schedule of prayers organizing your day and night. The novices woke at 5:20 to the sound of Brother Director walking up and down the halls, ringing a big school bell with a vengeance that the threat of eternal damnation might instill or lifelong sublimation could inspire. Nowadays we know from neurological research that the still-forming brain of an adolescent is not wired to function seamlessly in the morning. Even if such knowledge had been commonplace back then, nobody in charge of the bell's clapper would have cared.

I was given my own room. In accordance with monastic tradition, this room was called a cell—that is, a private space historically linked to venerable notions of sanctuary. As monks have been known to testify, your cell, where you reside in solitude, can be in and of itself a kind of spiritual guide. Though it was small, my cell would hardly be confused for the kind in prison. Neither did it trigger claustrophobia the way the velvet-curtained confessional box sometimes could. The ceiling was higher than the bottom of the net hanging under a basketball rim. The walls were about as long as the average altar, wide as the typical wings of a cross mounted in a church. It also had a full-length window looking out toward majestic hills and vineyards. My cell was furnished with a sink, a skinny mattress and a woolen blanket, a desk with a lamp and a chair, a compact bookcase, and a metal armoire, where I kept walking-around civilian clothes along with three black robes: one lightweight robe for the heat of summer, one medium-weight for most of the year, one scratchy heavyweight robe functional as a pea coat for the freezing winter mornings in the valley. On the desk I kept the beautiful (and then-newly published) Jerusalem Bible, which is the Catholic translation of the Bible. The book was presented to me at high school graduation as the recipient of the Pacem in Terris Award, so named after Pope John XXIII's earth-shaking encyclical that promised to upend Catholicism. That Bible remains to this day within easy reach of my desk. The inscription, done in elegant calligraphy, reads:

I have heard the cries of your soul, and have come here to comfort you. Open your heart to me and I shall fill it with light. Ask, and I shall show you the path of Truth.

Speaking of cries of the soul, there was that hand bell. A punch in the nose would have been a gentler wake-up. Then again, if you were in the market for gentle wake-ups, you wouldn't be sleeping here. After the bell roused me, I would splash water on my face. I would don a robe and wander groggily and grouchily as a hungover vampire across the grounds toward the white and gold chapel. This was a stunning, understated place of worship. The walls were white, the altar pure and simple. But I have never been a morning person, and my mood was often agonized. The novices recited prayers and sang the Daily Office. We spiritually prepared for Mass. For meditation, I walked among the grapevines, gazing upon the panorama. Now and then I would startle a deer as it nibbled on grapes and rose petals in the dawn.

I felt close to many of my fellow novices. There were eighteen or so in my class, a fair number of them Latinos from Southern California, more than a few from the tougher neighborhoods where the Brothers did some of their finest recruiting. One of my best friends from high school, Bill, had also come to the novitiate, and we teamed up with our new friends. There were plenty of good, raucous times. Basketball, football. Fraternal hours, where we learned how to drink wine with a vengeance not to be confused with discrimination. The so-called talent shows we put on in the common room were also goofy fun. We knew how to do shtick. I would sing and be the emcee.

We made the most of wacky opportunities, like the time at the local Catholic radio station when Brother Joseph led in praying the rosary, and in keeping them from laughing. When I was back for a visit at the high school, I ran into a girl I knew— actually, the first girl I ever took on a date. I was self-conscious in my Brother's robes. "I heard you on rosary hour," she said. All I could think was, what was a pretty girl doing wasting time listening to me on the radio praying the rosary? And also, how did she think I did?

We novices had plenty of heart-to-heart talks about the meaning of life and the purpose of our vocations, often with the aid of bottles of wine secreted from the fraternal gatherings. Once my father, during a rare visit, slipped me a bottle of Jack Daniel's before we went on retreat at the Russian River. The bottle was a dead soldier before the end of the first night.

The novitiate was a homoerotic culture, an aspect I was not equipped to consciously register at the time. That does not mean that homosexuality was rampant, or confirmably manifest. The closest I came to putting two and two together was the time I rounded the corner of the corridor going to my cell and saw something strange. There was one hard and fast rule: Nobody goes into anybody else's cell, ever. That day, though, undetected, I observed two novices skulk into the same cell, and the furtive way they did betrayed an illicit secretiveness. Those two novices were widely assumed by other novices to be gay, and they were both the subject of winks and jokes because of their perceived effeminacy. Now I had some circumstantial evidence, or so I concluded when I heard the door of that cell close with a tiny, surreptitious click.

I haven't seen most of my fellow novices for many years, but I remember vividly those closest to me: Bill, of course, and Robert, Eddie, Rene, Larry, Kevin, and Frank. Robert was a great pianist who liked to puff on a cheap, plastic-tipped cigarillo when he tickled the ivories. Bill has become a successful college administrator with a lovely family, and we remain friends. As for the others, I have almost no information, except with regard to my friend and rival, Brother Larry.

Larry was the Chosen One. He was tall and athletic with movie-star looks. He always looked like he was ready to play tennis. He was studious, smart, and articulate. He had an explosive laugh, which you hoped to detonate. Larry was the only one in that novice class whose vocation stuck. He went on to teach brilliantly in Brothers' schools, where he was a venerated member of the faculty and administration. Then, during the school field trip in whitewater with graduating seniors, he slipped out of his inner tube in the rapids and was carried off. After a few days, his body washed ashore. The year was 1980. Brother Larry was thirty years old.

★

BROTHER JOSEPH STOPPED GOING to confession—that is, taking the sacrament of reconciliation. This was the height of spiritual arrogance. Maybe it was the product of my confusion, my inability to distinguish one guilt or several from the totality of my life. Theologically, I was defenseless.

Even so, I sang praises of the Divine, worked the grounds and the fields, read the Scriptures with devotion, respected and cared for my fellow novices. But the truth was the truth: I was not a good novice. I would lie face down in the music room, hook on headphones, and listen, eyes closed, to Bach's Mass in B Minor and *Sergeant Pepper's*, Bob Dylan and B. B. King and The Doors. Lucy in the sky with diamonds. We'd love to turn you on. I feared I did not belong in the novitiate. After all, what kind of novice would invite a girl like Ella to a clandestine meeting at the novitiate? More than anything, I feared I could not leave even if I could not stay.

There was a magnificent bell tower in the chapel. You needed to climb up a very steep ladder, a good thirty feet up at least, and if you timed your arrival in the chapel, nobody would be around, especially late at night. I was never comfortable with heights, but something kept drawing me back to the bell tower. I could have been risking my life, but I had to see. What? See *what*?

Once I was at the top, the gigantic bells loomed, somehow resonating, clamoring in their silence. I looked out into the distance. There was the city far away, and a million stars trembled and thrummed. Van Gogh country. Clear night, murky soul. The usual combination for the human being I was. In grape-crushing time, the air was chewy and intoxicating, pushed along by the powerful, hot breezes rising up to the tower. Down there in the distance, I would think, there were other people. Were they like me? What did the future promise? What lay out there for me? Then something like a tide reversed, and I would feel dizzy and clear-headed all at once. The darkness turned bright. The evergreens on the hillsides shook and swayed dreamily. The bell tower seemed to echo. If there were a God, He was there. He had never been gone. He was keeping his usual low profile. Brother Joseph was eighteen and as close to Heaven as he would ever be.

★

BROTHER DIRECTOR WANTED TO talk to me after dinner. We were outside the refectory, and we were starting group walk, the postprandial constitutional stroll along country roads. When we repaired later to his office, Brother Director had a blunt message to impart. He had the jowls of a basset hound, the grizzled buzz cut of a colonel, the demeanor of an unsatisfied actuary. I am positive there was a wellspring of humanity and warmth, but I never gained access.

"Brother Joseph, you make too many jokes."

★

JUST FLEW IN FROM the coast and, Brother Director, are my wings tired!
I don't get no respect, I tell you, I don't get no respect.
That's what I'm asking you! Who's on first?
I'll tell you what's wrong with this parrot. It's dead. This is a late parrot. It is an ex-parrot.
Doc says, I've got some good news and some bad news. The bad news is that you have six months to live. The good news is I'm banging my nurse.

A thousand married Jewish men were surveyed as to what they liked most about oral sex. Ninety-five percent said it was the silence.

The Aristocrats!

Tough crowd! Tough crowd!

Always go to other people's funerals, otherwise they won't go to yours.

Brother Joseph'll be performing on our stage the whole weekend.

Don't forget to tip your waiter.

★

BROTHER HAD A FAIR point. I didn't ask the Brother Director, who was behind his desk in the glass-paneled office and functioning as my latest critic, if he had suggestions to pare down the number of jokes, or if it was a matter of my lousy timing. I didn't press him to define jokes or to help me understand "too many"— relative to what? Coincidentally, zero would be the number of times Brother Director ever pistol-whipped out of us a smile, a snicker, a chuckle, a laugh.

Brother Director had a voice that was smooth and soft as cashmere, which was not as comforting as it perhaps sounds. Hired killers talk softly, too. And though this is overstating it some, his was a Clint Eastwood/Dirty Harry soft-spokenness, subtly this side of a crack-up. I could say he never seemed to me to be an ideal candidate for the directorship of a novitiate, because he had no psychological sensitivity whatsoever, but I won't. Not because I give him a pass, but because I have no standing when it comes to determining what qualifies for being any sort of a good Brother.

"Brother Joseph," he had said, as I seem to recall, "you make too many jokes."

I don't remember anything else he said, though I am positive he said that. So after leaving his office and mulling over his judgment, I decided the time had come. I would leave the novitiate. I called Brother Director on the house phone and informed him. I probably said I needed time away to reflect on my vocation.

I called together my posse and we met in the chapel side room. I was miserable, because I loved these guys. I had to go, not that I necessarily knew there was something better elsewhere. We talked into the early morning. If this escape from an untenable situation was supposed to be a good thing, why did I feel so miserable?

That morning, when everybody else went to chapel for Lauds, the earliest prayers of the day, I packed. It was a lonely few hours till my father showed up at the back entrance, and he drove me home, whatever home meant. I was miserable, fearing I had let down my friends. What did Jesus call his disciples? He called them his friends.

It took me many years to realize that Brother Director was correct. I did make too many jokes. I was not cut out for the religious life, or at least this version of a religious life. I was not called, after all. And I had proof now, because I had left the order. But if I was not called to a Brother's life, I had to ask myself a follow-up question: To what sort of life was I called?

Liberal Education

M Y FIRST TRUE LOVE lived on a nice part of Riverside Drive, which is on the island of Manhattan. Though Riverside Drive and Manhattan were part of New York City, in effect it was a starship journey away from Humboldt Street and Greenpoint. We met at our East Coast college and proceeded to do four years together full bore—complete with spectacular break-ups and poignant make-ups coast-to-coast and on two continents, in airports, cafés, bookstores, classrooms, dorms, seashores, and concert halls.

I missed this truth at the time, but more than anything, the two of us were good friends who stood by each other during family and personal travails. Luckily for me in the long term, she was smarter than I was, but I did not grasp this—unluckily for me in the short term. This was all the essential meaning I could use: I had fallen in love, head over heels. That seemed like the single and capacious and clumsy concept that applied to the feelings I could not manage. Whenever she got on an airplane, I thought I would die. Yes, I was a diva.

Naomi was unquestionably the best first girlfriend any mostly red-blooded Brooklyn-born Catholic-with-a-sudden-question-mark could ever have had the good fortune to come across. As for the Catholic part, I did stop going to church, but oddly, this decision did not constitute a spiritual crisis. I had misplaced the religious need, if that was the word, at least for now. I had my hands full with other concerns. Naomi received

Subway to California

extra credit for being Jewish, too, which also made her exotic—
in my world if not in Manhattan, where I heard there were a
number of Jews.

I was not in Greenpoint anymore. Or California, either.
Was difference the ultimate turn-on for me and for her?
The ultimate turn-on is often the, well, ultimate turn-on. Still,
does anyone know the truth about such connections? She was
slender and I have never been known to miss many meals. What
connected us? I amused her. I wrote poetry. I was intense. She was
coruscatingly smart. She was sardonic. She was very attractive. She
was charismatic. She spoke French. As I may have mentioned, she
was Jewish. All signs indicated I had died and gone to Manhattan.

Naomi had friendly domestic help, people who wore uniforms
and made nice sandwiches and toasted bagels with lox and cream
cheese. A gastronomic breakthrough if I ever saw one. They were
kind to the California-transplant New York boy. Once I carelessly
used the word "maid," which was in poor taste, I discovered to my
horror. How was I to know the fine distinctions? Naomi's family
had fancy paintings on the walls of the beautiful apartment. If I
squinted, I recognized one from pictures in art books.

During dinner, she and her parents effortlessly alternated
between United Nations-ish English, French, and German. The
dinner table itself was gorgeous, maybe mahogany, under a lovely
chandelier, like the kind I had seen in movies. As for the table,
there were situated all manner of forks and knives and spoons
in close proximity to my plate, where food was beautifully
presented—food which was sometimes recognizable. Not the
spaghetti and meatballs my Nonna served. Not the unseasoned
pork chops my mother incinerated. As for the cutlery, an array of
Medieval axes and maces and scimitars would not have seemed
more terrifying. I was fearful I would never do the right thing,
that if I wasn't careful I would grab the wrong spoon for the
soup (why were there two spoons, why?) or knock over a wine
goblet with a hairy paw. They served wine with dinner, too, some

of it French. I lived in mortal terror of the moment I would commit a faux pas (like tucking a napkin into a shirt collar) and everybody would snicker and tell me to get the fuck out.

Naomi's parents were hardly snobs. They were kind, sophisticated, liberal, Planned Parenthood, intellectual, Jacob Javitz, New York Jews with tragic tattooed-wrist European family lineage and a subscription to the *New York Review of Books* and good seats for the theater and the symphony. Her father was an international lawyer, her mother taught sociology at a college. Their daughter was a private school girl with a cosmopolitan sensibility and a heightened political and aesthetic consciousness. What she wanted with a boy like me was a mystery. Sometimes I couldn't follow what Naomi was saying. I was dazzled by being cast in an off-Broadway play without a script.

Naomi sympathetically quoted her mother on the subject of me, my favorite subject. Her mother seemed to like me and Naomi agreed with what her mother said: Joe was the kind of boy who had obviously raised himself. When people raise themselves, she said, they often have a void they spend their whole lives trying to fill.

Was it that obvious that I was not to the manor or to the Riverside Drive born? I did not present any conventional clues of class friction and discomfort, like grease under the fingernails, the spear of straw hanging from the mouth, the dress bowling shirt. It had to be subtler. This idea of being a boy who raised himself baffled me. At the same time, it might be true. As for the void—well, that was on the money.

Despite the disgusting things I was doing—or yearning to do—to their beautiful, brilliant daughter, her parents were civil. People actually had conversation at dinner. I was tongue-tied more often than I care to remember. After dinner her father lit up tiny elegant cigars, French and German cigarillos. Those luxuries seemed the epitome of refinement I aspired to aspiring to. Her father opened his gold cigar case when he noticed my curiosity, recommending sagely it was not necessary to inhale. Soon I was holding one in my fingertips. It was fantastic. His daughter's boyfriend would one day himself pick up the habit, though the Davidoffs cost a small fortune. Later, when I applied for conscientious objector status in response to the Selective Service's interest in me, her father wrote a beautiful, generous letter of support on his personal stationery.

Stationery?

So *this* was how people lived? Who did I have to kill?

I could get used to this life. *Whom* did I have to kill?

Stationery!

I believed I would never belong, that I would never travel confidently in circles like these as long as I lived. I knew this on the night when her parents inquired about pot and about how all the kids were smoking it. Naomi's mom might have read the *Village Voice* and might have gone with her daughter to hear a folk singer in the East Village, and she called it Mary Jane.

"Want to try some?" Naomi brazenly asked her folks. She could cut to the chase. Naomi would someday assume a powerful post in the federal judiciary system.

Her parents ruffled and puffled and wiffled their lips and guffawed chuk chuk chuk and then, upon consideration of all the facts and hypotheses, and assessing the risks thereunto appertaining, indicated yes, they would try some of the cannabis weed. So we smoked a joint in the beautiful living room, which had stunning carpeting and rugs (some pinned on the wall!) but no television set, unlike the living rooms I knew. The folks laughed and laughed for no traceable reason. Naomi called her parents by their first names, and they did not object, so they all must have been stoned. Her folks laughed and laughed some more till they trundled off to bed. By morning light, Naomi was standing in the foyer looking into the living room, analyzing the subtle imprints and indentations on the plush piled carpet.

"Was somebody rolling around on the carpet?" she asked.

★

THIS NEXT PART HAS been put off long enough. With luck, we will get through this with a minimum of embarrassment for all participants involved.

When we separated for summer vacation the end of the first year, Naomi sent me a book. This was before she went to Woodstock that August with friends, including members of the male species. *Friends,* she said. She said they were *friends.* That was the word adumbrated. She joined the approximately seventeen million others, the number continually rising to this day, who claimed to have attended, but she went for real. She went with some *friends,* to be clear, including some friends who were not of the female persuasion, in case that was not obvious.

This wasn't the occasion of my first recorded outbreak of jealousy. I was provisionally acquainted with that emotional tapeworm twisting in my gut. The parasite was still in its nascent stage of development, however, and I earnestly strived to keep its growth in check. I had no notion the voracious beast had other ideas.

Back to that gift book. A book was innocent enough for two bookish teenagers. Girls had given me books a few times before, but they were all titled *The Prophet* by Kahlil Gibran. To me, that tome was conveniently short and vapid, much like my interest in those kind Catholic schoolgirls. Naomi's present was different. Somewhere in between the lines of the happy birthday inscription she penned, she intimated yes. Yes to the big, obvious question resonating, the question that had consumed us both: Do you want to? She was suggesting yes, she *did* want to. Maybe her yes was not a Molly Bloom yes yes yes, but I didn't know James Joyce yet, so I would have been tone-deaf to such an English majorish allusion. The fact remained: green light at the end of my dock (and I loved that other book).

The book she wrapped with the implied gift inscribed was a great novel by Thomas Hardy called *Jude the Obscure,* controversially published in 1895 and greeted by his enormous popular audience with shock and horror. I had never heard of the work or the author. As everybody but me knew, Jude the Obscure Fawley is a working-class kid with dreams of becoming a scholar. It took another working-class kid with scholarly dreams a while to get to reading this book. Maybe I was preoccupied rereading the inscription. As any English major could testify, the heartbreaking novel doesn't end anything like *It's a Wonderful Life.*

Soon we helped each other cross for the first time the rapids of the river of inexperience at the juncture where it diverginated. Naomi had taken the requisite care, contraceptually speaking. Previously, I had become intimately acquainted with the virtues of a cold shower, whose attractions rapidly paled. Because we cared about each other deeply and unironically, it was not something that had to be gotten through ironically, like prom night in the backseat of a car. Our selected romantic setting was an empty dorm room with a mattress on the floor before the school year began, in an otherwise empty building before the RAs planted their flag. We arrived on campus early to organize with other students for the purposes of ending the war in Vietnam. We had also arrived because we were in love.

At the grand moment she and I had been waiting for, there was the predictable amount of "you go here, no wait, that's me." And at some juncture, there was an endpoint, and maybe it was too quick but how would I know? (You always know.) Maybe there was a book to consult published in India or San Francisco with helpful pictures of earnest mustachioed men and acrobatic long-tressed women *in flagrante.* We were bookish, us kids.

Afterward, no cigarettes were fired up. No champagne cork popped. We could laugh about the clumsiness, now that we were experienced and grown up and by definition mature. Maybe the act was better for being about love, and for being anticipated for so long and so eagerly. Still, there was no question that this experience was better because it was excellent in and of itself. One lucky, lucky boy was I. It took me a long time, however, before I grasped how profoundly lucky.

Her flesh, my flesh. My flesh, her flesh. For a minute, it was all destined to be oneness. Oneness wasn't bad. It was better than advertised. And it produced bigger dividends than any twoness imaginable.

*

THE BLISS EXPRESS GOES off the rails. Others flirted with Naomi. This would qualify as a newsflash only on some planet other than Earth and in some institution other than college. She was of interest to other males, and males were omnipresent, like rodents in New York sewers. For instance, her rakish heartthrob of an English professor with a voice like syrup asked her out on a date in the middle of the term, which she told her boyfriend about, not expecting said boyfriend to explode with rage. She was naïve. I was irrational. This was long before lawsuits regarding sexual harassment. Being an idiot, Naomi's boyfriend could not tolerate this state of affairs. Poor word choice. She turned her professor down, a risky, brave move, and received a lower grade than deserved. But her boyfriend had bigger problems than *her* grade point average. Which was unkind.

Did my jealous spinouts drive me to crazy exhaustion? Yes. My obsessiveness and possessiveness did not get displaced onto other activities, like drugs that were within easy access. I liked drugs, and I enjoyed altering consciousness as much as the next longhair, but drugs were not all-consuming. I did my work devotedly, scrupulously. Was that obsessive? I was a schoolboy who did the reading and got his papers in on schedule. Nights were consumed by fretful, despairing, bitter imaginings, but I kept up *my* grade point average, as if it were a consolation. It is embarrassing to admit that it almost sort of was.

A jealous person has, in the psychologist Leslie H. Farber's words, "a despairing dilemma; he is driven to prove an infidelity he cannot tolerate and is unable to prove a fidelity he so obsessively requires." (Take that, Othello.) I was a sick young man, relentlessly giving over to my jealous fantasies, and wow, were they cinematic. Hardcore pornography had nothing on my day-to-day private screenings. I continually envisioned my love object literally in the grip of an X-rated exercise. And the details. The details. How crucial were the details, which I dotingly turned over as if I were waterboarding myself. As Farber put it, "Any particulars she offers, out of anger or compliance, will be seized upon and elaborated in his home movie, so that his obsession assaults him with sexual scenes he would avoid if he could. Though this home movie remains necessarily incomplete, its impulse is essentially cinematic in form (no still shots will do) and pornographic in content, having some resemblance to commercial pornographic films that portray, with a minimum of artifice, all the sexual posturings within reach of human bodies."

Love and sex. Secrets and deceptions. Naomi was sleeping with me. What would stop her from sleeping with somebody else? Every time I began with a new psychotherapist, the conversation started…

Wait, why were there always new psychotherapists into whose easy chairs I uneasily settled? Well, not so many anymore, but what about couples' counseling? The couples' counselors I met were usually big-haired, big-breasted MFCCs who had answers for everything, but despite that could well have been insightful. *Could* have been, that is, if one member of the couple didn't regard therapy as a branch of law enforcement. Every time the therapeutic conversation began the same way, with my rendering of the primal scene: hearing my father's rage over my mother's whorishness, and the recognition that she had betrayed everybody, including her son, and now that other marriage, another man, is in his imagination, unable to be dislodged, and my brothers are not my brothers anymore and it's all a big fiction, all a big lie. That's the primal experience my jealousy may be rooted in, but I'm not blaming my father and mother—I'm just connecting the dots, and that's what therapy is all about, right? Connecting the dots?

My love of Naomi was targeted as the first kill of my jealousy. I subjected her to degrading overemotional calisthenics, put her through the paces of suspicion, recrimination, self-justification, fear. Suspicion, recrimination, self-justification, fear. Those terms might as well have served as my college cheer. No wonder she would run for shelter as the sky darkened. I was a one-man year-round tornado.

Then Naomi did a semester in Europe, and I followed her there for an early spring visit. I took a flight to London, where they speak a version of the language, then a boat to Calais, where they don't. If I was not careful, I could get arrested for a criminally poor French accent. I met with Naomi, possibly in Paris, possibly in Rouen or Amiens or Poitiers. I remember the breathtaking cathedrals, the Jeu de Pommes, the Louvre. I read menus that memorably offer eel, a supposed delicacy in whatever region we are in, on which I took a shivery pass. Our travels together divided us.

On the flight back to San Francisco, I sat next to a beautiful art student who designed lingerie. The inevitable transpired. Is this a cliché, or what? I never confess to Naomi. Why would I? Once I had left for the States, her heels became round and she took up for real with a French boyfriend. Was this another cliché? She didn't get around to informing me right away. Could anybody blame her? Her assignation was unbeknownst for a while, though I congenitally doubt her. After all, I was cheating, too. What's good for the goose is good for the gander. I hate all the geese and especially all the ganders. Naomi and I wrote aerograms, we sent each other telegrams. Our sentences reeked of half-truths and lies. We broke up, thousands of miles apart in every sense.

Back at school for the new term, we avoided each other. But something drew us back together. Many months later we reconciled. But the wounds were too deep.

I was so jealous—so fraught—so anxious—so terrified over being humiliated again, over the prospect of Naomi's again sleeping with somebody else, including possibly somebody without French citizenship, that I initiated a preemptive strike. I slept with somebody else. This plain statement suggests the presence of much greater logic and perverse integrity than was currently in play. I could never believe, not really, not truly, that anybody would ever want to have anything sexual, erotic, romantic to do with me, so when somebody indicated an interest, I was confused, wanting to please, and after all, this girl who was flirting was going out of her way to do something gracious and altruistic and disgusting, so I would do whatever she wanted. I went with her after the anti-war meeting in the basement of the chapel. We walked over to her apartment, a nice girly-girl room with fluffy pillows. And it happened. I cheated. I performed ineptly. Whatever that meant. As if it isn't obvious what that meant.

More importantly, I betrayed Naomi when she came back to me, sullied as she was by her Gallic boy toy and the whole bris-eating nation of France. Yet the deed was done, I didn't die. Well, maybe a bit. Not that I expected to be struck dead, but that would have been all right, too. As far as that sorority girl was concerned, that was the end of our non-relationship, pretty much. I left her room. The sun was coming up. It was awful to see. I wandered back to the bed of Naomi. She never asked a question. I was a trustworthy guy who wasn't like that, after all.

Next time I saw that other girl, months later, I was leaving an arts lecture. She was sitting in the last seat on the aisle. I said nothing, she said nothing. She was holding an apple. A big red post-lapsarian Garden of Eden where's-the-serpent apple. She gave me a big bittersweet smile and tossed me the forbidden fruit. It spun in the air for maybe ten thousand years before it smacked into my palm. I wanted to laugh, wanted to cry. I went outside in the snow, a clear starry night. I couldn't bite into her apple, a magnificently bright red apple. I threw the apple as far and as high as I could. In the battle of images, she had crushed me and I would never forget her.

As far as my first girlfriend was concerned, she probably knew. I was wrong when I underestimated her. She went on to become a criminal defense lawyer. She probably knew everything. Which makes it something of a miracle that Naomi and I somehow remained friends.

★

SUCH A SCHOOLBOY. IN my freshman year, they placed me into an Honors seminar taught by a famous poet. The poet was cool and blustery as a Nor'easter and smoked corncob pipes. He had numerous opinions. He let you know how illustrious he was. He probably wanted to teach well, but one time he assigned a truly stupid paper topic, something about using a dictionary. Unbelievable.

The Honors student believed he had a fascinating take on the ridiculous subject. When the professor handed back the paper, there was a D penned in scarlet. I went to office hours. I gently suggested that, with all due respect, perhaps the professor had missed the point of the essay. The professor didn't think so. "Well," I argued, "I was writing a parody of a bad student paper." See the attitudinizing, famous professor poet? See the poor sentence structure through your corncob smoke? See the self-consciousness, sir? Isn't it obvious?

Strangely enough, I was telling the truth. It *was* intended to be a parody of a bad paper, which was my idea of the suitable response to an inane paper topic.

I took my D and went away.

Once the professor brought into class a couple of his friends who were visiting campus: a current A-list movie star and his radiantly gorgeous then-wife, a fabulous actress doing a celebrated star turn in an Ibsen play on Broadway. Naomi and I had seen the play. Oh my God: she was absolutely stunning up close. And Rod Steiger and Claire Bloom looked about as unmarried as any married couple could look and not be driving in a Benz down Sunset Boulevard. Somebody had a question for the tough guy: "Why?"

The man ran with the *why*. Why be an artist, why be an actor, why be a man? It was a terrible question, it was a great question. The man improvised the hell out of the question. Because there was no alternative, that was why. Art was the justification, and it was self-justifying. Who else would ask a dumb question like that?

★

NATURALLY, MY PARENTS HAD refused to fill out financial aid forms when I applied to college. My father disdained personal revelation to strangers, which was another thing strangers had in common with everybody in the family. Since the applicant wasn't going to go anywhere without financial aid, I forged the papers and tricked my mother into signing them—which was a big achievement considering who she was. ("No big deal, Mom, forms.") I recall invoking the word "grandiose" in an application essay, which I thought meant grandly inspiring. Probably too appropriate. I must have done a fair job of lying, because I received a handful of scholarship offers.

I followed the money. I chose the college that gave me the most. It wasn't as if I had the luxury of doing otherwise. Looking back, I might have chosen another college, but that was not a consideration—I was priced out by a few hundred bucks. I was on my own in the college search, never having had much in the way of counseling in high school, when they were promoting my religious vocation. Why did I apply to this college in the first place? My pal Frank and I were driving around one night, and Frank made a suggestion: "Why don't you go to Syracuse?" Syracuse *was* inarguably far away, and Frank's was all the college counseling I required.

Poor decision-making process or no, I ended up in by far the snowiest college in America—more than ten feet of snow a year. It was also a school overrun by excellent, celebrated writers in a famous creative writing program. I, of course, was clueless about the program's existence. But once again, I was lucky. A few of those writers taught me all a young writer could need, even if their lessons took long after college to sink in.

My favorite was George P. Elliott, a great, underappreciated author. His fabulous book of short stories, *Among the Dangs*, had been nominated for the 1962 National Book Award in Fiction, where it competed with, among other finalists, Heller's *Catch-22*, Salinger's *Franny and Zooey*, Yates's *Revolutionary Road*, Malamud's *A New Life*, Maxwell's *The Chateau*, Singer's *The Spinoza of Market Street*, and the winner, Walker Percy's *The Moviegoer*. Talk about a Murderers' Row.

George and I kept up correspondence for years after college. He nominated me for prizes and fellowships, some of which I won, introduced me to his agent. He pushed his student to question the zeitgeist. He generously marked up my manuscripts.

When I was in graduate school, a clerk in the English Department accidentally handed over to me my personal file. I was on my way to TAing a class before I realized what this trove contained. First chance, I took a look. This folder contained, among other materials, the recommendations that had been submitted in support of my application for the graduate program in which I was enrolled. The grad student hesitated—for maybe a minute. Then I allowed myself to read George's letter. I still feel guilty. As opposed to the other typed, two-page letters, George's letter was composed in his distinctive hand in blue ink and was exactly one-sentence long. It was a compound sentence, with two independent clauses. Eighteen words, one comma, and a period. It was the most generous thing any teacher ever said about me. It doubtless got me into Berkeley.

In 1980, George died of a heart attack, age sixty-two.

I have retained George's wonderful letters. In wistful moods, I have been known to resume the correspondence. I imagine writing, asking for advice, showing off, reaching out for the wisdom George had at his command. When I published my first novel, my biggest regret was that I could not send him the first copy.

★

As Brother Joseph I had reported to the local draft office, which was required by law. I was granted a somewhat rare deferment from military service: I-Y. At the time, this designation was reserved for an exclusive club that by statute included homosexuals and members of the cloth. According to what then prevailed as common sense, these were men "qualified for military service only in time of war or national emergency."

Now in college, I needed to be reclassified. I applied for conscientious objector status. I met with the resident Quaker advisor on campus, a burly fellow with a rabbinical beard. He was smart and helpful and encouraging, though he conveyed the fatigued sense that he had been going over this same ground for a thousand years. Quakers might understandably feel that way about the promotion of peace. On this score, there is that unforgettable moment in Vonnegut's *Slaughterhouse-Five*:

"You know what I say to people when I hear they're writing anti-war books?"

"No, what do you say, Harrison Starr?"

"I say, 'Why don't you write an anti-glacier book instead?'"

What he meant, of course, was that there would always be wars, that they were as easy to stop as glaciers.

I was officially applying for I-W status: "Conscientious Objector performing civilian work contributing to the maintenance of the national health, safety, or interest, or who has completed such work." My six-page essay to the draft board had a cover statement, which I signed and dated, February 9, 1970: "I am, by reason of my religious training and belief, conscientiously opposed to participation in war in any form and I am further conscientiously opposed to participation in non-combatant training and service to the Armed Forces. I, therefore, claim exemption from both combatant and non-combatant training and service in the Armed Forces, but am prepared to perform civilian alternative service if called." It must have been Quaker boilerplate, but it spoke my mind.

My essay quoted Jesus and various theologians and philosophers, with the goal of establishing my bona fides and telling the story of my religious background and training. It is the account of an earnest young man struggling to articulate deeply held conviction. It's composed in a non-ironic voice that I recognize as a true enough echo of my own today. I furnished three letters of support: one from Naomi's dad, one from the dean of the College of Liberal Arts, and one from the English professor who had once given me that D. I was humbled to read that they all testified to the applicant's sincerity, honesty, and conscientiousness.

The professor wrote me a cover note when he sent his letter, a letter which contained references to Gerard Manley Hopkins, a Jesuit priest who wrote spine-tingling poetry. "There is nothing untrue in my letter save only, perhaps," said my defender, "the first sentence of the second page." This was the sentence he referenced: "Mr. Di Prisco and I do not happen to belong to the same church."

The draft board elected not to consider my application, and here's why. When the lottery was established, the number I received was 222, which for all practical purposes assured me of never being drafted, and therefore guaranteed I was going to receive a student deferment, a status of II-S. I could not legally apply for I-W status because that was higher than the II-S, which I was already granted by reason of the lottery. What would have happened had my lottery number been lower and I had been drafted as I-A, or had been denied CO status? Would I have refused service? Would I have risked imprisonment? I believed I was ready to go to jail, if it came to that. There was no question that I would never serve in Vietnam.

★

THE ANTI-WAR EFFORT CONSUMED me. To further the crusade, I ran for student body president on a radical platform, hand-selected by the then–student body president David Ifshin. Dave was brilliant. He talked so rapidly you would wonder how he took in any oxygen. It was not long thereafter that he was famously and illegally flying to Hanoi alongside Jane Fonda (with rumors of romance trailing them). There he went on the radio with her to express American student solidarity with the Viet Cong. Afterward, Dave formed an improbable friendship with a POW named John McCain, who had been forced by his captors to listen to those broadcasts. Dave was influential in liberal Washington political circles until his early death from cancer. McCain delivered a heartfelt eulogy. Where did that principled fellow named John McCain ever go?

I helped Dave coordinate campus marches and protests, and I had a public profile that on one occasion inspired the substance of the lead Sunday editorial in the city newspaper—an editorial about me, amazingly, and my alleged ties with the Peace and Freedom Party, supposedly a violent, radical organization. I was never a member of the party, and never a member of the SDS, the Students for a Democratic Society, which was also demonized, seemingly appropriately, by the FBI. All the campus publications endorsed my candidacy. Pretty girls wanted to talk with me about my educational policies. I had all sorts of policies I wanted to share with them, not all of them educational in nature. Sometimes we would sit on stairwells and talk and sometimes get around to that subject. I would hold forth in my campaign stops, and I meant every word. My staff published my philosophies in long documents titled "Academic Revolution." My photos appeared everywhere. I resembled a happy frog with a beard. This was before *Sesame Street,* but I could have served as a model for a disconsolate Muppet. We distributed two campaign buttons. One read: "Reject the Insanity! Vote Joe!" The other said: "Too Much Outtasight, Not Enough Insight! Vote Joe!" Exclamation points ruled the day!

One night, these twin brothers called and offered me a lot of campaign money—I cannot recall how much, except that it was plenty—if I would appoint them to my cabinet. I told them to fuck off. I didn't like their attitude and presumption. In return, they backed my opponent. Real politik in action. I won the first round by a margin insufficient to avoid a runoff. Perhaps I should have taken the money. Maybe just this one time the ends justified the means. Had I taken the money and garnered their support, I might have won. The day of the election, most of my supporters were where I wanted to be: New Haven, at the protest that helped turn the tide of American public opinion.

★

ON A WINTER NIGHT we took over the administration building. It was going to be peaceful, not like takeovers at other colleges, where guns appeared in the hands of guys wearing stupid berets. I always hated the beret in any incarnation. And also guns.

Hundreds of students gathered. On the way to the administration building and our date with destiny, I marched with the publisher of the student newspaper, a bright fellow who would later become the publisher of a major metropolitan daily and eventually a billionaire in the dot-com boom. We knocked over garbage cans with half-hearted glee. This may not qualify as a surprise, but such an act was not satisfying, and we both quickly stopped our asinine vandalizing of the campus.

When the sun rose, the steering committee was entrenched in the chancellor's office, lounging with legs over the arms of his big chairs. We had been up all night. We did not do any damage to his office, though some guys did rifle his drawers, searching for the good cigars. The chancellor was a prolific, championship smoker. There was one crazy guy who had other ideas. "Let's set something on fire! Let's let them know we're for real." Nobody bit.

I had met the chancellor before anybody else in the room ever heard his name. I had been the one undergraduate representative on the university chancellor selection committee that, after a national search, recommended him to the Board of Trustees. It was intriguing to be inside the decision-making process along with muck-a-muck captains of industry and the faculty power brokers. They were smart or they were rich, or they were both. They politely listened when I graced them with my opinions.

I believed our choice was the right one, and the board concurred and coronated him with fanfare. He was a formidable man, tall and pink-faced, with the hint of a country accent that encouraged people to relax around his considerable intelligence and Machiavellian savvy. Since he assumed office, the chancellor had allowed me to meet with him so I could graciously enlighten him about the student point of view, access to which I believed I singularly possessed. He would come to appoint me to other university committees, including one conducting a search for the dean of the liberal arts college.

He also appointed me to serve, again as the one undergrad representative, on an emergency taskforce investigating charges of racism in the athletic department, which was the subject of a recent blockbuster front-page article in *The New York Times*. The campus was up in arms when the African American players rose in unison and quit the football team. The opinion on the quad and in the locker room was that the benighted coach had to go.

Our committee scheduled a meeting with the famous, grizzled football coach. That afternoon I had an exam, so I was late. When I did walk in, there was one seat available, directly opposite the granitic-jawed coach with a Semper Fi buzz cut. His head was down and his eyes were burning holes in the table, clearly pissed that we made him do the dog-and-pony. He was carrying on. The world was going to hell in a hand basket. His record spoke for itself: his Heisman Trophy winners, his ability to work with all student athletes. He was no racist, he was no racist, he was no goddamn racist. No, the atmosphere on campus was to blame. He had been coaching for decades and he knew what was up on the gridiron. All these protesters, these wet-behind-the-ear protesters. This was a great country, and his program was a great program, and they were miserable punk radicals. Then he slowly looked up and temporarily halted his diatribe. Our eyes met. He smiled sarcastically and pointed at me and said: "There's one right here."

After lengthy deliberations and interviews, our committee issued an excoriating report that might have set the land speed record for the use of the then-fashionable term "institutional racism." The coach resigned. Something tells me he "resigned."

★

IT WAS SIX IN the morning when the chancellor ambled confidently into his "liberated" office, sat down at his desk big as a luxury automobile, lit his trusty cigarette, inhaled, exhaled, and took the measure of the motley crew. He was cool and composed, almost perfectly concealing any semblance of rage he could have defensibly felt. His administrative assistant approached his desk and awaited instructions.

"Anybody need coffee?" he asked us.

Who didn't?

"Doris," he addressed his assistant, "looks like six, no, seven coffees. Cream and sugar? Joe, you want cream and sugar? Okay, Doris, two black and five with cream and sugar." The coffee materialized in time for us to be taken behind the woodshed.

"First of all," he drawled, "you have made me look bad with the board of trustees, so as of this minute, you're all expelled."

Many years later, I would be the chair of a board of trustees for a little school, nothing like a major university, of course. Back in college, I had no idea how serious looking bad to the trustees would feel to the chief executive officer. Looking back, I find it astounding how restrained the chancellor was.

I also need to mention another thing I find astounding. I was taken aback by the expulsion. What the hell else did I imagine was going to happen? Did I believe we wouldn't be disciplined? Honestly, the thought never occurred. Did I believe our action was going to change university policy? That instantly the chancellor would see the light? Hard to believe, isn't it? I suppose I thought we could be arrested, and in that way I could take my eternal place alongside other famous protesters who were members of my heroic pantheon: the Reverend Martin Luther King, Jr., Mahatma Gandhi, Henry David Thoreau. Time in jail was what history dictated. The hottest places in Hell are reserved for those who, in times of moral crisis, remain neutral. A famous Italian poet said that. Screw neutrality. The war was evil, it needed to be stopped, and the university needed to…

It is now unclear to me what I or any of us thought the university could or should do. I am sure we had ideas and proposals and demands. Big word back then: demands. The school had contracts with Dow Chemical. Okay, that was bad, Agent

Orange being what it was. Ivory tower, schmivory tower—the whole world was watching, and the political apocalypse was at hand. Up against the wall, motherfucker. And you know, if I had rationally calculated the risk of being expelled, it would not have kept me out of the administration building that morning. It might have spurred me sooner. Besides, the issue was too grave for me to worry about my petty little life. Another thing. Would they really expel somebody with my grade point average?

So the question about me remains. Naïve? Brave? Principled? Altruistic? Stupid? All of the above? I would probably now go with F, All of the Above.

The chancellor did not invite the local constabulary into the inner sanctum of his office. For the record, some of us called the cops pigs. Not me—I didn't do that. I didn't like name-calling, and it didn't seem necessary or a boon to our cause.

What was it he said again?

"As of this minute, you are all expelled."

Oh, right.

All around me flowered the crushed, disappointed countenances of my sleep-deprived, pallid peers as the news filtered down from the tops of their ponytailed heads to the bottoms of their salt-encrusted snow boots. Everybody fell silent. The chancellor wasn't finished. He was warming up. He let the silence build. He let the news sink all the way in. Then he expanded upon his previous declaration:

"You're expelled, that is, unless we figure out how we can all save face."

Brilliant. Such a brilliant move. I didn't think so at the time, but this move validated my belief during the selection process that he was the best person for the chancellor's job.

He said we were going to come up with a joint statement to release to the press, and afterward we were going to march over to the packed-to-the-rafters chapel in the heart of the campus. A thousand unruly supporters of the takeover were milling about.

"I'm not going out there alone," he said. Another brilliant move. He was going to speak, and we were going to stand behind him. Did we have all this straight? Good, then. And once we polished off the joint statement, we were going to leave his office in a peaceful manner and meet in the chapel. We could work with that.

That morning, I went on television for the first time. The takeover was the lead. I was interviewed by the peppy morning crew in between weather reports. There was always lots of big weather to report in the region. I am proud to say I did not mention that you don't need a weatherman to tell which way the wind blows. The smiley-faced interviewers were not hostile. They allowed me to make my case. I imagine that, if I didn't convert anybody, at least I didn't set back the cause. When it was done, I washed the make-up off my face as fast as I could.

After the takeover, the war went on, the university went on, and I myself went on to receive my college diploma. By past university practice and tradition, I would have been named class salutatorian. Whoever had the highest grades was valedictorian, of course. If, for instance, the valedictorian happened to be female, though, the salutatorian was to be non-female—the male, that is, with the highest grades among male graduates. This year that would have been me, or so the Registrar informed me. Daffy custom, it could be argued, and I might be inclined to agree—in theory. I was not a grade-grubber, but most of us grade-grubbers are similarly deluded. What cost me was the C in my Greek class on the Iliad. Homer is thrillingly accessible in the original Greek, it turns out. But I was too preoccupied with politics and I mailed it in, and honestly, that C was a gift. In any case, the commencement rules had been changed that spring. Nobody ever remembers the salutatorian, but something tells me the university did not want somebody like me up on the dais armed with a bullhorn.

Soon after graduation, I signed a contract to teach at my old high school and they paid me $4,900 for the year: in my eyes, a small fortune.

They say there's no going back, no reliving the past. Based on what I know now, I have to say they could be right. As for me, my first teaching experience happened the year—no matter what the meteorological records may indicate—when the rain rained down for three hundred and sixty-five consecutive days.

Stinson Beach and the Great Whites

I SLIPPED THE QUARTER into the slot of the payphone, heard the dial tone, and punched in my parents' number. It was 1975, when phone booths still existed. It was the same number my parents had had forever, since I had a room in their house. Calling them at five a.m. seemed like the thing to do under the circumstances. I knew I was going to be waking them up. This wasn't a time for sleepy heads.

I was at Kaiser Hospital on Geary Boulevard in San Francisco. The fluorescent lights turned the whole place yellowish-blue, like the inside of a neglected aquarium where somebody had stolen the fish and scooped out the water.

The phone was ringing. Good.

It was a cold November outside, and the sky was sparkling brilliantly. I remembered that from earlier in the evening, when I took some air and cleared my head. I walked through the dicey neighborhood and passed by The Peoples Temple, not far from the Fillmore Auditorium where I once saw the Allman Brothers. Red-shirted disciples of Jim Jones stood on the steps at full militant attention and somehow glared through their sunglasses. Exactly three years later to the day they would be drinking the Kool-Aid, committing mass suicide in Jonestown, Guyana.

That morning nobody lurked within view, not a bleary-eyed sleepwalking intern, not a custodian with a mop and a cigarette dangling from his lips. Candy machines loomed nearby, wrappers and soda cans littered the floor. The phone kept ringing. My parents were asleep. They had the right. But now they needed to wake up. I was hungry, I was thirsty, I was tired, I was happy.

Ring. Ring. Ring. Ring. Ring.

My mom was the designated phone-answerer, the switchboard operator.

"Hello?" She sounded like she was expecting the call, as she should have been. A teenage, positive mood swing inflected her tone.

"It's a boy," I said.

I could visualize her big smile. She liked the babies. The babies returned the compliment and liked her, too.

"He was born an hour ago."

She called out to her husband. "Joseph says it's a boy!"

"A boy?" my father said loud enough for his son to hear. Back then, pregnant couples didn't get to know the sex of their child in advance.

"And he's healthy and everything. He's perfect."

She asked about the baby's mother.

She was doing okay, considering her labor went for twenty-nine punishing hours.

"Twenty-nine hours!" Her voice lowered an octave: "They do a Cesarean?"

"No, the operating room was ready, but the Pitocin drip did the trick."

Letting a woman endure twenty-nine hours of labor effectively amounted to medical malpractice—not that the new dad appreciated this at the time. Every so often her labor petered out. Contractions weakened, then would intensify, randomly, unproductively. We had started in the midwife's Marin County residence, where we had intended to deliver. When dilation ceased, we were swooped up and sped to the hospital. The two guys in the ambulance looked to be eighteen, and earlier that evening had been acquainting themselves with a bong. To this day, I do not want to imagine all that might easily have gone tragically wrong. I do not want to remember that we were lucky, and I still want to sue those medical "professionals."

In the background I could hear my father: "Ask him how big!"

He was a healthy boy, seven pounds and change, and the Apgar score was excellent. Ten fingers, ten toes. The caller was exhausted and sleep-deprived himself—not as much as the new mom, of course, who was, I would freely stipulate, a champ during the ordeal. The new mom and new dad had had plenty of problems in their relationship, but we were united around this experience, for the moment, anyway.

My dad grabbed the phone. "Got a name?"

Not yet. What I didn't say was that the new parents were not in alignment on that one. I didn't embellish. If the baby turned out to be a girl—well, I cannot recall what ideas for a name we might have had. I wanted an ethnic Italian name, something that could never be truncated or adapted for a nickname. I wanted it to be a mellifluous name a girl could breathe into my son's ear, and mean it with the full sweet force of a whisper at a romantic moment. I knew the perfect name, and I was hoping I could sway the boy's mother in that department. I hoped as much though I had not enjoyed a record of success swaying her in any department lately, a pattern that I later concluded would continue forevermore. I was staunch as a pit bull, however, like me a member of a misunderstood species.

She was pushing a two-syllable Irish name, as Irish as any in *Angela's Ashes* and traditionally employed in Elizabethan pastoral poetry for wooly-minded shepherds. I mentioned this fact to her, in the interest of furthering the discussion. More often than not, speaking as a graduate student of English literature doesn't help a guy's cause.

We would leave the hospital without a name on the birth certificate. When all was said and done, the mom got the call on the boy's second name (the pastoral shepherd) and, for good measure, a third name (her family name). The father got to select the first (Mario), and we both agreed on the last, my family name. No ritual ceremony was organized to celebrate this event. It would take twelve years before Mario himself decided he wanted to experience his own baptism. When the news about that imminent occasion spread, somebody waggishly mused in my vicinity, "Despite your best efforts, your son became a Catholic." That observation didn't seem entirely right. But it didn't seem altogether wrong, either.

Over the years, Mario gravitated toward his father's close friend who was a priest. Father Shane is a mystical monsignor and a big-hearted Southerner who can out-preach any fire-and-brimstone Baptist, as well as being a psychotherapist and a lifelong Italophile. In other words, he was the perfect evangelist. He became the boy's spiritual guide and ultimately dispensed the sacrament. Mario asked my oldest friend, Bernie, to stand as the godfather, and my dear friend from graduate school, Katharine, to stand as the godmother. I was proud of him. It was no coincidence that this was when I, after a sixteen-year sabbatical, headed back to church, following in my son's footsteps.

I have no recollection as to what else my father talked about the early morning my boy entered the world, only that this moment constituted a significant marker. I caught a glimpse of my father in a new light. Being a father at age twenty-four put a new perspective on what it must have meant to my father to have a son—a son like me. I could put no words to that feeling, and I can barely put words to that feeling today, but it was true. It must have been hard for my dad. Did I ask myself then what my father was feeling when he was standing at a similar juncture in *his* life? I did not. But at least the two of us were joined around this experience: we were both fathers. Fathers and sons. Sons and fathers. The day your son is born you know deep down that many fathers and many sons are worthy of a long Russian novel. That night, I had a burst of sympathy for my dad. And something akin to appreciation. And something inside was telling me that this might be the closest we would ever be to each other.

Meanwhile, the newborn was resting at the breast of his exhausted and exhilarated mom after such a long journey. Everybody involved had come to the end of a very long journey. Another longer and twisting journey was about to begin.

★

A COUPLE NIGHTS BEFORE the birth, around midnight, I was behind the wheel of the 1962 Volkswagen Bug, which was a faded shade of robin's eggshell blue. My partner was in the passenger seat, her water broken as of a few minutes ago, her contractions commenced. We were going over the underratedly elegant San Rafael Bridge, heading into Marin County. Any bridge in the vicinity of the Taj Mahal of bridges, the Golden Gate, would suffer from an inferiority complex. It was the middle of November, an electrically bright moonlit night. The Bay was black and shiny like a stallion, and the velvet sky was cloudless. We were on our way to having a baby.

We had attended birthing classes as students of the Bradley Method, so we sort of anticipated what was on the horizon. The Bradley Method was purportedly different from the Lamaze Method. Bradley was branded "husband-coached natural childbirth." I would learn what has been obvious to birthing moms since babies were first being born, namely that "husband-coached" anything during labor is an open invitation to wife-coached homicide. There is, however, the possible dream exception of the "husband-coached" epidural, which I wished had been administered to me.

Epidurals, however, were not the order of the day. She had learned how to breathe, prompted by her birth coach (me) before my head could be bit off. Our birth would be natural. We had decided on a home delivery—not at our home, for some reason, but the home of the RN midwife in Marin County. I am certain that pellucid, unassailable logic was informing each and every one of these moves, but I cannot currently reconstruct it. Nowadays, whenever my sensible, professionally accomplished adult son hears about this plan, I can almost hear his perfect teeth grind as he marvels over how incredibly stupid his parents were. It is hard to argue. But his mother and I were working on what we took to be the most enlightened contemporary thinking. For instance, our team of obstetricians was very well respected in the community: pleasant, forward-thinking, sure of themselves. With any luck, some of that élan would accidentally rub off on this father-to-be.

"Don't drink a lot of alcohol," the OB advised his patient, "couple of drinks a day tops."

Chalk that up as useless counsel. The hippie-chick mom-to-be was a teetotaler.

Graduate student dad-to-be butts in: "How about cocaine?" That sounds really bad these days, I know, but there was a lot of coke around then, going for next-to-nothing in those neatly folded gram-size bindles, which were widely assumed to be joyous packets of powdered energy that generated such animated conversation—endless, world-stopping, brain-napping, spirit-crushing conversation. Who could possibly know that what seemed like party candy would end up being granulated morbidity snort? Oh, maybe an obstetrician who graduated from a certified medical school?

"Cocaine?" considered the doc. "She can do some coke, in moderation."

Moderation—that was what was advised with regard to the crystalline alkaloid $C_{17}H_{21}NO_4$ that Sigmund Freud prescribed to patients while setting aside some for his hirsute unconscionable self, with results history has shown to be the fruits of quackery.

Again, I wonder if I can still sue those clowns.

When she became pregnant, we were living together in a cabin on the side of a hill with no neighbors and a potbelly stove for warmth—and boy, did we need that for the cold nights. I had played my generative, biological, evolutionarily dictated role of producing and encouraging along the tiny swimmers who made a successful beachhead. Happy times perfectly eluded us. There were some good moments, sure. I recall watching Monty Python with her. I recall going to stores together, shopping for groceries, when I felt useful and connected. Tofu and Brussels sprouts and snow peas were in bounteous profusion.

Stinson Beach is about as lovely a stretch of coastal land as there is in all of California. I was in the English Department at Berkeley, a ninety-minute drive away, with a miniscule graduate fellowship, while also working part-time as an English teacher at a private middle school, in total making less money than the illustrious, locally born Native American named Ishi. I was driving a 1967 blue Ford Thunderbird with a so-called landau roof (which meant polyvinyl chloride) and a set of impressionistic dents (not by me but the duffer I bought it from) on the doors, which resembled cans at the discount grocery store. Three days a week I'd drive over the hill on the two-lane, curling, maddening Highway 1, often behind tourists with bumper stickers that said, "I May Be Slow But I'm In Front of You." On the plus side, the car was equipped with an FM radio, a big deal for me.

I remember picking up a letter in my post office mailbox. It was from a very good university press, offering to publish my first book of poems. This publication offer was incredible. I thought everything would turn around now.

I could say my own experience of family had not given me much to work with, but nobody stopped me from coming up with a plan and a design, and I never did conceive one. I have to admit that I never once thought about what a family should be, or could be, for that matter. I don't know why I never had fantasies of happy homes and happy children and happy dogs gathered around the hearth, but I never did.

Here is the final poem in that book that came to be published, a book that I dedicated to my son's mother. I make no apologies.

I was a young man expecting a baby and I was standing outside looking at horses grazing on the hillside, and hawks soaring overhead, and I could almost imagine that somebody else in my place—a better person than I—would be happier with the hand he had been dealt. The most complimentary review it received, which appeared in *Kayak*, my favorite poetry magazine and one of the most influential poetry journals in the country, quoted admiringly the whole thing. The poem is titled "_____ in the Pregnant Garden":

> *Twenty-five days and we'll have zucchini,*
> *In two months more there will be snowpea,*
> *In three months more a child.*
>
> *The world is too violent to usher in a*
> *Squash, so many generations of*
> *Stony uncultivated fields and plots gone to seed.*
>
> *Today, though, Sunday between us*
> *Under the sun, the one season for giving*
> *Birth, you pick away at the weeds,*
>
> *Wander marvelous among the artichokes,*
> *Bitter lettuce, peppers, and California poppies,*
> *Radiant, about to bloom.*

How could somebody not want to be with somebody who would write a poem to her? Pathetic, I know. Don't remind me.

★

STINSON BEACH, A HEARTBREAKING town. I liked the beach, where I walked the dogs, the highpoint of the day. Every so often there would be reports of Great White sightings and panic would spread on the shore abandoned by would-be swimmers.

Who worries about a white shark nuisance when you are depressed? Shark bites can sound like a welcome relief. Who cares about a spectacularly beautiful ocean and hawks soaring over the hills when your life is falling apart? Nothing makes a difference to people having a baby who know they are not going to make it together, no matter how hard they try, though try I would and try maybe she would. I pity the industrious, gifted family therapists who shook their heads as they applied buckets of glue to the leaking hull of the good ship *I Give Up*. One family counselor pulled me aside, breaking the rules, and said, "Joe, leave her." That made sense. That was a plan, or a half of one. I didn't leave her. It wasn't that simple. Together, apart. It didn't make a difference.

It was all bad. While driving my father's car on Highway 1, I got into a head-on crash at a curve. Nobody went over the side into the sea, and nobody was cited by the Highway Patrol. It was an accident. A tiny consolation was reading my books outside the hillside cabin at a small, weathered red table. Sometimes the gentler horses stuck their necks over the fence and I would rub their noses, feed them apples. I was studying the Renaissance, also the Metaphysical Poets. This is good company for a bad time—horses and Andrew Marvel, dogs and the sea.

We moved from Stinson to the East Bay for reasons no longer recoverable, but they were certainly finance-related, for every single decision was finance-driven. As for my not being a husband and her not being a wife, I did all I could to rectify that omission. I asked for her hand in marriage, and meant it sincerely. I didn't get down on bended knee, she didn't tear up. It wasn't made for TV. She rejected the offer. We were slipping and sliding on the icy steps to domestic disaster.

★

I SUPPOSE I SHOULD give thanks that she would not marry me— and I would be astounded if she did not feel the same way. We met while walking our dogs under the BART train tracks in Albany. And she, age twenty-nine, became pregnant quicker than you could say "About that birth control..."We were not a match made in heaven, or in Marin County, or anywhere else. I could call her passive-aggressive, and she could call me jealous, and she was right, of course. In the end, I was not her cup of chamomile.

Who could know the two of us would be intertwined for the rest of our lives, and that the wounds, so nicely scarred over, could be pried open whenever the need arose, using the emotional equivalent of a screwdriver or kitchen knife, or whatever else was handy around holidays and so-called family occasions?

Who could know we'd be intertwined forever?

Who? Besides everybody?

We could not have done a worse job of giving birth if we had decided to be the most incompetent parents on the face of the earth, with the possible exception of Michael Jackson and his spouses, without all those inconvenient millions and cosmetic surgeries. And despite this, I think we did not do a totally terrible job of being Mom and Dad. It goes down as a minor miracle, considering how much vitriol we two so-called adults produced, how little money we had, how little we had in common, etc. Sometimes you also can get lucky, as we did, producing a child who was better, much better than we could have hoped. Or as Mario was alternatively and affectionately known and revered: Baby Jesus.

Once when he was in high school he and I had a heart-to-heart. My son mused how lucky he had been. That was the word he used, *lucky*. I was moved he felt that way, but I knew there were times I had done less than I should have, and he had deserved much more. We were all lucky.

★

SHE THREW ME OUT of the house before our son turned one. Denying me access to my son will always constitute her unforgiveable deed. At the same time, I get why she did it. A celery stalk would get it. I found a room for rent in Berkeley, in a separate part of the house from a divorced mom and teenage daughter. There was nothing wrong with these people, probably, but I was more than miserable, and seeing the two of them made me feel more depressed. These were months when I can recall the same song always playing on the radio, a mind-rottingly catchy tune by Elton John. To this day, when I hear this song on an elevator, where it belongs, I want to cry. I was broken-hearted, missing my son, but there would be no reconciliation. On one level, that was a wise, judicious, prudent decision. On another level, I screamed silently at the ceiling every night.

The years went by. I hate it when the years go by. And they were going by like flocks of birds dive-bombing my head. I pulled together some money and retained a good lawyer. I sued to legally establish paternity. There were no forms in the courthouse for what was termed "inverse paternity." Nobody ever sued for that. It was normally the other way around—women sued men to assume responsibility. My lawyer said the judge loved this, and that seemed to be true. I was awarded joint legal custody.

It wasn't enough. I yearned for more access to, more time with, my son. She dared me to take her to court. My lawyer said I had a case for physical custody, now that judges were taking claims by fathers more seriously. But he also pointed out something that the boy's mother's lawyer had undoubtedly told her, namely that testifying would be traumatic for a young boy, squeezed between parental loyalties. I decided not to sue. She won the way she usually did, by being passive-aggressive, by daring me to play chicken with our son's emotional health.

New drama unfolded over the years, this one involving—let's say Stanley was his name. That drama begins before the break-up.

Stanley and I had become fast friends at a writer's conference, when I was immersed in the pregnancy to the extent that I could barely pay attention to the workshops and the competitive infighting young poets are renowned for. Stanley and I believed we were above all the pettiness. Stanley was wry and big, long and lean as a great room crossbeam, and he looked and talked like a dockworker—scarred face, dentures, beer can at the ready. And go figure, but this is the truth: He wrote poetry like an angel. The two of us were kindred spirits among the male poet testosterone-challenged pale-skinned types, who were equally divided between dandified aesthetes wearing pastel headbands and tough-guy poseurs in denim work shirts bought at Macy's. I placed myself in both camps.

Stanley was different. He really was a tough guy, an alpha. His whole bearing suggested capacity to do damage—to others and if necessary to himself. His body listed like he had finished the eighth round, and whoever was in the opposite corner would be crazy coming out for the ninth.

The mom-to-be was distraught that the dad-to-be was gone, even though I had a scholarship and she had encouraged me. Come-here-go-away was her go-to move.

By now you have observed that I reference her state of mind as if I had entrée. As you are doubtless concluding, I did not enjoy any such privilege. I would need to be another Ali Baba scuffling with thieves to trick his way inside the cave. I never decoded the open sesame. So discount a serious percentage of everything I say about her, from the non-identification of her name to the content of her heart.

At that writing conference, as with all such forums, there was the usual nocturnal intramural action. The queen bees flirted with Stanley and me. Nonetheless, I can be a sentimentalist, so whenever I see the published books of that lovely novelist who was batting her eyelashes at me my heart still skips a tiny beat. I missed my pregnant partner, and she said she missed me. I left the conference and went home early. Stanley did not leave. But nothing happened, he swore, with the now-famous poet he was romancing, or was being romanced by—and sometimes, honest, isn't it hard to tell? Stanley and I resolved to stay in touch, which we did.

Stanley and his wife had a child, a gorgeous, sweet guy, and the three of them would come over sometimes. When Mario was born, they were helpful, bringing tuna casseroles and beer, the touching sweet stuff young parents do for each other.

Then came a series of shocks. Stanley's wife, who had the same first name as Mario's mom, was diagnosed with advanced-stage lymphoma. The cancer mercilessly ravaged her. Within a few months, she was dead. This turn of events was unbelievable in the way that such things can seem unbelievable to you when you are twenty-five years old. I was not yet accustomed to the ordinary devastating depredations of real life. Stanley's wife was a kind and smart woman, funny with an edge of sadness, like a movie you watch when you battle insomnia and images on the screen blur. The loss was devastating for all of us. The night she died Stanley said she visited him in spirit form and comforted him till the time came for her to be on her way. Everything indicates that he was telling the truth as he knew it.

A couple of years later, romance bloomed for Stanley and Mario's mom. It wasn't long before the two of them moved to an undisclosed out-of-state location. All I heard through the grapevine was that she took our now two-year-old son and Stanley took his, and she didn't tell me where they went or furnish any further details. What's the old joke? *My wife ran off with my best friend, and I really miss him.* Not quite.

The sequence of events grows cloudy. She and Stanley broke up after a year or so of cohabitation in, I would eventually find out, the Arizona desert, and she moved back to the Bay Area. At least my boy was back in California, where I could cultivate the dream of more and freer access.

Eight years pass. I get a call out of the blue.

"You still comin' after me?" That was no-nonsense Stanley. The two of us had not talked for a long, long time, since bitter words were exchanged.

"Probably not." I didn't feel the anger of betrayal anymore.

"I need to know." He had a Boston-inflected voice that had been soaked in a six-pack of Guinness and a bottle of whiskey.

"Why can't you live in suspense like the rest of us?"

"'Cause if you're still comin' after me, I'm comin' after you first."

Stanley was the sort of guy who meant it when he said something like that. He also apologized for what he had done. He had broken a code, and he knew it. He was sorry, and he implied he could say more if that was necessary. It was not.

"OK, I'm not comin' after you," his former friend decided.

"Good. Something else. I just had a baby. I mean, my wife had a baby, a boy." They were living in Baltimore. The new wife was news.

"Congratulations, Stanley."

"I'm naming the boy after you. I was going to name him after you even if you were comin' after me. So I'm glad you're not comin' after me. This way, I can name him Joe instead of the other name I had for you. I figure not too many kids'd wanna be named Asshole." He also issued an invitation to come to Baltimore. "I got a job teaching writing in the prison. They got good crab cakes in town. I want you to be the kid's godfather."

That wasn't the only out-of-the-blue communication I ever received from that once-upon-a-time couple.

One day, some thirty years after secretly moving to Arizona, Mario's mother mailed an astonishing note to me, here printed in its entirety:

Dear Joseph,
I have wanted to say this for a very long time.
I am sorry for taking Mario and not telling you where he was. There are no words for the pain of not knowing where your child is.

I wish you well.

Thirty years. I have yet to figure out how to respond.

★

THE SUMMER MARIO WAS ten, he and I traveled to the East Coast. We went to museums and baseball games, we stayed with my college friends, we met the new godson. There remains one valuable souvenir, a postcard my son sent me after we got home. It's the famous NASA photo of the Earth as seen from outer space. From that vantage point the Earth looks particularly beautiful. As the postcard and the whole trip showed, sometimes you need to look through the other end of the telescope.

August 10, 1985
Dear ~~Mario~~ *Dad,*
    This card will remind you of all that we did when ~~your~~ *were 35 years old and went to Baltimore, Washington and New York. I loved going there with you because you are easy to travel with. I hope when you have your grand children and remember this great trip*
Love,
Mario Di Prisco

★

YEARS BEFORE THAT JOURNEY with my son, my mood had been different. That was before my relationship with Mario stabilized and I had regained paternal access. That was when my parental, domestic, romantic, spiritual, and professional life was in a shambles. I was twenty-eight years old and adrift. This was not a new feeling, to tell the truth. Even new shambles, I believed, would be better than the old, familiar shambles. It was too late to run away and join the circus, I supposed. Racecar driver?

My Honda hatchback was a major limitation in that regard. Firefighter? Fear of heights. And death. Enough said. I became a professional gambler.

This was a surprisingly small leap for a baby daddy studying for a doctorate in English literature at Berkeley, penning the increasingly infrequent poem, being fairly permanently broke, donning flannel shirts, and feasting on veggie stir-fry for dinner. In due course, I would be wearing silk suits purchased by my backer along with one pink suede Neiman-Marcus jacket, my uniform of choice while wagering big bucks in casinos around the world, and afterward drinking comped Dom Pérignon in Las Vegas, Monte Carlo, the Caribbean, and South Africa.

I keep the pink suede sport coat to remind myself where I once was. Deep, deep in the farthest reaches of my closet is where I can find it, a coat so bright it almost glows, radioactive. The other day, I tried it on. It almost still fits. Funny how so much about those years almost still fits.

Sailing to Las Vegas

I T ALL BEGAN WHEN I worked in an Italian restaurant. Everybody should work in an Italian restaurant at some point. Not a Babbo or Del Posto or Spago or A16 or Marea or Maiolino or Prima. The right kind of restaurant should be rough around the edges, with sausage and mushroom pizzas ordered family size, a place without a page of thousand-buck Barolos on the wine list. A place where waiters cannot bank on a twenty-percent gratuity, or any tip—some place where a customer might dash out without paying, and you're going to have to tackle him on the sidewalk. A place where sliced sourdough is served in baskets covered with a paper napkin. Nothing corporate, though, nothing like pretend Italian restaurants manufactured for television ads. The right kind of Italian restaurant prepares you for anything, whatever your course in life turns out to be.

I started at that sort of restaurant when my younger brother, who was the manager, and a great one before he was strung out, got me the job. While I was still living in the house with my child, I needed the money to pay the rent. After I was booted, I kept working. I didn't formally leave graduate school, but nights were often dedicated to delivering the spaghetti with meatballs or the cannelloni and not to the marvels of the Metaphysical poets. It was a very popular restaurant not far from Cal, with lots of table turnover, so it was a good opportunity to line the pockets of the average waiter, or even the pockets of a below-average waiter like me. And everybody should work as a waiter once, too. It humbles you, whoever you are. Humble pie has a distinctive taste, like Vegemite, that is impossible to forget or desire ever again.

My fellow waiter Mickey asked a big question one night. "You want to make some real money, Joe?"

Mickey wasn't a waiter because he was broke. He was rich, but without ready access to his money, which he stashed in a Swiss bank. Mickey, all five foot one of him, was in his early thirties, a block of marbleized muscle, blond hair, baby face and baby blues, a big smile full of brilliant white teeth. As a condition of parole, he was employed by the restaurant owned by the stylish, brainy, entrepreneurial Johnny Francesco.

Johnny was a complex, enigmatic man, with a streak of tragically Italian sensibility wide as the mighty Arno. This waiter he had hired could not anticipate this, but Johnny and I would become close one day—not the stuff of *The Great Gatsby*, but at least *The More Than Relatively All Right Francesco.*

As for Mickey, he was fresh out of San Quentin after doing five years on a first conviction for distributing serious-weight heroin.

"Don't say that *word!*" Mickey would freak whenever somebody did.

"What word should I say?"

"Say *shit, stuff, smack, H, horse,* I don't care, only don't ever say that word."

On this night, we weren't talking old business. We were talking new business and real money. *Real money*, what could that mean?

I was a worse waiter than graduate student, but I was paying the rent with the cash picked up on the tables combined with meager teaching assistant or fellowship money. Mickey was possibly a more inept waiter. If Mickey had been brought up in another world, and not on the streets of East Oakland, he would have been a stock analyst, an inventor, a politician, a lawyer. Maybe a professor. How he tolerated the slugs, lopps, punks, and knick-knackers—or so he liked to characterize them—who contaminated his tables was a mystery. It was a wonder he didn't knock somebody's head off when they complained about the minestrone or left a measly tip. The minestrone polarized the clientele. Some loved it, some were disappointed. While we're on the soup subject, controversial minestrone is another marker of the right sort of Italian restaurant.

As for real money, Mickey wanted to introduce me to the great Al Francesco, brother of the great Johnny Francesco. Despite their names, the Great Francescos were not a magic act or lion tamers, though their line of work was not completely unrelated.

His fellow waiter had never heard of Al Francesco.

That was okay. Al had never heard of Joe Di Prisco, either.

"You're not a waiter," Mickey declared, but not in an unkind way. He was voicing what disgruntled customers in my section waiting for their bread, their house wine, their fettuccine alfredo uttered all the time.

"I'm asking you a question, brother. You want to make some *real money*? You're a smart guy. When you gonna stop knick-knackin' around?"

Good question. What did I have to lose?

In the English teacher trade, that's called a rhetorical question, as in nobody expects someone to answer it. As it turned out, that question would become anything but rhetorical.

Mickey and I would go on to be cellmates—well, roommates in Vegas—and Mickey was one of the smartest people I ever met. He had a sentimental as well as a ruthless side. Whenever he had a personal problem, almost always with reference to the latest heartbreaker of a girl, Mickey would pick me up and we would go for a ride in the metallic blue Corvette. We would drink cocktails and talk. Mickey would offer to lend me a few bucks if I ever needed. And there was always plenty of coke for sharing.

"How much is real money?"

It must have been a relatively slow night because we were talking in the waiters' station and nobody was flagging us down, abjectly pleading for water, food, fork.

"Few hundred thousand in cash a year."

No, I didn't have to kill anybody. But I would have to kill on the blackjack table. Al Francesco was starting a new blackjack team. His was the biggest name in the world of counting cards, internationally feared, legendary. One night he cleaned out a small French casino. There was a snapshot of Al leaving the place with a black satchel stuffed with francs. He was grinning like a fat man in a funhouse mirror. Now Al had come up with a revolutionary new idea. Mickey signed up for the new team, and he was recruiting his fellow waiter to join.

If Mickey explained the essence of the big idea, it was instantly lost on his listener, who didn't understand the first thing about gambling.

"It's not *gambling*. It's counting cards. You're not gambling. You are doing statistical probability analysis."

Maybe Mickey understood what he was saying, but the potential recruit was in the dark. My scores on the math part of the Graduate Record Exam must have elicited guffaws when my graduate-school applications were read.

When Mickey got worked up, sometimes his eyes glistened through the rhinestone-studded aviator glasses he usually wore. They accessorized nicely with his twin diamond pinky rings.

"Come on, man, waitin' on tables, teachin' school? Quit knick-knackin' around, brother. Ain't nobody gonna fuckin' hand it to you on a fuckin' silver platter." Mickey spoke in mob movie dialogue, never more effectively than when he was being sincere.

His recruit had better break the bad news. I'd been keeping this to myself long enough.

"I never played the game."

Mickey may have not met anybody who had never played blackjack.

"I don't even know the rules of blackjack," I added. Mickey beamed. "Perfect," he said.

★

AL FRANCESCO'S PENTHOUSE APARTMENT featured splashy, panoramic Bay views of majestic bridges and was accentuated with plush casino hotel–style furnishings. Everything was white, with glass and porcelain everywhere. To childproof the place, you would need to padlock the front door. Al's home was pristine and uncluttered, except for a table with teetering stacks of books and numerous decks of cards and charts. Mickey and I were invited out onto the balcony, where there was a telescope set up, lens pointing down.

Al invited me to take a look. Al's suggestions were not suggestions.

On the other end of the telescope a very attractive woman was sunbathing in a bikini at the side of the pool.

"Nice view, huh?"

There was a blackjack table set up in the kitchen, and there was a crockpot stewing lunch. Al fancied himself a chef, not without cause, and this was the era when everybody possessed one of those artifacts called a crockpot, then ubiquitous as a moon rock. This was the same cultural epoch during which most of the buttons on a man's shirtfront were as functional as Dodo wings. French wine was uncorked on the counter. Al was living the dream life as the most unusual type of gambler there is: a successful one.

"Mickey says you're smart. What I hear from him and my brother Johnny, maybe you'd fit in with the new team I'm putting together. I know your brother and your dad, too."

My pedigree was coming in handy for a change.

"I never played a hand of blackjack in my life."

"Yeah, Mickey told me." Al chuckled. "That's okay. Might be better you don't know the game."

I thought I should clarify: I had never gambled a dollar in my life. Al turned his head to hear better. He was fairly deaf in his right ear.

"Good. Blackjack's not gambling."

How much I had to learn, I had no idea.

"So you would be a good candidate. Means I can teach you the right way. You don't come in with no preconceptions."

No reason to argue with a man who might make me what I could hypothetically conceive of as being rich.

"Blackjack's a simple game. Simple. I didn't say easy, I said simple." He repeated himself for emphasis a lot, but with him, it wasn't irritating or patronizing. Al Francesco was impressive, except with regard to the mispronunciation of his last name *Fran-ses-co*, instead of saying the Italian *Fran-che-sco*. But that's all right, because that's not his real name anyway. It *is* the name they put on the wall when he was made the inaugural member of the Blackjack Hall of Fame, and whenever his blackjack peers speak of him, they do so in hushed, reverential tones. Any Hollywood movie referencing blackjack, such as a production involving MIT students who think they invented the counting as well as the calculus and possibly the microcomputer, depends upon the Big Player schemes first conceived by Al, a guy straight outta Gary, Indiana, a town where the economy depended upon the local guys' proficiency at helpfully lightening the load of trucks overladen with toasters, leather coats, and televisions.

Al had a reputation for being able to throw a good punch if the occasion dictated. If half the stories were half-true, you wanted to be on his good side in a bar fight. Even dressed as Al was that afternoon in his tennis whites, he wasn't the kind of person whose parking place you would try to steal. At the same time, with all that was left of his hair flaring along the sides of his head, he looked like a cerebral, charismatic bantam rooster. First impression for this recruit: Al was a smart guy. Second: This could get interesting. Third: Thanks, Mickey.

"Blackjack's about beating the dealer. Beating the dealer. It's not about making blackjack, though there's nothing wrong with making blackjack."

The subtlety was lost on me, who in the first place didn't know what constituted "making blackjack." In my defense, beating the dealer is a subtlety lost on nearly every loser throwing away his money on tables in the casino. It wouldn't be long before I got it. Not if Al had anything to do with it, and Al most definitely did.

"I'm going to give you some books."

Now we were talking. Books were things I had seen before. "Read them."

I didn't think there was any ambiguity about what you were supposed to do with a book, but I was not going to question Al—not for a long time, anyway.

★

Soon Mickey and I were back at the penthouse, and the professorial Al Francesco held forth. He was good at that. His task was to instruct the two of us and the other four members of the team in the principles and practice of counting cards. The six of us came from different backgrounds, though nobody besides Mickey and his running-mate Woody was an ex-con. My teammates were all pretty good guys on balance, and they were prepared to quit their day jobs to move to Nevada or wherever Al wanted to base his operations.

Tim was the brainiest and braggiest. He didn't carry around his college transcript, but he made you think he could impress you with it at a moment's notice. He had technological ability, and despite his personality flaws he was highly skilled. These days he has a seat on a stock exchange. Ali was a jelly-bellied, handsome, mustachioed Iranian who bellowed like the twin cams of his sports car and called himself *Persian*. Mickey and

Ali were rivals, and Ali could get under his skin. Ali would say something like, "I go to restaurant now." Mickey would flip. "I go to *the* restaurant now," Mickey would scream. "I go to *the* fucking restaurant now! You been living here for twenty years. Say fucking *the*." Ali's belly would shake with laughter.

Blackjack is different from, say, craps or roulette or the slots, where the odds are killer, especially the slots. Poker, a great game, is all about playing your opponent. Sure, you figure percentages in poker, but as much as anything else, you make crucial decisions based on a psychological reading of the table. With blackjack, it's you against the house, and the house has no strategic options. You continually recalculate the odds based on the cards that are played. Once a card leaves the deck, it's not coming back, and the drift of the deck determines the size of your bet as well as your moves. You seek out favorable situations and then pounce. To put it simplistically, you yearn for decks relatively rich in tens and aces. Another way to put it is that decks relatively poor in fives and other small cards are good. That's the essence of counting. No wonder the bored rocket scientists were descending in legions on Vegas. Computer models were easy to generate and the software churned through billions of hands. There was excellent information, and there were powerful systems for counting. But counting cards in real time was harder. For one thing, casinos were taking countermeasures, such as barring counters—or gamblers thought to be counting. They were not being sporting about it.

I told my dad about my new direction. He liked to play blackjack. He liked to bet anything. He was happy for me. "Lots of luck," he said.

The counter's sacred touchstone text is Edward O. Thorp's classic *Beat the Dealer* (1962). Popular counting systems—Revere, Humble, Hi-Opt—followed the pioneering lead of the Thorp Ten Count. All books on blackjack after Thorp are essentially footnotes to his. The counting system that caught on with sophisticated counters was the Lawrence Revere Advanced Point Count. Al was going to teach everybody that system. In all card counting, each card has a value, and you track the net value of the deck as you go along. The suits are immaterial. Here are the Revere card values:

2, 3, 6 count for plus 2.

7, plus 1.

4, plus 3.

5, plus 4.

Aces and 8s, zero.

9, minus 2.

10 (all the face cards, plus the 10s), minus 3.

You keep count of all the cards, and maintain a separate count for 8s and aces. A lot of numbers to process, yes. But humanly possible. Not easy, but doable.

Back then, single-deck (52-card) games were available. That is the best sort of game for a counter. Multiple-deck games were proliferating, because casinos believed it was harder to count multiple decks, which are dealt out of a contraption called the shoe. It isn't necessarily harder to count multiple decks, but it can take a lot longer to find and maintain an edge. Counters depend on the house going deep into the deck or the decks, no matter the number, one or four or six. The situation has deteriorated since. Nowadays, it is not rare to find a blackjack table that employs a "continuous shuffle" device. That is, every single deal becomes effectively the first hand. It's futile to count cards with the "continuous shuffle," because you never get information upon which to act strategically. Better to bet on flipping coins.

Here's a random, simple counting example with a single-deck game. Let's say you're playing heads up, alone against the dealer, as most counters strived to do. You keep a running count. Incidentally, there is a running count as well as a true count, which is based on the level of penetration into the deck. The cards are dealt and you count their values. You keep track of two sets of numbers: the raw total of your hand, which determines wins and losses, and the card counting value, which determines a player's decision-making.

Let's say this is your hand: a 7 and a 9. You have 16. The dealer shows an up card 5. The counting total is separate from the hand total, remember. The running count in this hand therefore is +3, which you calculate by adding up all the values (+1 -2 +4 = +3). Now, 16 is not a great draw, but that is not most significant at the moment. Remember, the goal is to beat the dealer. What is more significant is that the dealer shows a 5. You would never hit a 16 against a 5 in a plus count, which is what you have. For one thing, there is a good chance you would catch a card that would take you over 21, and you would bust out and lose. For another, given the appearance of that 5, there is a high percentage the dealer is going to bust out—that is, go over 21, so you win. In the counter's sweetest dreams, the dealer always has a 5 for an up card.

If you were fortunate enough throughout your life to play exclusively a plus deck, which is mathematically impossible, and if you played infallibly, which is psychologically impossible for the typical counter, it would be virtually inconceivable—over the long haul, let us stipulate, and in theory—not to win. By the way, that principle of playing solely positive decks is the key to Al's brilliant Big Player Concept: the soldiers at the table count cards till the count gets juicy, and then they surreptitiously signal to the BP who has been waiting in the wings for such a signal and who barges in and bets big. The BP looks like a true gambler throwing around money, when in reality he is jumping into advantageous counts. Casinos have wised up, and it is illegal now to send signals.

With a card-counting system, there is a number for every conceivable situation, every imaginable combination of cards. The situation is dynamic. It changes with the appearance of every new card, with each passing moment. You have 337 possible card combinations (your cards vs. the dealer's up card) to memorize—for hitting, for standing, for doubling down, for splitting, etc., depending on casino rules. Using Revere, for example, your ace, 2 against a dealer's 2: double down when the count is + 17. 7, 7 against a dealer's 6—always split (that is, play two hands). And so on and so on for 335 more situations. Strategy numbers must become second nature.

You do all this figuring while playing the hand at the same time as making small talk with the dealer and schmoozing with the pit boss and flirting with the cocktail waitress. That's called your cover, which also includes how flashily you dress and how many diamonds sparkle on your fingers. If your forehead wrinkles when you are thinking hard or your eyes squint and you appear to be strenuously crunching the math, you are on the fast track to being barred. Freshly minted counters have been observed moving their lips while keeping the count. Casino pit bosses appreciate the tell.

In real time, the casino places all sorts of obstacles before you. You can come across a grouchy dealer who doesn't like your action. It happens. So he speeds up dealing, *rat tat tat*. In the course of an hour heads up you might play as many as 180 hands of blackjack. Fast game, with lots of money on the table. If your smallest bet is $200, sometimes escalating into the thousands depending on the situation, that's a lot of money at risk. By the way, the interesting part about speed dealing is that the dealer might hurry up because he is under the impression you're counting. He goes faster, assuming that will force you out of your rhythm. But the funny thing is, it is easier to count cards when you are cruising above the speed limit. No time for mentally wandering into a synaptical rest stop. By the way, the constant repetition and the rapidity of the game were perfect for an obsessive player—a heretofore underappreciated and undervalued advantage for somebody with a compulsive disposition.

★

THERE ARE NUANCES UPON nuances upon nuances to card counting that would require hundreds of pages of explanation—and that would barely scratch the surface. Al taught his new team how to count, and it took a long time. Everybody quickly internalized the fundamental truth that blackjack was a game you could beat if you were disciplined and informed—and if you counted without error. And if you had the financial backing to withstand the normal swings of statistical probability.

As powerful as counting cards was, Al had come up with a better idea. He didn't make all that money and get into the Blackjack Hall of Fame by being complacent. The casino knows what to do with the self-satisfied player: give him enough rope to hang himself on his own assumptions and arrogance. And the casino also has at its disposal a deadly weapon: It can bar you anytime it pleases, without your having recourse.

As powerful as Revere was, though, Revere was not the last word, according to Al.

What if you could be apprised of the exact content of the deck you were playing—and not simply the positive or negative drift? What if you could analyze the situation such that you acted upon the precise information as to every single card remaining?

For instance, no matter the count, plus or minus, what if you had an 8 and a 4 in your hand, a total of 12, and the dealer showed a 4. Basic Strategy, which is simple to learn and does not entail counting cards, dictates that you stand—that is, take no more cards. A moment's reflection indicates why that might be prudent. If you catch a ten, you bust. And besides, the same big cards can break the dealer's hand, so let the dealer bust first. What's the game again? *Beat the dealer.* What about playing that hand according to the Revere Advanced Point Count? According to Revere, you would stand if the count were 0 or more. But let's say the count is 5 or higher. Counting dictates you stand, but what if you were able to act on the knowledge that there were, say, four 9s left in the deck? In that case, you stand a fair chance of catching one of those 9s and making a winning 21. A risk well worth taking, in other words. But how would you know there were four 9s remaining? No counting system equipped you with such detailed information, and unless you possessed a photographic memory, you would not have such data at your disposal. But what if you could play with a hidden computer? And what if that computer were to be surreptitiously manipulated? That would be something, wouldn't it?

That was Al's new concept.

★

WE CALLED THE COMPUTER George, as in George who slayed the dragon, the figurative dragon being the casino safeguarding in its cave immense riches, keeping such treasures away from the clutches of lowly counters. A rocket scientist named Kevin had shared the prototype with Al, and Al leaped, financing the operation along with his partner, another renowned blackjack player named Ken Upton. Kevin was a devout Christian with a weakness for fast food, both of which attributes may have offended Al's atheistic, epicurean sensibilities. But he was a genius, and Al knew a good bet when he saw one. Kevin's voice was soft as new slippers on Christmas morning, and he spoke in complete paragraphs—reasoned, densely packed paragraphs—and that could also have seduced Al. The gambling world is much more diverse than is assumed. Upton, on the other hand, was closer to the stereotype—if, that is, a prodigy who starts Yale at age sixteen and quickly becomes the vice president of a stock exchange and is as trustworthy as a snake on a plane is somebody's stereotype. Upton, incidentally, went to college with the professor who would one day ultimately be my dissertation director.

Kevin's baby George would be inserted into specially constructed shoes. The shoes were equipped with four switches, one above and one below each of a player's big toes. The switches had values of 1, 2, 4, and 8. Using those four switches in a certain sequence, you could input all the cards to represent the hand you were dealt and the dealer's up card. George could process more information with each new big-toed input as the hand went along, continually recalculating odds and strategy. On the sides of the shoe soles were ports for the insertion of lasers, which enabled the shoes to communicate, and which compelled players to place their feet flat on the floor in close proximity. In the shoe's instep was a buzzer, a vibrating device that gave a Morse Code–like readout that translated instructions to hit, stand, double down, etc. You might hear the buzzer in a quiet church. Nobody in a noisy casino stood a chance.

The shoes themselves were constructed in the Mission District of San Francisco by a crew of cheery and blasé Latino cobblers, only one of whom spoke any English. The cobblers were acting on the specs issued by Al and Kevin, but they were kept in the dark as to the shoes' true purpose. In this way, they were innocent as to what they were unleashing upon an unknowing world. No wonder they chortled at the spectacle of the crazy gringos who came in for fittings and re-fittings of these Frankenstein-monster brogans. Later on, Kevin, working with Tim, would fit in the Georges and the battery packs, and install the laser light function. In case there is a doubt, these heavy-as-lead, steel-shanked, handmade shoes would not double as your dancing shoes, not even back in disco days when platform shoes were the fashion. When we left with the shoes the last time, the chief cobbler told us in halting English: Don't tell anybody where you got the shoes. Everybody has a reputation to protect.

Al laid out the business proposition. The players would get a cut of the winnings as the money rolled in. "When you win the first fifty grand, first month or so, we distribute the winnings, start a new bank. Your net piece of the action increases with each new bank. Pretty soon, we'll be betting big, big money." The fundamental principle of team play is that with equally competent players you level out the risk, thereby reducing the element of ruin. Assuming everybody was playing at the same level, which was an enormous assumption, it was a matter of getting more and more money into action on the table and raking in the profits, which would be shared.

Before long we were toe-tapping along the switches. Right off the top, even with their halting command of counting, we had a glimmering of how powerful George was. At the same time, George was no small challenge to learn. It took a lot of practice to manipulate the switches accurately, and a lot of time—about three months of dedicated study and repetition. The team camped out at Al's and he fed us lunch and dinner. We were excited. We were going to be monsters. That summer we were realizing we were soon going to be making some of that real money.

"I'm putting my winnings into real estate," somebody said, before the bubble.

"Maybe, maybe. But I like equities," said another. This was long before the crash, or the other crash, or the big big big one after that.

"I'm going to buy a new car," ventured a third. He was shouted down. He was told to regard the money as capital to invest, not cash to blow on a consumer item.

"How about you, Joe?"

"Me?"

"Yeah, what are you going to do with your money?"

"I would have it, the money."

"You never *have* money. If you only have money, you never *keep* it, brother."

I wanted rent and child-support money. And some time to write poems. I didn't think that would make sense to anybody else.

THE TEAM PUT DOWN stakes in Reno, where we assumed residence in a rented, furnished house. The plan was to move on to Vegas eventually, maybe Atlantic City, which had reopened casinos with tremendous fanfare. Al served as den mother, chief cook, dishwasher, house cleaner, motivator, coach, guru, and mentor. This had all the makings of a situation comedy—a sitcom that gets cancelled after two episodes.

For the first time, the new counter and former waiter and embattled graduate student would go out to play for real in Reno. After a few practice sessions in casinos, I was now using live ammunition. I was undaunted. For some reason I was never nervous playing big money. I could not explain why, but it was true. I had $5,000 in hundreds in my leather jacket, and I felt ready to play whites, as the hundred-dollar chips were called in the Reno pits. (In Vegas, they're blacks.) These were very big dollar amounts at the time.

As I walked toward the entrance of a casino, I experienced a footwear problem, however. A heel broke and the battery pack popped out onto the street. Nobody seemed to notice or care. Perhaps stranger things happened in gambling towns. I limped back to the car and headed for the house. Tim worked some magic with a soldering gun and, in an hour or so, all was good as new. I hustled back to the Strip.

My first dealer was a wise guy. Not an uncommon descriptor for a blackjack dealer. He was a little too sharp, a little too smart, to be a working stiff in a two-bit casino. A few minutes later, as he was shuffling up after the first deck we had played against each other heads up, the dealer gazed pityingly at me, the poor guy right in the middle of the table, second base as it is known. First base was nearest the left hand of the dealer, third base, the right. The wise guy volunteered some free advice for the young fellow—with a secret state-of-the-art computer determining perfect decisions and clueing me into the best strategies and who was down a couple of thousand.

"You ought to take up another game."

"Really?"

"'Cause blackjack ain't it for you."

Perhaps it is amazing how ignorant dealers can be. A lot of people think otherwise, probably for the same reason they think cab drivers reliably recommend the best restaurants. Most dealers wouldn't know a bonehead play from a brilliant one. For cover, sometimes you ask them for advice. "Should I double down on this 11?" you ask, knowing full well this is a no-brainer. "I wouldn't," they idiotically reply. Pit bosses are the same way. Sometimes they try to stare you down, which doesn't intimidate a seasoned player. The best thing to do with a pit boss who does that is to engage in conversation. Stop playing and chat. *How's the wife and kids? How about them Niners? Hey, does that cocktail waitress have a boyfriend? I have been losing my ass all fucking day long.* And don't put up any money. They soon deduce that this isn't working for the casino, so they wander off. Remember, pit bosses are nothing but former dealers, and they carry over their prejudices and preconceptions into their new job as a suit. They like to convey that they understand counting, but by and large they are clueless. All they can do is watch the spread—your betting variation. If you spread too much, anything over 1 to 3 or 4, they bring on the heat.

After my first session at a blackjack table, they did not roll up a wheelbarrow for me to carry out all my winnings. In fact, my pocket was lighter than when I came in, though I had almost closed the gap, almost got back to breakeven. Back then a casino in Reno was a good place to renew my spiritual aspirations, because it was a deeply sad and seedy place packed with small-timers. Big money played Vegas. When playing in Reno, there also existed the possibility that you were battling a cheating dealer. Al was vigilant if not paranoid in this regard, and he scouted the terrain and gave the team tips for spotting one. He demonstrated how a talented cheat with a deck could sneak a peek at the cards to come, and make sure the player got a bad one and not the ten or ace that was his due. The dealer would deal a second or a third card in the deck, and not the top one that would make a player's hand. Some people, Al cautioned, a word to the wise, some people spend all day analyzing financials—or reading books, like me. Other people spend all day refining their sleight-of-hand. Some of them are hired by casinos as mechanics, to come into work quick and snuff out a rally. Watch out for new dealers suddenly appearing, especially those who are exceptionally friendly.

Some dealers are entrepreneurs. I once had a dealer who played heads up for a while, and he was not the most charming guy in the world. Later I bumped into him on a break on the casino floor, and, without prompting, the expressionless man whispered the following: "When I have crap for cards, I lean forward. When I have a pat hand, I lean back." He said it so quickly that one wondered if he had actually said anything. Then the dealer strolled off. Casino security has tightened up considerably since then, but that was still a brazen and certifiably insane thing to do. Theoretically, by knowing the composition of a dealer's whole hand, and not just the up card, your odds get astronomical. And what the dealer was implying, of course, was *you take care of me, by tipping generously.*

I played against my would-be ally, and paid attention to the lean back or forward. Despite the information, I didn't do appreciably better. The dealer got frustrated. The player got frustrated. The table filled up, and the dealer went on break. I never saw the guy again. And I assure you I looked. Maybe he tried the scam with somebody else and security caught on. It could be similar to baseball: When they steal the catcher's signs and relay the pitch to the batter, the batter theoretically has the edge. But some players don't want to know. They prefer to bat on their own.

As for unscrupulous, somebody might wonder if playing with a hidden computer in your shoe was kosher. Let's contemplate this question carefully and weigh all the factors and...hell yes, it was kosher. In fact, such activity was, at this time, not illegal. When it comes to scrupulosity, perhaps a more relevant question is, how scrupulous are casinos when they bar anybody they *say* is counting? Casinos are less likely to bar you while you're winning: you have their money, and if you leave they won't have a chance to take it back. They are more likely to bar you when you're losing: they have your money and intend to keep it.

★

EVERY GAMBLER'S NARRATIVE SEEMS to be informed by a notable and, some would say, agreeable sameness. So does every counter's narrative. There are hundreds of such narratives, some published to acclaim and sales. Many are self-published to no apparent acclaim or sales. Others are passed down orally, like Al Francesco's.

The archetype of the counter hero shapes up something like this:

"I couldn't get a date, and I was busted and devoid of prospects, legitimate or ill. Pretty girls never gave me the time of day. Guys pushed me around in the gym. Then one day it changed. I learned to count cards. Before I knew it, I attracted the notice of rich guys, who staked me with beaucoup bucks. Singlehandedly I took on the mendacious and nefarious casinos and I was raking in the chips. I was living large in flashy hotels around the world, driving a leased Lamborghini, popping champagne, snorting lines of coke off the taut bellies of one luscious babe after another. When the girls leave, I give them walking-around money. They don't ask. Nothing sadder than a pretty girl in tap city. Those were the days when I was making more money than I could ever use, so I pissed it all away, despite being the smartest guy in the room. Working the blackjack pits, I made people stop and admire me and my diamond-studded cufflinks while I performed amazing feats before worshipful throngs. The night comes when I am pulled up by casino security. They take me to a padded room and pummel me in the kidneys, where bruising doesn't show, but which hurts like hell. My backers disappear like I'm a leper. They refuse to take my calls. One day I wake up in rehab, my sinuses torched, jonesing. From then on I vow to live a simpler life, involving meditation, exercise, sound nutrition—and teaching people to count cards when they can't get a date and when guys push them around in the gym…"

★

AS FOR RENO, THE strip of downtrodden casinos is tawdry as can be, but I liked the high mountain town full of pretty lakes. The snow dusting the higher elevations in the distance was breathtaking. My beloved dog Rupert kept me company, and the two of us went every day to a sweet park, which nobody besides us ever seemed to frequent. A flock of quacking ducks landed on the water every day at precisely five o'clock. I came to look forward to the ducks, and my dog and I kept a watchful eye on them. One day, they did not alight, and I never saw them again.

When the sun went down, it was almost always nippy in Reno. I would play nights occasionally, but my preferred time was early morning, which is, saints and poets say, also the best time for prayer and poetry, two activities I was not emphasizing much those days. The night shift was weary after working since midnight, and I was fresh, having woken at five or six. I needed to make sure I got out of the casino before the day shift started. One good rule of thumb was never spread your action across two shifts. Keep your exposure to a minimum.

One unanticipated benefit of the Reno move was its proximity to my son. He and his mother had moved to a small town in Northern California, about ninety minutes away. She and I were going through a tranquil period, and she encouraged me to visit, which I did on many Saturdays. That was when casinos were packed with weekenders, and therefore harder to get a good heads-up game. I kept my powder dry. Mario and I could spend time together. His mother made dinner or lunch, and we all sat down at the same table. Win-win-win. I was glad. I was going to say it was like the good old days, but that wasn't true. The good old days never happened, or if they did, they passed in a flash. Sometimes, I admit, I fantasized reconciliation.

It wasn't long before problems arose with the team. Unaccountably, everybody was losing, big and consistently. George's equipment was erratic. Shoes would break, wires would snap, switches would fail. Seemed like one or more of us was always out of commission. Smoke from the soldering gun often wafted through the halls, and we were using up Super Glue by the bucket. And when the shoes *were* in commission, George wasn't delivering. Things looked bleak.

It's embarrassing to mention the next part, but I was the one dependable winner. In fact, as our months in Reno approached an unhappy conclusion, I was still up by a significant number. Sure, I had booked my fair share of losers, but on balance, I was a winner. And nobody else had booked anything but a net loss. Expenses were mounting by the day and we were bleeding cash. One day Al wanted to talk to me.

"I've met with everyone," he said. "Ken's in town."

"Upton's in town? Haven't seen him."

"Yeah, but listen, we have other investors, too. And everybody, everybody thinks we should drop George." So much for the velvet glove.

"That's crazy."

"We're pulling everybody up. Show's over. We're done."

"We're only getting started. We're still working out the kinks."

"I went to bat for you, I did."

I reminded him I was winning.

"OK, you're right, you won, but everybody else lost their ass. Their ass."

I couldn't believe what he was saying.

"Everybody is going to join Ken's team in Vegas. They'll be counting Revere and working with the BP concept. Ken's great at that. There's a lot of money to be made." Only not with George. "I know you're going to have a lot of work to do, getting up to speed with Revere, but you can do it. Then you join Ken's team. You can make a ton."

"So George is finished?"

There was yet another shoe to drop in a house teeming with dropped shoes.

"Keith thinks he may have made a slight programming mistake. Slight mistake. We might have not had the edge we thought we had at zero. Maybe we overbet. Maybe we were too cocky. Remember we tried flat-betting, and that didn't work. We're going back to the drawing board. There's some new wrinkles we might try."

"When can I start?"

"You're not going to play. There's a guy who's a big loser at the tables, name's Doc. Keith's going to teach him and he's going to be the only player with a George."

"Doc, huh?"

Al put me on notice. "I'm getting upset, Joe."

"Me, too."

"We're going to come up with a new bank, a hundred thou, and Doc will be a major investor, which is something you can't do, Joe."

Cheap shot, but fair enough. I couldn't resist: "This Doc guy, you watch, he'll never make it. You gotta be broke and hungry to put up with learning George."

That was the day Al confiscated my shoes and I traveled back home with my dog. Six months down the drain. I went back to waiting tables and reluctantly practiced counting cards every day, which maybe would come in handy someday if I needed to try out for Upton. I was not overburdened with options.

★

EVERYBODY ELSE ON THE team relocated in Vegas. It was November. I got a call one day from Al. Upton's team had lost two banks in quick succession. Why did this matter to me? The team needed new life. Al was irritated with me all over again, but this time it was different. "You should be down here helping us when we're down."

I heard him out and I told him I would think about it.

"How's your Revere?"

"How's yours?"

"Get down here, Joe."

Mickey called me shortly thereafter, so those two had coordinated. "If something don't change I'm gonna have to go to Switzerland and pick up some of my Kruggerands. They're all fucking losers here, brother. You should come to Vegas, man. We need you. Get your ass here. Upton don't respect me. I can count like a motherfuck, but he don't respect me. It's fucking ingratiating, you know what I mean?"

I did, I truly did.

Mickey had something else to tell me, too. "Look, man, you're a fucking winner with George. Everybody knows that, 'specially Al. I think you and George have, I don't know, man, a physical relationship. Maybe George got a toe fetish for you."

He didn't drink much back then, but maybe that night was an exception.

"You gotta get next to Johnny." He was referring to Al's wealthy older brother, the restaurateur, horse owner, and entrepreneur. "I hear Johnny's kinda interested in backing George, he just don't want to get into Al's action. You should talk to him, you can probably work out something good for yourself."

I had nothing to lose. I called Johnny and I brought up the idea of reviving the comatose George. Johnny was noncommittal. Did it really work, and how come the team busted out in Reno? I told him I feared the other guys couldn't take the pressure of real-time playing, that maybe they made errors as a result. There was another big question. Did members of the team skim cash? Al made us all take polygraph tests, so there was certainly some doubt on that front. I remember being hooked up to the lie detector and not liking it. In fact, I stumbled. The tester said he noticed a possible variance in my responses.

Here's what I recall about my skimming. Once after a long session at the Riverside in Reno, a winning session, I got up from the table, and as I walked off I placed two bucks down on a single number on the roulette table. The number came up, at thirty-five to one, and I walked away with $70 in my pocket, which I never declared in my winnings.

I told Johnny. He didn't seem bothered by my admission. He had a bigger concern. He said he never liked Reno, that we should have started in Vegas, where there were better rules. We spoke a few more times. He was hinting around the possibility that he would put up a new bank for me and George. He would have to work out the details and the splits with Keith and Al. He and I were getting nowhere, however, till I offered to put up some of my own money. It wasn't much, but the gesture did the trick.

"That's okay, I don't need your money. I just wanted to know if you were serious."

So this was a go?

"You heading down to Vegas?" he asked.

I wasn't till that instant, but then I said I might be.

"Maybe I'll see you there."

I left my dog in the care of my brother and his dog, and packed up my cards and books and clothes in my gold aluminum suitcase, specially suited to safely transport the technology in those pre-

9/11, pre-luggage-X-ray times. I got behind the wheel, having equipped myself with a couple of fortifying grams of coke for the twelve-hour drive to Vegas. If it didn't work out with Johnny, I would try out for Upton's team. What choice did I have?

I arrived, and things got pretty wild.

★

IT APPEARED AT FIRST to be like old times in Vegas. The team, the rented tract house, the rented furniture, the sitcom setup with Al as dysfunctional mom and dad. But soon after I arrived, Mickey hopped a plane to Geneva to pick up some money. And then Johnny sent out signals that maybe, just maybe, he was ready to saddle up. Kevin was resisting, kicking and screaming, but I talked with him at length and tried my best to convince him it was a good idea to work with Johnny. Al and I had dinner with Upton, who told me definitively that we weren't going to play George, that he wanted me to try out for his BP team as a counter. He didn't care what Johnny wanted or didn't want—it was his decision. Even though I won with George, they were going with Doc, end of story.

Days passed. I knew the worm had turned when Al gave me an address and told me to head over there right now. Doc was waiting. Why was I going there? To pick up my George, which Doc had been using. Or in his case, not using. Doc had gone down in flames. He couldn't do it. That was the most satisfying drive across town I ever took.

Mickey returned from Europe, but one night soon thereafter, while crossing the Strip, he was hit by a car and spent a few days in the hospital.

Then Johnny arrived in Vegas. He had flown down in his private twin-engine plane. He was carrying a black leather purse. You could get away with such a fashion accessory back then in Vegas. The deal was done. He was the bank. Kevin had relented. Upton shut up at last. I was going to be the only player. My piece was better than it was under the former agreement, and what other details they had worked out I was not to know. Thankfully, that was my last piece of business with Upton. He went on to publish a book that gave up all the trade secrets of the BP. What accounts for his killing the goose that laid the golden egg? Desire for fame? Narcissism? We will never know. A few years later, age fifty-two, he died suddenly in France. Rumor was he OD'd.

"Ready to play?" Johnny asked. He was wearing a white silk sport coat and a black shirt. His clothes never seemed to wrinkle, no hair was ever out of place. I was as ready as I would ever be.

He pulled out five thousand from his purse, which contained a lot more than that, and handed me the money. By nightfall we were up $23,000.

★

JOHNNY DIDN'T SEE THE point of my keeping residence in Vegas, and I concurred. We based our operations instead in the Bay Area. We could always hop in his plane on short notice and get to Nevada in a couple of hours. We'd stay in some motel for the weekend or sometimes a week, and then come home. For the next eighteen months we played everywhere we thought we might have an edge. We even went back to Reno and tried again, achieving the same mixed results as before. Vegas, on the other hand, worked like a charm. Certainly, we booked some losers, but we also killed a few times. We went on gambling junkets to Aruba and Monte Carlo, both of which wound up losing propositions. Johnny had bought me a couple of suits for international play, and one day in Vegas he talked me into trying on that pink suede jacket. I couldn't say no.

One day he told me to go to a pawnshop in San Francisco. It was run by a genial, amusing fellow we'd met on a junket. "He's going to give you a ring." I looked mystified. Johnny figured out why. "No, no, no, he's not going to call you, he's going to give you a ring." He had asked the guy to lend me a diamond ring for cover, and he did—a very nice one, by Vegas standards anyway.

This man would eventually make big local news when the FBI arrested him with great fanfare. I knew he was a horseplayer and bet on sports, but he was a bigger fish than I knew. When the Feds busted into his pawnshop they confiscated $8 million in cash. That was some kind of business to be doing in hocked guitars and vest watches. Either that, or the real business lay elsewhere.

The reality was elsewhere. In 1994, he pleaded guilty to illegal monetary transactions. He had laundered the money for a huge bookmaking operation. He served six months in prison and paid $570,000 in forfeitures and fines. The $8 million evidently disappeared.

At some point in 1979, the FBI began to circle Johnny and me, among others, not that we knew it. We did pick up that there was a lot of heat building with regard to bookmaking and related activities. Matters escalated after what went down with Whitey.

Everybody's favorite bookmaker was a physically imposing, quiet, gracious fellow named Whitey—not to be confused with Whitey Bulger, another story, another coast. They say when you bet with a bookmaker you need to win two bets: your original bet and the bet you get paid. On this score, Whitey was a class act, unimpeachable and reliable. He'd square you up right on schedule, every week. He was a regular at Johnny's restaurant, for obvious reasons, and he and Johnny were friendly associates. I did no business with him and our exchanges were curt but amicable.

One day, police discovered him and his wife in their suburban home, murdered execution-style. Whoever did it didn't want there to be any misunderstanding. They didn't touch the stacks and stacks of cash that were found all around their bodies. This wasn't a robbery. It was likely done by out-of-towners, and they were sending a message. What message? Was Whitey muscling in on somebody's territory? Was somebody muscling in on his? Did Whitey have something to do with fixing games? That was the word on the street. He was friends with a pro star athlete who may have been a heavy better. If he did fix games, he could have pissed off the wrong guy who didn't possess inside information. In any case, for years after, when certain people were pulled in by police, the first question they were asked was, "Who killed Whitey?" His murder has never been solved.

★

I PICKED UP A few classes in the English Department. My lofty academic title was something like adjunct acting assistant instructor. Cal was still on the quarter system, so there were convenient openings in my calendar and I could plan my ten-week teaching to enable travel. I had missed teaching, and it provided a steady if inglorious income, making big bucks teaching the evils of comma splices, the virtues of sentence variety, the correct meaning of the word "disinterested," the difference between fewer and less, and how you said different *from* and not different *than*. One convenient classroom in Wheeler Hall had a payphone right outside the door, where I could place a bet on an afternoon baseball game if I got an inspiration. Sometimes I left Wheeler and sped over to the airport, where Johnny was revving up his plane.

The most successful trip was the one we took to Sun City, South Africa. It is a very long journey to South Africa, so Johnny wanted to break it up and start out with a stay in Italy, my first. We traveled with his wife, Anna, and the three of us landed in Florence.

Johnny and I spent one memorable rainy afternoon at the Uffizi. I recall standing alongside him while we studied a painting that caught his eye: Botticelli's *Birth of Venus*. He asked me if I knew anything about it. I was distracted by the ravishing movie star who was hovering in the vicinity, but I did my best to illuminate the painting and hoped to impress either her or Johnny with my vast knowledge of the Renaissance. I failed because I did not have such knowledge, but Johnny pretended to be enlightened. The painting, as everybody knows, represents Venus rising from the sea on a shell, about to step onto the shore. As the great art historian E. H. Gombrich writes in his magisterial *The Story of Art*: "Botticelli's Venus is so beautiful that we do not notice the unnatural length of her neck, the steep fall of her shoulders and the queer way her left arm is hinged to the body. Or, rather, we should say that these liberties which Botticelli took with nature in order to achieve a graceful outline add to the beauty and harmony of the design because they enhance the impression of an infinitely tender and delicate being, wafted to our shores a gift from Heaven." That was a theme, gifts from Heaven, that we were all working.

I now had money in my pocket, and I bought a linen sport coat and pants at a famous tailor in Firenze. The coat was midnight blue and double-breasted, the current style, and the pants light blue. I also bought some blue shoes, which forever after my son would mock me for wearing. I was the belle of the ball. I had never spent money like this in my life. Later I would give the jacket to my wife, who looked better in it after she had it tailored to fit.

We never made as much money in one casino as we did in Sun City over the course of a few days. The cards kept coming my way, hour after hour. As a result, I was miserable. Johnny was miserable. Why? We should have made a whole lot more. We should have shut down that casino. They were dealing, they had good rules. I felt invincible. But then the casino did what the casino can always do: it barred me.

"Thanks for your visit to Sun City, have a safe trip."

I didn't know I was planning on leaving.

"We'll be needing your room, pack your bags."

We got on the hotel bus (no more limos for the now-exposed counter), which would take us to the edge of the hotel property, where our rooms were located. Anna was standing outside the bus for some reason, and Johnny and I were in the back, steaming. Then the bus started moving off, without Anna. She was waving frantically at the driver but was ignored. I called out to the front of the bus to wait, somebody needed to get onboard. The bus kept moving. I called out some more. Catcalls greeted my request to stop. South African catcalls.

I went ballistic. All the frustration of years of playing and being barred got to me. *Don't take no shit from nobody,* as somebody once said. And I was swept up by all the self-righteous anger I felt toward my apartheid-loving hosts. I had taught Nadine Gordimer and J. M. Coetzee, and up close anybody could feel that this was a country under psychological siege. Everyone was battered, from the oppressed blacks to the oppressive minority whites in absolute power. Everywhere we went in South Africa, stores or restaurants or airports, in every sign that said Whites Only, we could feel the desperation, the pressure, the inevitability of the revolution that was going to take place.

Not so incidentally, did it ever occur to me, in advance of the trip, that it was morally questionable to go to Sun City, to contribute to its economy? I have to admit, no, it did not. I could say I had every intention of reducing its GDP by winning at blackjack, but that is a self-serving justification. I am guilty as charged.

All this to say that, in the back of that bus that night, I don't know what I screamed out, exactly, when I lost it. I do know I denounced the country and all its people in a stream of coarse expletives my mom and all of Brooklyn would have admired. Some men in the front started coming toward me with a mind to settling the disagreement, and I was in the mood for a little brawl. Sometimes, the difference between being punched and punching is inconsequential. People stepped in between me and the South African patriots. Cooler heads prevailed and the brawl did not materialize. The bus came to a stop and Anna jumped on, and the bus moved along in silence. It felt pleasant, to silence the country.

"Matey, you all right?" gently inquired a friendly Aussie nearby. "Have a bad night in the casino?"

Sure, okay, I can go with that, why not?

He nodded knowingly. "Next time, don't rile up the natives."

Johnny looked at me with a cracked smile: "Never seen you like that."

Before we headed back to America, we went on a safari at a wonderland dude ranch, near Kruger National Park. No hunting—not that kind of safari. I saw the Big Five. Lions. Elephants. Rhinos. Cape Buffaloes. Leopards. South African wine is fabulous, and the venison, too. But all I wanted to do was play blackjack and make money. Being in a foul mood, I got into unwinnable debates with the locals.

"You Americans," said one fellow, coming back at me in his Soothe Effrican accent, "you think you know everything. You think you have a right to tell us how to run our country. Let me ask you about Vietnam, let me ask you about Martin Luther King."

He had a point—not as good a point as he thought, but it was a point.

We drank numerous bottles of South African wine that night. And later, going back to our huts, we saw a lion lope across the lawn on the way back to the veldt. Thank you, king of the jungle, for not eating us alive, unlike the casino.

When we got back to the States, we made a few more trips to Vegas, but the handwriting was on the wall. After Sun City, my blackjack days were numbered. Casinos shared the intel. Every time I sat down at a blackjack table, I was barred within minutes.

★

I SETTLED BACK INTO graduate school, picking up whatever Composition and Intro to Lit sections were available, working on my dissertation. *Working* on my dissertation? More like staring at the computer screen where I had some first-draft pages of a dissertation.

One day I saw a certain graduate student in the halls of Wheeler, and we struck up a conversation. Chemistry. It wasn't my favorite subject in high school. It was my favorite subject today. I asked her out. She said yes. When I arrived at her apartment a bit late, bad traffic, she left a note that she had gone out. She wasn't going to wait for me or for anybody else, get it? I should have known better than to ask her out again. But I did. I had my reasons. Well, I had one really good reason. As far as I could tell, she was the most alluring creature I had ever met, and I was thinking with an organ other than my brain.

They say you find out everything you need to know during a first date or when calling to make your first appointment with a psychotherapist. What do you find out during a first date that never happened? Maybe more.

"You met your match." We used to say that to each other. But that's just another pose of mine. I was no match for her. Then again, I didn't care that I wasn't. In poker, if you can call you can raise. If you have the nuts, be a man. If you don't, leave it up to others. I did more than call. Before I even had a clue as to what kind of hand I had, I was wondering what all my chips would look like in the middle of the table.

★

JOHNNY WAS ROLLING IN it, and he was in an entrepreneurial frame of mind. He would eventually hire me as the general manager of two new from-the-ground-up splashy San Francisco restaurants he financed. The GM money was too good to turn down. True, I had no great management skills, and hardly any understanding of running a restaurant, but Johnny promised to teach.

With the first operation, almost immediately there was trouble. I got caught up in a dispute between Johnny and his Italian American partners that turned litigious and vicious. A loyalist to the other partner and I squared off in the kitchen one Super Bowl Sunday afternoon. I was Sunday-punched but I got in a few licks of my own before the combatants were separated. In case this isn't obvious, a restaurant kitchen is not a smart place to get into a fight. Knives, pans, mallets, and other implements of culinary destruction are within easy reach. I received a mild concussion, according to the doctor at the hospital who stitched the cut under my eye. Johnny's partners fired me, which they couldn't legally do, and that's when the lawsuits started flying around. That wasn't the worst part. While the former partners took their places on the legal battlefield, and everybody was hemorrhaging money, somebody got the federal government involved.

One day, I received a phone call from a federal agent who identified himself as Dave Williams. He informed me that the Federal Bureau of Investigation was putting me on notice that I was the prime suspect in a RICO investigation. That was the term: prime suspect. And RICO stands for the Racketeering Influenced and Corrupt Organization Act. I had been called lots of names before, but until then never a racketeer. The agent asked me to come over to the office in San Francisco. I said certainly, that I earnestly wished to clear up any misunderstanding. The agent and I talked for a few minutes more—I would not care to characterize the exchange as cordial— and I took some notes. This is the last thing he said to me:

"Don't leave town."

Just like old times: the FBI and people named Joe Di Prisco. I wonder if some other FBI agent had said the same thing to my dad when he was about my age, before he promptly left town.

I didn't instantly grasp all the implications of the FBI's presence in my life, but I sensed a call from the FBI did not rank as a promising social development. I would later find out just how not promising a RICO investigation was.

The RICO statute is complex, and its applications for law enforcement have morphed over time. It was conceived as a tool to prosecute the Mafia. According to RICO, you are a racketeer if you commit two or more serious crimes—like murder, bookmaking, bribery, embezzlement, extortion, kidnapping, money laundering—over the course of ten years in the furtherance of an ongoing criminal enterprise. If you are found guilty of racketeering, you are liable to pay fines of $25,000 plus doing twenty years in prison per count. These are complex cases to adjudicate, and controversy has dogged the courts since the law passed in 1970. If you are indicted under RICO statutes, the government has the right to seize all your assets that are presumed to be fruits of the poisonous tree, which makes hiring a defense lawyer a tad problematic.

I was the prime suspect in a *RICO* investigation? Me?

A few minutes after I hung up the phone, once I stopped trembling, I picked it up again and dialed my attorney.

"Wait a second, let's go over this slowly."

"Good."

"He actually used the term RICO?"

"Yes."

"And he told you not to leave town?"

"Those were his very words."

"Shit."

"That bad, huh?"

"And what else did he say?"

"He also said I was the prime suspect in a RICO investigation."

"Fuck."

"Okay."

"Joe, do you know what this is all about?"

"No."

"You have no idea?"

"Maybe."

"Get in here."

Turns out *don't leave town* and *prime suspect* are the magic words in the federal criminal justice system. Billable hours commenced with a vengeance. Criminal enterprise? Murder, kidnapping, extortion? I was the prime suspect in a syndicate? Johnny's attorneys and my attorney met with him and the other attorneys in the conference room of a white shoe San Francisco law firm. They strategized, speculated as to where this investigation was going, and the answer was no place good anytime soon.

Afterward, when we were alone, my attorney asked me how well I knew Johnny. I said we were friends. I certainly believed we were friends. My attorney was skeptical: "I wouldn't trust him as far as I could throw him." His client didn't share the attorney's mistrust, but everything did indeed look like it was going to go sideways fast. I later found out that my phone was tapped and they had filmed at least one meeting I attended in a deli—filmed it from the roof across the street. For six months, I was actively investigated.

Gradually, it became apparent that the Feds were dreaming a big dream. They thought they had discovered the East Bay Mafia, whose existence would have constituted extraordinary news to the identified prime racketeering suspect.

Of course, everybody in the inner circle in which I found myself—Italian restaurants, blackjack, sports wagering enthusiasts—had lots of vowels in their names. Again, the FBI was seeking to establish a pattern of criminal behavior in furtherance of a criminal enterprise. If I had ever met with the FBI I would have said this was the pattern: there was a consistent pattern of randomness, if not chaos. The vowels were but one part of the problem. Nonetheless, visions of sugarplums were dancing in their federal heads—only these sugarplums were bookmaking, corporate defalcation, money laundering, skimming, and drug dealing, all allegedly organized by the same syndicate of individuals. Johnny swears one night he was watching the late news and he heard the newscasters say that federal law enforcement officers were descending on an East Bay restaurant to break a local organized crime ring. That didn't happen, however.

And as for me, I was the prime suspect in a RICO investigation. On advice of counsel I never appeared at the FBI office, and I never left town. Where was I going? My card-playing days were over. They interviewed lots of people and showed them my photo and shared details as to my financial assets—considering my assets, that wouldn't have taken much time. All in all, I wouldn't put this experience up there with the most fun times of my life. Along with the others, the FBI interviewed my brother John and my father. I did not talk on the phone anymore about anything related to the case, but I did meet with John, who appeared concerned. "The guy opens his fucking briefcase," my brother said, "and he's got his fucking piece in there. Guess he's trying to intimidate. He's good at that." John's then-girlfriend was interviewed at the same time, and said she had to take two Valiums to calm down.

My dad, predictably, said nothing about the substance of his interview, which was his nonverbal way of tacitly indicating his fundamental position: Nobody was hanged for something he didn't say. I would have loved to have been a fly on the wall for that conversation between him and the fed. My father was born for that sort of non-exchange. If he was curious, he never asked me a single question. True to form, he probably did not want to know something if there was indeed something to be known. He wanted maximum deniability in case there came a moment when there was something that needed to be denied. *Acqua in bocca.* Mum's the word.

Innocent as anybody may be of some charges, nobody is innocent. Maybe they were going to make a federal case out of the blackjack team or the restaurant deals or Mickey's involvement, and who knew what else? Here is some free advice: If you can arrange it, you don't want the federal government investigating you. Their resources are effectively infinite. They have nothing but time to get into your business, and when they want to bring down the full force of the law they have no qualms. You are by definition the bad guy. You deserve it, what with all those vowels in your name. You may even be the prime suspect.

The FBI also has a powerful weapon at their disposal that nobody else can use. If a Brooklyn detective, during an interrogation, asks you where you were on Sunday night when the gun went off, and you say at church for a novena, and you pretend to believe a novena is a kind of cream-filled pastry, that is one thing. If, on the other hand, an FBI agent asks you a question of probative import, and you lie, that constitutes obstruction of justice and is in and of itself a federal crime. Oftentimes, in big cases, they fail to prove the underlying charges, but they prove that somebody lied to the Feds, which is why people like Martha Stewart end up in the slammer.

Here's what tough guys (or soft guys' tough attorneys, like mine) say when they stand up to the Feds: "You are on a fishing expedition." But here's the thing: When you go on a fishing expedition, sometimes you land a fish. My attorney figured they were throwing their lines into the last restaurant deal, but what else? Nobody knew.

★

ONE DAY MY ATTORNEY calls. "Good news, Joe."

He was a fine attorney. I let him play it out.

"The US Attorney just indicted the Hells Angels on RICO charges."

My attorney represented bikers in the past, so maybe he was getting new business.

"Good for you, maybe," I said. "Why's it good for me?"

"It's great for you. They do one RICO case at a time. They

think they got their big fish. Means as far as you are concerned, the FBI's picking up their toys and going home."

Which is exactly what they did.

★

DURING MY RUN AS GM of the second restaurant, Johnny fired me. That was the only time in my life I would ever be fired. The instant I was terminated, I understood I was not general manager material. I had vaguely suspected as much. This self-recognition shocked me in the sense that I should have realized it long before, before I was doubled over in the coffee station with stomach pain brought about by anxiety or maybe an ulcer's calling card. And if the high point in my restaurant life was a fistfight in the kitchen, the Mario Batalis of the world were not going to worry about any competition from me. A restaurant GM's life: You are there to greet the produce purveyors at first light, there to put the money in the safe at close of business at the end of the night, there at the bar down the street to take it down a notch for a nightcap. Or three. You hire, you fire. You sweat out the details. You romance the clientele, you make people feel important. The margin is miniscule, success is a long shot. Your lowest-paid employee, such as the dishwasher, can do something to erase a whole night's profit. A true GM loves this—he revels in the action, the pressure to perform.

Johnny made a sound decision. He needed to protect his investment. He had a right. As the guy in the silk suit tells his boxer in the fight-fix movies, "This ain't your night, kid."

The restaurant would go out of business eventually, so maybe a bad GM wasn't the sole problem.

There was one thing left for me to do. Get back to grad school and finish up the dissertation. My friend Mickey was sympathetic. He fixed me up with all the cocaine I could use.

The Modern Language Assocation and Other Nightmares

M Y GRADUATE SCHOOL GIRLFRIEND and I attended the MLA convention in New York. The two of us had lived together before and after she was appointed assistant professor at a most prestigious university. She was on the fast track to academic renown.

For academic literary types, the convention is a chance to network, dazzle your colleagues countrywide, and drink other people's cheap booze. It's also a meat market for seekers of employment. That was where I was being interviewed for tenure-track jobs, even one at Harvard, where they must have been feeling generous. For her part, she was there to advance her professional ambitions, including delivering a talk and mingling with the power brokers in the academic world, their status something to which she fervently aspired. She and I had temporarily separated, purportedly to allow some distance to heal the expanding fissures in our rocky relationship. Ours was a volatile connection. As far as I was concerned, we were destined to be together. Still, we traveled separately to New York and took different rooms. No point in putting extra stress on the inherently nerve-racking ordeal that is the MLA.

★

HER HOTEL ROOM WAS at the end of a long corridor that could have come from some New York noir detective story: the door faced out, at the end of the corridor, so you could see it at a hundred paces. The effect was akin to looking through a telescope, or down the barrel of a gun, both of which oddly related.

Once I reached her door, I distinctly heard the ping of bedsprings, the whoosh of sheets, the slap slap slap of flesh, the wet music, the rhythmic incrementalizations.

I looked at the number. Yes, this was the room. From where I was, I could hear emanating from within those easily identifiable sounds: the squealing, the rustling, the lubricated and lubricious rumpus, like a small mountain lake rhythmically lapping against the pilings of a pier. A moan now and again, just this side of sweet agony. I had the capacity to recognize these sounds with confidence. This took no great skill. A deaf man could identify these sounds. Those were the sounds people made during acts of intimacy. In this case, it was my girlfriend who was making love, I had reason to believe, and she was making love not to me, because I was outside her door, and she was inside.

I started pounding on the door and, when it went quiet inside the room, I kept pounding and pounding more and more vehemently.

I stopped breathing, or wanted to. *I think I will keep knocking and at some point possibly kill somebody.* Silence on the other side of the door. I kept knocking, louder and louder.

Parenthetically, let me observe that at last we have incontrovertible proof I was no masochist, for a masochist would have felt transported by this rich development. I would have been orgasmic, though in a different way from how she was.

Let me in, I probably improvised, brilliantly.

She would one day be an internationally celebrated scholar, but a C student would have done what she did: she elected not to open the door.

Then I noticed I was no longer alone in the hallway.

"Come with us."

Somebody must have said that. Maybe somebody grabbed me by the arm. I was relieved to be taken away. I was no voyeur—or listeneur, if that is a word, and it should be. I never thought of myself in such low-grade felonious and sickening terms, but perhaps voyeurs think of themselves as excellent observers and availers of unexpected opportunity.

"Don't continue to make a scene," I was told, or something along those lines. That must have struck me as sensible advice. One does not normally want to make a scene. And one never wants to *continue* making a scene, which sounds frenzied. But a *scene*? A scene means throwing people through windows, off roofs. A scene means punching out somebody who sorely needs to be punched out. It means getting out of the car to have a discussion with the guy who flipped you off when he cut into your lane. A scene involves hysteria. And yet, hysterical does capture my mood that December night in Manhattan.

"Hysterical" is a word the literary theoreticians made a big deal about back in the day. The vexatious etymology was thus: *hustera*, Greek for uterus, suggesting that womb-related issues made for glasses breaking, furious tears, breathing into a paper bag, and other uncontrollable female mood swings. Nowadays, there exists a more clinical vocabulary to piss off a woman. You might call her, for instance, bipolar. Probably that word amounts to hysterical and meets with the same degree of success. But the language of biology is in ascendance these days. It sounds so dispassionate and clinical. "You are so hormonal." Unfortunately, that turns out not to work very well either.

But to return to the scene I may have been making: they threatened to restrain me if I offered resistance. Their voices were calm, confident, maybe disgusted by the spectacle of a pathetic young man making a scene in a hotel like this. They were there in numbers. They were wearing suits and ties, not bellhop uniforms.

Seeing no other option, I walked with them down the corridor, where we took an elevator down and down. It was an evening full of seeing no other options. Ah, the pathetic entourage of the cuckold. Little-known fact: under such circumstances, rose petals are not strewn on the path.

Silence blanketed us in the elevator. Not really silence. It was a noisy elevator, but there was no talking. There was that rushing between my ears that meant I was in the throes of a mental slippage. And how long had I been out there, pounding on the door, telling her to let me in? I had no idea.

Yes, I did. I had been there all my life.

*

EVIDENTLY, THE HOTEL BASEMENT was where they washed the dirty laundry as well as interrogating losers like me. Connections were too obvious to be made explicit. It was warm and stifling, and bleach fumes filled my head. Outside, it was winter in New York, that lovely time of year. The toys gleamed in the store windows. The holiday decorations sparkled. Kids were the other day having their pictures taken with Santa. Down here in the bowels of the hotel, security officers were snapping my picture, too. They did not ask me if I had been a naughty or nice. They were taking notes. They were formally putting me on notice. They said I would be arrested if I ever set foot on hotel property again. I did not tell them I had been thrown out of nicer bars than this. For one thing, I wasn't sure if that were true. I was half-hoping they would throw me around. It would have been perversely satisfying to feel the objective correlative of being kicked in the balls.

I learned something invaluable in the process. I wish I hadn't learned anything, valuable or not, which suggests yet again that education is not an absolute value. But okay, I didn't care, now that I had nothing to lose, now that my worst nightmares had been realized. Which made this a dangerous moment for anybody to be around me. Here was the invaluable lesson. I was alive. I didn't die. I looked into the belly of the beast that was my jealous nature, and I did not expire.

At the break of dawn, my brother Eddie took me to the airport. Eddie was unfailingly reliable, a good brother everybody should have. I caught the first flight back to San Francisco. The flight was a ghost town, and I kept on the trench coat and gave a thousand-yard stare to the nice flight attendant, who had to realize I was an unstable compound. But sorry, sweet flight attendant asking if she could do something for me. I was thinking along the lines of forty lashes.

How did I get into this particular fix? It started at the University of California, Berkeley.

★

THIS WAS ANOTHER BAD time. I was in graduate school, teaching or taking classes or doctoral exams. I was running restaurants or being fired when I tried to. I was betting the games, football and baseball. A new thing. I was betting more on each game than I was being paid per month by the university. I was working on a very serious coke habit. And I was in love with the worst girlfriend imaginable, and I was the worst boyfriend imaginable. As for being a dad, I was not going to win any parent-of-the-year awards.

My friend Katharine used to ask a fundamental question of herself, and of me. We would talk for hours about love and relationships over bottles of inexpensive, graduate student wine, and she would inquire relative to one doomed love affair of hers, "Is this a love I can use?" Hers was also a love destined to fail. *Is this a love I can use?* I would have given anything to know for sure.

What I didn't know about love could have filled up several Gothic cathedrals, and a cathedral was where I should have gone and Gothic was what I felt. One time, this love I couldn't quite figure out how to use but couldn't live without wouldn't let me into her apartment. Yes, a pattern. Outside her door, not being let in. We had been fighting on the phone. We knew about fighting. It's what we did best. Anyway, she was in her apartment (we had yet to move in together) and I hung up the phone and fifteen minutes later I was downstairs.

I buzzed. I buzzed some more, she wouldn't let me in some more. I was standing before a wood door, heavy and nicely situated, right there where a door should be. I was studying karate at the time. I wasn't talented in the martial arts, but it is amazing the techniques you acquire even in less-than-advanced classes. A little knowledge is a dangerous thing. In this case, my knowledge constituted a threat to doors. I didn't imagine any alternative to the next move, which was this: if she wasn't going to buzz me in, the door needed to come down. I stepped back and kicked the door in the exact center. I didn't do the karate yell, but it was a perfect kick and it might have earned me another belt at the dojo. The door seemed to shimmer and shiver and hang in midair, the dust particles glimmering beautifully in the shaft of light that sliced through the hallway. Then the door fell. I took this opening to leave. My work was done, and maybe my relationship. But it was not done, not by a long shot, though doors, it would turn out, would be a motif. As for that night the door fell, we made up later. Of course we did.

I was not much of a scholar. And neither was I a pharmacist. But I did know the books and the drugs that I liked. And the nexus between the two was forged during those years.

The Berkeley English Department was only rivaled from time to time, and only occasionally, by one or two other graduate programs in the national rankings. I had gone to grad school to get my doctorate so I could get a job teaching college and writing poetry, and I vowed to leave if graduate work thwarted the writing. A couple of years into graduate school

I had published a first book. It would be a long time before I published the second. Academic work was not the reason. I had gone astray, in this and in so many other respects. And I? I took the road academically more traveled, and that, that has made all the difference. Or not.

I roped an eminent professor and brilliant critic into being my dissertation director. I made the formal ask when our paths crossed in the locker room of the university gym, and maybe in such a vulnerable milieu the professor was too kind (or tired from working out) to beg off. It wasn't this professor's fault he didn't have a lot to work with. Nonetheless, I gave him my word-processed pages. The professor would look at me with befuddlement and inquire as to how I was producing such ham-sandwich prose. I was a professional writer, or so my director told me one day. I should write better. Once he sent back a draft of a chapter he was not going to finish reading. It was a mess, according to his lights. At the top of one page the professor scrawled, "In the middle of this so-called paragraph..." The critic was right. Perhaps I was a mediocre graduate student. Perhaps I was a Triple A prospect, maybe good for a cup of coffee in the bigs, not a prospect for the major leagues.

My graduate student career, such as it was, took place during the seventies and eighties, in the transitional period between the life of letters and the professionalization of literary studies. It went from reading, talking about, and teaching books to theorization about reading, talking, and teaching. Theory triumphed and theoreticians were spiking the ball and doing cartwheels in the end zone. Between the time I entered grad school in 1973 and when I got a PhD in 1986, I had failed at playing cards, running restaurants, being a poet, being a good father, and being an academic. During this same period, the entire landscape of literary studies had ineluctably changed. And so had I.

Majestic adverb back then: *ineluctably.* Whatever it meant, I had become another soon-to-be dead white male looking for a job. How somebody of my background became the bell cow of the privileged and repressive male hierarchy eluded me. A good possibility it eluded me ineluctably. I was obligated to endorse these conditions. I was supposed to take one for the team. Sure, I was made unemployable in the process, but progress is hard, people! Let me concede this, though: More than a few of my fellow Berkeley grad students were brilliant men who went on to glorious academic careers.

This was the Frog Jazz era, and the merry ass bandits included Foucault, Derrida, Lacan, and Barthes. Barthes was the only one of them I thought could write. To quote the great scholar and power forward Charles Barkley, who once complained he had been misquoted in his autobiography, "I may be wrong but I doubt it."

Why would anyone choose to live and work in such a universe of gauzy, gummy discourse? People pretended to understand those theorizers. Maybe they did. Books were out. *Texts* were in. The writer was no longer a human being but a manufacturer of historicized artifacts, and everything a writer wrote was not merely intrinsically unreliable, an old idea, but a material product, a fake new one. The consequences for graduate student parties indeed seemed grim. I once went to such a gathering. Later I was reminded that the first thing I said upon arrival was: "I feel at home. There's so much pain in the room."

Opacity had become the new black.

Opacity had become the new erection.

The erection was problematic.

Not to worry, everything else was problematic, too.

There were also problematics to be discussed, whatever they were.

Opacity was the new orgasm.

The old orgasm—hey, nobody needed to mention the old orgasm, which men alone used to privilege, an old noun now verbed into avant-garde incomprehensibility.

Doubtless, these are the feeble grousings of a masculine and/or male PhD student whose professional prospects were dimmer than that of the British Raj, for presumably the same reasons.

The imagination was colonized. It was a short journey to genitalizing the politicization of the eroticized. Such terminology hung like dead fruit on department trees.

This Way to the Egress: that was the famous sign put up by P. T. Barnum. His customers, assuming the egress was an exotic animal, supposedly doubled over with laughter when they were bamboozled and found themselves out on the street, needing to pay up again to come back inside. The sign should have been posted on the door of every English department.

★

THE ENGLISH DEPARTMENT REQUIRED oral examinations in fields of study such as Shakespeare, twentieth-century British, American poetry, etc. Completing your orals was the essential rite of passage. You spent a year or so preparing, reading everything in your fields. I myself consumed a great deal of coke to get ready, for I was dedicated. At the time I was living with my brother John in a rented suburban tract house. John was sharing a bedroom with Laurie, whose picture once appeared in *Playboy* and who was as tall and beautiful and skittish as somebody could be who once lounged in Hef's vicinity.

Graduate students are hard to live with, partly because their lives are so attenuated and abstracted. Living in the 'burbs with John and Laurie was a cure for that malady. I couldn't do abstract near John. Here's how unabstract domestic life had become. When I ventured out of my room one day, I saw Laurie down the hall, skimpily dressed in something from Victoria Secret, pissed at me for something. I was probably richly deserving of the rage that produced the following gesture on her part: pointing a handgun in my direction. She was calling me Joseph, a bad sign, and she was now waving the gun around as if it were a garden hose. Indiscretion is the better part of valor, I realized. I non-confrontationally skulked away. Her bedroom door slammed shut and an argument between her and John echoed through the house.

Nobody mentioned this occurrence again—for twenty-five years. At John's funeral, Laurie was in attendance, and the subject of the gun came up at the reception afterward at my house, at which point Laurie broke down in tears. She had hoped the gun had been forgotten. "John made me crazy. There was so much coke." Good reason for a gun to make a dramatic appearance. Better reason for gun control.

As for the occasion of my oral exams, I wore a black leather vest. The garment had the semiotic value of a billboard that announced: *Too Cool to Be a Grad Student*. My interlocutors included my dissertation advisor, who was designated to serve as corner and cut man for the bout, along with the committee chair, an eminent and dashing Victorian scholar, an admired poet professor, and the not-nearly-as-famous-as-he-deserved-to-have-been short story writer Leonard Michaels, who would one day come to be happily married to my friend Katharine. There was also an outside-the-department examiner, as was university convention: an assistant professor of Portuguese. I would someday come to spend a fair amount of time in Portugal, because my wife's family had taken up residence. This is a country where, in my experience at least, absolutely nothing works—the banks, the keys, the televisions, the roads, the restaurants, the birds, the dogs, nothing. If I had known then what I knew about the Portuguese later, I would have been armed to the teeth for that outside examiner.

The exam went on for two-plus hours. I was asked questions that ranged from batting-practice fastballs to knee-bending curves. I can remember practically none of it, except for the performance of the Portuguese professor, who peppered me with questions about nineteenth-century British theater. After Oscar Wilde, there is not a great deal to talk about, in the humble opinion of this ignorant, leathered graduate student, relentlessly being grilled. And the Portuguese prof asked about T. S. Eliot. Nobody talked about Eliot those days, as in nobody, his presence now safely in the rearview mirror, nor was Eliot technically covered in the selected fields.

Then I went outside into the Wheeler Hall corridor while the committee deliberated. I walked up and down the corridor. This seemed like a good time for a cigarette. I have smoked exactly one cigarette in my life, and that was after a baseball game. It was a Kent a teammate offered. I can visualize the purple-on-white packaging. I vividly remember throwing up immediately and exuberantly. Nonetheless, a cigarette would have been the thing to occupy me on this occasion—and maybe even the projectile vomiting, as it gradually dawned that something was amiss inside the room. Forty-five minutes after leaving the exam, the charming Victorian lit professor charmlessly beckoned me back into the Star Chamber.

Once they all took their places around the table, the professor stroked his long shiny locks, disgusted. "One person on this committee thinks you did not pass your exam in nineteenth-century British literature, which is the field I examined you on." So the examiner not so subtly signaled that it wasn't he who had failed me. I was met with looks of support from everybody except the Portuguese assistant professor.

"Now what?" I wanted to know.

"We have a split decision. The university will review our reports and determine if you have passed your orals. I feel confident that you will be passed."

"This whole process will take a long time?"

"Months." He practically whimpered with revulsion and derision.

So somebody thought I didn't demonstrate enough knowledge about a field. But I thought I knew plenty about the field in question, and proposed a remedy:

"Let's do the exam again."

The committee chair's eyebrows rose, and he said this was unprecedented, but he glanced around the table and everybody agreed why not, including the grudging Portuguese assistant professor. The discouraging prospect of everybody's generating paper probably cinched the deal.

"Let's do it," decreed my dissertation director, now the cut man tending to the ego lacerations visible on the lightweight grad student.

The exam recommenced. This was the first question I was asked, which I will never forget:

"How many chapters are there in Matthew Arnold's *Culture and Anarchy*?"

This was an important book in the nineteenth century by a writer crucial in the nineteenth century and to a graduate student taking doctoral exams in the twentieth, and Arnold was very much for one (culture: "the best which has been thought and said") and adamantly against the other. And so was I, even if I wasn't always sure which was culture and which was anarchy. At the time of my exam, I recalled exactly how many chapters were in that famous book. I supplied the correct answer. Honestly, I had to find the book on my shelf to answer that question today. But from that lead-in, I proceeded, answering one wicked, obscure question after another, though never quite achieving the best which has been ever thought or said.

Don't take no shit from nobody, somebody once said. Another hour of the third degree, during which time the Portuguese professor asked not a single question, I was done again, and banished again into the hall. One minute passed, maybe less, and I was summoned back to the previous site of ignominy.

"Congratulations," the chair said, and I shook everybody's hand, including that of the assistant professor, who had obviously been the designated meathead. Read my mind, the examined student wanted to say to the assistant professor, read my mind, but right now I had other plans. I had an eight ball of coke in my pocket.

★

I MIGHT AS WELL name the woman on the other side of the hotel room door. I think I will name her Gerri, because that is not the name of anybody I ever knew, so on those grounds alone, it feels like a fit. Our relationship started with erotic fireworks and ultimately ended along similar lines that night in the hotel. Only it was different that night, as I was not setting off those fireworks—or setting her off, for that matter.

It would constitute sound public relations if I stipulate that she is a good human being, that she has friends and family who will vouch for her, that she saves puppies from abuse and works in a food bank and writes checks for underserved children and inspires her students to heights of hermeneutical thinking and so on, and I have no reason to think otherwise. But she will need another defender and her own book.

Socrates himself picked up on the theme of love as an illness, and though he did not steal it from me or my friends, if he were still around he might be quizzing us nonstop on the subject. I did love Gerri and I would have done anything for her. As proof of my craziness, here's this: She was unkind to my child and I tolerated it, I rationalized it, I implicitly sanctioned it. I put this down as yet another lowest point in my existence.

During our relationship, the old obsessive jealousy patterns snapped into place, like belts on the electric chair. Even jealous men can be betrayed, and I was pretty sure she was cheating all along, well before our special Christmastime in New York and despite attestations of innocence. She was attesting as much even as I was discovering inconsistencies that indicated the absence of innocence, which is logically impossible to determine because absence (which is a vacuum) cannot indicate anything (which is a presence). To be unclear, I was teaching introductory literature and comp classes at Cal, where you had to pretend to comprehend stuff like that.

So my strategy for coping with the continual stress of almost certainly being cheated on was the obvious one: I beat her to the punch. It was an old trick of mine, tried and untrue.

Sex as a preemptive defensive maneuver was surprisingly entertaining if not sweet. Like finding money on the street or in the pocket of some coat you haven't worn for a long time. Smart as Gerri was, could she have picked up on my carefully stage-crafted disappearances and threaded together the various implausible explanations of my whereabouts to conclude that I was stepping out on her? But would she have cared? I don't think she would have. That didn't help.

The more I slept around, the more I was convinced she was sleeping around. Did I mention this was a very sick relationship? That I was writing a dissertation on Mark Twain because it was her idea (and true, Berkeley had the Mark Twain Papers, a gold mine of primary materials), and because she always had the better professional ideas, being the most ambitious person I ever knew. I think about all the hours spent mulling over her infidelity. "Mulling" is not close to being the word. And all the hours spent practicing my own infidelity, dates when I said I was at meetings, lunches when I said I was teaching or dinners when I said I was working on my dissertation.

Here's a favorite recollection on this score: I once had dinner with a delectable fellow graduate student. As we finished a bottle of wine, maybe two, she said, "You remind me of William Hurt." That dates back to when the talented actor was a huge star of hot motion pictures featuring steamy babes and frantic sexual escapades defying the laws of physics by taking place anywhere and everywhere including, if memory serves, the ceiling.

[Chekovian pause inserted, to permit the incredulous reader to sneak a peek at the author photo... The photographer may be internationally celebrated, and a wonderful former student of mine, but even her magical powers couldn't make me a movie star.]

Hearing the William Hurt comparison, I had evidence she was drunk, so I must have improvised, "Really?"

"Yes," she said, and without pause added: "My boyfriend said if I had the chance, I could go to bed with William Hurt."

I could go on. For instance, I dated briefly, very briefly, a mud-wrestler. A female mud-wrestler, in case there is any question. Obviously, we shared common ground. But never mind. There is a list somewhere, because compulsive types live for lists, but I can't go on.

Never once did I seriously entertain the thought that I was out of my mind, which is as surprising to me as it is to anybody else. There were those phone calls with Gerri that abruptly concluded. There were those long stretches of time where she was not accounted for. There were those professional lunches of hers that struck me as being anything but. She would proclaim her innocence, but not proclaim it too forcefully so that I could say, "The lady doth protest too much." She was brilliant. There were those looks exchanged across rooms at parties— not exchanged with me. When I think back on all the effort to sleuth out the truth, and all the energy I invested in imagining what I would do when I found out the truth, it is remarkable, to me, how the whole matter was definitively resolved. It was not of course resolved that night in the hotel, as is shown by how I am afflicting you—and also myself—with the tale.

Would it have been better for me, and maybe for her, had she opened her hotel room door? Would I have felt the need to assert my devalued manhood by slapping somebody around? Punching somebody in the nose? Were you aware that as recently as 1974—that is, a few precious years prior to my mauling in Manhattan—a man who killed his wife and her lover in Texas when he caught them *in flagrante delicto* was deemed not to have committed a crime? No, it was determined that under reasonable-man rubrics, he was acting legally when responding to such provocation.

She had in the past provoked me and I responded violently. Things were said, objects were tossed around. One awful night I was frankly open to the possibility that one of us was not going to see the sunrise.

As for the night in question, was I going to hurt her euphemistically identified "companion"? That indeed sounded like a pleasant prospect, but we have all found ourselves in situations that seemed destined to end in violence, and yet did not. I have associated, by happenstance, with men who physically hurt people as a profession. To a man, they say it's harder to inflict damage than it might appear, despite being paid for the job. No wonder you need to pay premiums to take somebody out.

Did I need to see it all with my own eyes? And see what? Where to train the camera? What difference would seeing make? "Give me the ocular proof," says my old jealous pal Othello. If this were a scene in a novel, we would all figure the chances were very high that I did know the person who was with her in that hotel room, and perhaps that I still do.

"Give me the ocular proof": When Othello says that to Iago, he is speaking for me. Iago is ever willing to provide whatever images the general wishes to see. As soon as Othello questions Desdemona's integrity and admits the possibility of her sexual betrayal, he is driving a vehicle on black ice without brakes. Since he had an unrealistic and idealized conception of her from the first, she was destined to disappoint him. And since he had an unrealistic and idealized conception of his own honorability, he was destined to disappoint himself. Iago can access porno channels for Othello all day and all night long. Othello yearns to not believe his eyes because he cannot believe he can be betrayed.

"Wouldst thou see her topp'd?" Iago says, and if Othello had not shared my disease, he would have shivved him on the spot.

Imagining such things makes them real, or real enough to torture and to tantalize. That is the best trick known to the green-eyed monster.

Beyond that, here's the thing about proof, ocular and otherwise: There is never enough proof. Because when you are searching for proof of betrayal, you are already betraying yourself. I had all the proof any red-blooded man could need, and it wasn't adequate. It wouldn't have been enough to break through the door. And why didn't I? It was nothing but a hotel door. Maybe I really didn't want to see. Maybe I was like one of those guys you see on the street calling out somebody, and it's after midnight, and he's hoping somebody holds him back before he gets his nose smashed. As the tough guy says in a Tarantino movie, "You gonna keep barking, little dog, or are you gonna bite?"

The reason proof is never enough is that you don't want proof. You really don't want proof. You want there to be no need for proof. Because there isn't one love that is based on proof. You desperately want to deny what you know to be true and what won't be denied. There isn't one love that is not based on trust—insane, futile, crazed trust.

And please excuse the query, but would somebody tell me why I was still in love with her? I think if I had been granted access to that hotel room—"Come on in, Joe, how's it hanging?"—I would have wished away the proof. I might have wanted to dismiss the reality before my eyes and see what I wanted to see, namely a kindness and a goodness at heart, which was precisely what never existed between Gerri and me. I probably would have listened to her if she said, "This is not happening, you merely think it is happening." And that would have been a perfect illustration of our love affair. For the two of us, it was about passion and power, rage over wasting my life with her and revenge for her not loving me in any way that I would want to call love.

Gerri was too good for me. I survived the moment of listening to her fucking somebody else. Who could have figured that? Not me, a jealous man, that's for sure.

★

GERRI ALSO LOVED COCAINE, so we had a ménage à trois. Some users think that coke brings out the worst in people. Probably what is certain is that coke brings out the *most* as well as the *least* in people. It did for Gerri and her cuckolded boyfriend.

I never did any coke around my son, but what does "around" mean in this context? *I* was around my son, and that was bad enough. And it seems that once my son, early middle school, came across an ounce in a baggie at a summer house party Mickey threw, and asked me what kind of tea was made with white powder. Somebody must have come up with that lie when the kids at the picnic happened upon the baggie. I was terrified. It had come to this. Another low moment in my life as a father. At a bare minimum, this moment shows that in my world and at this historical juncture coke was everywhere and in quantities that could potentially lead to indictment on felony distribution charges.

I could argue that as coke habits go, mine was mild. It was not Hollywood Hills feral, that's for sure. But in my experience, there is no such thing as mild when it comes to this drug. There were bad weeks and very bad months, let's put it that way. What Robert Stone called the "birdies or bats" dread that comes with the arrival of dawn after a night of it. The *it* that produces zombie natter and zombie love, zombie argumentation and zombie play, zombie time and zombie freedom, zombie sadness and zombie sleeplessness, zombie phone calls to other zombies picking up their zombie phones in the middle of the zombie night. Sticking your head through the chain-link fence zombitude to get at some. Putting your arm into a meat grinder zombishness. And you have a sudden crashing moment or recognition: Okay, Joe, that's it for the night. Call it quits, okay? There's no end in sight if you keep going there. Take a look. No, not in the mirror, that's corny. Take a look into yourself. You are wasting your life. You're right, you're certainly right, who am I to argue?

But then, but then, but then the spoons come out and the tiny mirrors and the razor blades and it all starts up again, until later, much later, when it is all gone, you decide that this is the time that will be the last time, this time will be the last time you waste a night, a day, a week, this time will be the last time, the very last time, and you feel your heart race around the track inside your chest while you are standing still, your heart twanging and twanging and twanging like a self-perpetuating tuning fork. What kept me going back and going back to the nothing that was there and the nothing that was not? Now would be a good time to refer to the endorphin release chart in the back of the book, if this were that sort of book. And I could present the experiments done with rats in cages, who chose cocaine over food and water if given the choice and whose imminent death was consequently foretold. This substance was the breakfast of champions, where all the champions were losers. And where *make me love my misery* hit on me all night long.

★

Cocaine cocaine cocaine. Cocaine? Cocaine, cocaine cocaine cocaine cocaine cocaine cocaine. Cocaine. Cocaine cocaine. Cocaine cocaine cocaine, cocaine. Cocaine cocaine cocaine cocaine: cocaine cocaine.
"Cocaine cocaine cocaine cocaine," cocaine Cocaine.
"Cocaine cocaine!"
"Cocaine."
"Coke?"
"Cocaine…"

★

IT WAS THE SUBJECT of every jittery sentence. Also the object. There was a time when it was also the verb. The adjective and the adverb, too. The prepositional phrase. The main clause and the subordinate clause, and always the insubordinate clause. A time when it was better than oxygen, better than food, better than poetry. It was everywhere. It was a bad time, and coke was the perfect bad drug for that time.

★

LONG AFTERWARD, KATHARINE WROTE me an email reviewing her recollections of that New York night in the hotel and its aftermath:

"I was in Berkeley. David was out of town and had left me his Nissan station wagon, but had walked off with the key that opened the gas tank, which I hadn't brought into consciousness until the fateful drive to the airport to pick you up. But, I get ahead of myself.

"You kept saying, 'I'm going to kill her…I'm going to kill her…,' which clarification was mixed in with a disrupted tale about indescribable yet indisputable sounds coming from Gerri's bedroom. I mumbled something about 'ocular proof' and kept suggesting to you that it would be best not to kill her because then you would have her with you for the rest of your life. I said, 'Come home…as soon as possible,' which generic plan we were able to agree upon. Later, you called to give me the flight number and time. It being pre-9/11, I was to meet you as you got off the plane.

"I set off for the airport on a drizzly, late December day and was on the Bay Bridge before I noticed that the gas indicator in David's car was on empty and I did not have the key to open the tank. It was before cell phones. I thought about praying my way across the bridge, then seeking a gas station. But I was terrified of what you would do if I wasn't there when you got off the plane, which please God would be late. By Treasure Island, the gas gauge was creeping below zero, but the tin box of a car forged onward. I accelerated because I couldn't stand allowing a long unraveling of events—that is, a cautious, slower, less gas-guzzling drive to the airport in which the uncertainty would be prolonged. I rushed to judgment. I made it across the bridge, then past all the SF exits, starting to boast in my head that my gamble had paid off and that there was really more gas in the tank than indicated. I made it to the airport exit when the car started chugging—but, I was so close—chugging up the last rise, then I raised my foot from the gas pedal as I started to coast down the ramp to the airport. Gravity contended with friction. I stepped on the gas pedal again as the car started to slow—cars rushing by still at freeway speeds—no response, coasting, slowing, me rocking forward and back in the driver's seat, steering and shearing, trying to avoid the gas-soaked monsters on every side. David's car stopped in traffic. I jumped out and started running for your terminal at the other end of the airport.

"I flash past a clock that indicates that I am five, then ten minutes late. Finally, I am in the terminal and the board shows your plane arrived early. I sprint to baggage claim and there you are, unraveling, not searching for your bags on the carousel, the last, lonely, unclaimed receptacles.

"The next memory is of sitting in a gas station inside of David's towed car waiting for them to pry off the gas cap, fill the tank, and then sprinkle more gas on the parched engine head to coax the car back to life. It is raining and through the slush of the windshield wipers we are taking stock of what is looking more and more like thirty-plus years of misspent service in the armies of the misbegotten, misbehaving, Aristotelian acolytes of pity and fear, longing for a transcendence in which the searing fires of the faith are indistinguishable from sexual betrayal. We are both in our Christological year, thirty-three, as you remind me. But how thorny the roads, how bloody and bowed are we, the ardent pursuers of this uncomfortable faith. Which word leads our meandering minds to the possibility of redemption or, at least, consolation through leaps of the same: Father Shane, the Church militant, glows in our joint imagination.

"We make it back to Regent Street, by way of a liquor store in which you procure several medicinal palliatives in the form of fifths of Old Bushmills. You are soon extended on my futon couch, gargling whiskey.

"Father Shane arrives. We tell the tale, its exquisite details, its roaring anguish, its multiple meanings, its unfathomable depths, its rituals… We look at Shane to judge his comprehension, his recognition of the horror…the horror…longing for the crystal truth, the core meaning he will deliver. He is silent…we drink… we tell a bit more…we wait… He shifts in his chair, composes his frame, tries to assume his ghostly mantles… 'Perhaps sex is better pursued within marriage…not before,' he says.

"There is a beat of silence. Then you say, 'Shane, I wish I had thought of that.'

"I laughed until I cried. You laughed…in that way you have. I thought, we're not going to die tonight.

"That's what I remember.

"Love always,

"Katharine"

★

BACK IN CALIFORNIA THE answering machine is full of Gerri's messages. But I don't stay at my apartment. I stay with Katharine, who is performing a mitzvah. Of course, her mitzvah began by picking me up at the airport. Which produces a strange, tiny coincidence. I catch myself recalling the first time I landed in San Francisco, when I arrived from New York in 1961, and how I met my father at this gas station. Funny thing, but Katharine's car is at the same gas station. That was the first and the last time I returned to my California starting point.

Have I been pursued by symbols and metaphors my entire life?

Gerri insists on meeting with me when she gets back to California. I agree for reasons too belabored to be obvious. She offers herself up, a sacrificial victim, to expiate her sins. She wants to get back together. I can do whatever I want. I can be cruel. I can sleep with anybody. I can have sex with her right this instant. OK, I agree to the last point, because I am a skilled negotiator. Afterward, I watch her leave my apartment. I still do not understand how she has such power over me. I don't think it's possible for me to love somebody as much as I hate her.

So where does this end? I have no recollection of the sequence. It ended, the way life does, when you least expect it, and maybe for the same reasons.

As for the woman who occasioned these labored reflections, I haven't spoken to her since. I did, however, see her once more, in LA International Airport, many years later. I was at the gate, making a connection to San Francisco. My wife and I had gotten off the plane from Paris, and she had gone to the women's room. I had the most terrible hangover. I didn't know such a thing was physiologically feasible, but I had slipped from inebriated directly to hung over in the course of the miraculously bumped-up-to-business-class flight. I was seated, coat and dark glasses and hat on, and there she was. If she saw me, she did not let on. I felt a thrill. The thrill I felt was that I was not with her. Best hangover ever.

Looking back, I probably never mattered as much to her as I believed I did, which is a narcissistic blow for me or her or both of us, but there it is. Because of my misconceived commitment to her, I sacrificed a great deal. She is not to blame, I concede. I am. I lost valuable time with my son. I lost sight of my responsibilities, including those to my beloved dog, who was put down at a very advanced age without my being at his side. I suffer to think about him and about how cowardly I was and about how I let him down and I beg him to forgive me. In the last few years, when I put down three other very good dogs, I thought of Rupert and begged he would forgive me.

Gerri's first book was based on her dissertation, which I had done my solemn boyfriend duty to comment upon as it went through drafts. Her book's title is one I gave her. I can still hear her reading aloud from the famous poem that makes this resonant claim: "Yet each man kills the thing he loves..."

> *He did not wear his scarlet coat,*
> *For blood and wine are red,*
> *And blood and wine were on his hands*
> *When they found him with the dead,*
> *The poor dead woman whom he loved,*
> *And murdered in her bed.*

Yes, she most definitely loved playing with fire. I guess I did, too. So it may well be true. I didn't really kill her. You only kill the thing you love.

I was sent a copy of her first book by the press. She would go on to publish many more books and be celebrated as an important scholar in her field. Her curriculum vitae is impressive by any standard. She has achieved all the success that perfectly eluded me, so I am vulnerable to the charge of sour grapes. Beyond that, all this happened so long ago, isn't it time I get over her—and also myself? Fair point.

In the Acknowledgments of that first book of hers, I received some formal thanks from her for my help. My name does appear in one sentence, actually in one independent clause of a sentence that acknowledges my assistance. Then there is a semicolon.

You are acquainted with the functions of this notorious piece of punctuation. If you're like me, you avoid semicolons on something like religious grounds—the grounds being that it is a lazy, bogus connective. One can write a hundred fine books and live a full, complete life and never once use a semicolon, something I advised my students many a time. In my frame of mind her semicolon looked to be fashioned of neon and was this big:

;

After the semicolon, her new partner's name appeared in the other independent clause, cleverly acknowledging how the man did not help at all. Ha ha. "Help," what a lark, ho ho. Two names, two men, simultaneously linked and separated by a winky circumsized foreskin of punctuation.

I don't remember where I put her tome. That last sentence is the only untruth I am conscious of stating in this book.

High School Redux

I WAS TAPPED OUT and thirty-six, which is close to my father's age when we boarded the subway to California. Being broke, like the imminent prospect of being hanged, concentrates the mind. The pleasures of mind concentration are often overrated.

My latest casualty was the scholarly career. I had failed in attempts to secure an academic job. I had written a dissertation, and it was not half bad, according to the four people in North America who signed off on the magnum opus. The poor doctoral dissertation: what a lonely document, lounging around with the other pouty microfiche-accessible books, never permitted to perch invitingly on some shelf, where somebody might accidentally lift a page.

Mark Twain was my topic, or more narrowly, that period of the author's life, the 1890s and after, when he went broke on some bad business bets and when his loved ones died, one after another. In this stage of that illustrious author's career, he wrote unsettling, strange, revealingly psychological books—books that made him famous and rich all over again. They made him more famous and rich than ever, in fact, which was saying something—and which slipped him once and for all into that bedazzling white suit. Mark Twain's subject matter of this period seems more than accidentally reflective of the autobiography of one damaged and wishful doctoral student.

Here is good cocktail party patter for a certain type of academic gathering. At the turn of the century, there was virtually unanimous critical and popular agreement as to Clemens's greatest literary achievement. What was the consensus as to his most inspiring and transcendent book? *Huck Finn? Innocents Abroad? Tom Sawyer? Connecticut Yankee? Jeopardy* buzzkill to all of those. No, for the turn-of-the-century reader *the* great book of Mark Twain incontestably was...*Joan of Arc*. Yes, Mark Twain wrote a book titled *Joan of Arc*. Or more accurately, *Personal Recollections of Joan of Arc by Sieur Louis de Conte*. Sieur Louis de Conte is her page, but the not-so-hidden clue of Samuel Langhorne Clemens' identity lies in the page's initials. Partly a hagiographical exercise and partly a vehicle for Clemens's rage against the establishment, it is an odd novel—albeit entertaining enough for a PhD student who studied a book that few people alive have heard of, much less read. Because the novel was written by a genius, it was worth the attention. That book formed the basis of probably the best chapter in my dissertation.

My dissertation done, I had interviewed for an assistant professorship at some famous and good colleges and universities, at a time when there were no jobs going to anybody—except, that is, for my brilliant peers at Berkeley who would go on to one day rightfully assume their endowed chairs. I was invited for a campus visit and formal interview at one small and reputable liberal arts Northeast college. Looking back, I realize that I blew this opportunity by wondering out loud too much about what it would be like to live three thousand miles away from my son. Truth was, that was all I could think about. I liked the people there, and learned how to correctly pronounce THOR-eau's name during a lunch with the chairman, but I glimpsed doom in all their eyes. At the time I wished I got the job, because I would have had no choice but to take it. My life would have been very different had I been more professional in my pursuit of an academic career. But that was not meant to be.

So there it was, May 1986, and I was awarded the doctoral hood in a ceremony at Cal. There was nothing but a slow trickle of cash flowing in from work as wine and management consultant at the old restaurant. I needed to get out of that business. I saw an opening in the newspaper classifieds for an English teacher at a high school in San Francisco. Remember the quaint classifieds? What the heck, I said to myself, if anybody's an English teacher, *I* am—and an English teacher who happens to need a jay oh bee. I had taught high school before, and did anybody have any better ideas?

I applied to this high school I had never heard of: University High School. I figured this was one of those toney expensive schools of the sort I never could have attended. There was a last-minute summer opening. Somebody took a job in the English department of some university, dog in the manger that he was. So I licked a stamp and sent in a letter and got a call in what seemed like minutes. I interviewed with the new Head of School. The Head was gracious and preppy, all in tweed and sporting a bow tie, and talked the whole time. Having interviewed lots of people during my days in the restaurant business, this employment candidate determined this was probably an excellent sign— either that, or the kiss of death.

When the school called with an offer, I said let-me-think-about-it-for-a-while-hell-yes. I was relieved by the prospect of an income, and I confess that I believed they were lucky to get me. That's crazy thinking, isn't it? Hiring me was the new headmaster's first personnel decision. I will always be grateful for the offer. But was it a bad omen? Perhaps. Before too long, the headmaster himself was out of the job, having been discovered to have falsified his résumé and having lost the confidence of trustees and faculty who had reservations about his competence. Somewhat curiously, these doubts did not revolve around his first hire.

Little did this newly hired teacher know at the time that I was about to start working at one of the finest high schools in the country. I did not realize that hundreds of applicants had applied for the job I blithely accepted. I could not realize that many of my soon-to-be colleagues would turn out to be bright and kind and dedicated, and that I would teach students of remarkable ability who were delightful. How could I anticipate that I would so much enjoy teaching adolescents?

I taught for a total of twenty years—from middle school to high school to college. Far and away, the best classroom is, in my mind, the high school classroom. There is nothing you cannot teach receptive high school students. But as for the school's being lucky to have me, it would take a short while for me to realize I was the lucky one. Who could have guessed that one day I would come to write the lyrics to the school song? To this day they sing it at commencement.

I vowed to do a good job. To that end, I stopped drinking for two years, not even a glass of wine, not even on the weekend. I never did one line of cocaine ever again. The transition to another life was not seamless, however. In the first month on the job, I requested permission to miss school. I had a funeral to attend.

★

MICKEY AND I NEVER fell out of touch, and Mickey had bailed me out a few times when I was in financial straits. At one point he had taken on the role of financial backer for a heavy-metal band, and he asked his former waiter friend to be in management. They put my name on my own business card. The band was called Little Big Man. "I'm management." That is something fun to say to Security and to girls who want to go backstage.

Unfortunately, Mickey had gone off the rails, due to his addiction to freebase cocaine. The other night Mickey had walked into the home of the Twins, a couple of pretty Oakland prostitutes he liked very much and was feeling possessive about. Possessive? Romantic? Sky-high? It was hard to tell the difference with Mickey. When he showed up at their apartment, though, two guys were hanging around. At some juncture, it seems, harsh words were exchanged, and Mickey pulled out a knife, apparently with the intention of doing some harm. They scampered away down the stairs. Mickey was tweaking, free-basing without cease for days. You do crazy things on crack—I could testify on that subject if I had to.

Later that same night, Mickey was asleep in bed with one of the Twins. That's when one of those guys sneaked into the bedroom, plunged a chef's knife into Mickey's chest, and killed him. The murderer was sentenced to seventeen years.

To this day I catch myself thinking about Mickey and missing him.

Once, my brother John had teased the two of us at the restaurant, when we were talking and not doing our jobs. To be accurate, the language he used was "not doing your fucking jobs."

"What are you guys always talking about?" my brother asked.

"Shit, John," said Mickey. "I love Joe."

Mickey and I had nothing in common. We were friends.

★

Similar to what the Catholic Church did when I was a child, this high school threw me a lifeline.

Hardly anybody who knows me believes the next part, but it is true. I once taught a course on Women's Literature. Nobody was teaching such a course in 1987 at this school, and I was not having intellectual qualms about the idea—yet. After all, why weren't those female writers in the other literature courses where they belonged? Oh, those were the canon-reformation days, those heady times. Not that there is a connection, but that was also when there were big shoulders on jackets, so everybody looked like an admiral out of Gilbert and Sullivan's *H.M.S. Pinafore* at a Castro Street or East Village Halloween party.

This was the first question, first day of class, comprised entirely of senior girls, from someone with a famous surname who would eventually become one of my favorite students. She asked, "Who do you think you are to teach this class?" And I felt an instantaneous, chaste crush on this girl. "I hope to find out," I said. Truth be told, I wanted to do something unexpected to establish a reputation. That's also why I wore a tie and a sport coat every day, unusual if not unique in a faculty whose sartorial tastes caused them to dress in T-shirts with environmentalist slogans or jeans or Birkenstock chic.

One day papers were due in this class, and I collected them as students departed the room at the end of class. I was in Room 19, the most desirable room in the school, with a big conference table, nice views of San Francisco and the courtyard. Helena didn't turn in a paper. She stayed in her chair, and after a while the two of us were alone. After some back and forth, and my keep-your-agreements, respect-deadlines remarks, it was clear none of this was hitting home.

"I couldn't do it," said Helena. She had been planning to finish her paper on *The Awakening,* by Kate Chopin, which she loved, she said. It is the best French novel ever written in English, one wag of a colleague once said, but he was right. (Spoiler alert: Do not read the rest of this paragraph if you don't want to know the ending, which I have to give away for reasons that will become obvious.) The short novel ends with the protagonist taking a swim from which she intends never to return.

I liked Helena. She was quiet, thoughtful, smart, and troubled. It wasn't her fault her family was immensely affluent and loved her.

"I was at the hospital all night." She rolled up the sleeves of her sweatshirt. Her wrists were bandaged. Her eyes darkened. She slouched down farther.

I was on the other side of the table. Last class of the day, halls empty.

"Your parents know?"

"Yes."

"I'll need to talk with them. It's not that I don't trust you…"
I was winging it.

"No, don't talk with them."

"Does anybody at school know?"

"No, and I don't want them to know."

"I'm worried about you. I need to know…"

"Keep it between us, please."

I did not know if I could agree to this.

"You can talk to my therapist," she volunteered.

I needed at a minimum to determine if my student was in danger of hurting herself some more, and if she was being taken care of. Helena and I sat in the room for a long time. Teenagers are past masters of silence, but so was I, being Brooklyn-born.

At the time I myself was romantically involved with someone who was a psychotherapist. Jess was, and undoubtedly still is, a wonderful human being, and it was too bad we ended the way we did. When she told me that she wanted to tinker with me, meaning adjust my psychological and emotional self, I knew one or both of us were doomed. She stood a better chance if she'd wanted to detonate me and start all over again with the fragments. Still, she was crucially helpful with Helena. The main thing she helped me understand was that her reaching out to me wasn't necessarily about me, and that the student was looking for help, though incapable of asking for exactly the sort of help that she needed. Adolescent girls make attempts on their lives more often than boys, but boys are more successful in their attempts. Boys are more likely to use a gun or a car to achieve their goal. Girls tend to employ less drastic means. So Helena was something of an outlier, and certainly not in a good way.

Doing the due diligence, I called Helena's shrink, her very chic and expensive Pacific Heights shrink. To this day whenever I think of him, and recall his condescending timbre, the word "putz" leaps like a gazelle across my mental veldt.

I asked the doctor if he saw this coming.

"Saw what coming?"

Gee, maybe you can see coming this punch in the face?

"Did you imagine her making an attempt on her own life?"

It was not indicated by her previous behaviors.

Ah, I see now, Doctor Putzhead.

He briskly advised the teacher that he had discharged his responsibilities and that he could go back to grading his inconsequential papers, buh-bye.

"Are the parents in the know?"

With an exasperated sigh he said they were.

I hung up and instantly knew my work with Helena, unlike my relationship with Doctor Putzhead, was only beginning.

I met with Helena during the next free period, on top of the school building where picnic tables were set up for meetings on nice days. After the small talk...but teenagers don't do small talk. All talk is big talk.

"Look, Helena. I am having trouble with where we are."

Doe-eyed stare in reply.

"What I mean is, I think we need to let people at school know what has happened. People around here can help, you know. That's what they're here for. So I'd like you and me to go tell the school counselor and the dean."

Maybe there was a pause of two seconds, but not much more.

"Okay."

"You said okay?"

"Okay."

I took the money and ran. I hustled over to the dean's office, and the brilliant, big-hearted dean masterfully marshaled all the resources of the school to help Helena. And she responded.

Only later did I let myself fully indulge in my terror—something the idiot shrink should have understood. In the first flush of this experience, I dared not let myself feel that. Oh, such a beautiful life that could have been lost, such a waste. She must have turned in the paper eventually, and I bet it was excellent, but that is one thing I can no longer recall.

★

FINDING TIME TO WRITE while trying to make a living teaching was a Sisyphean task. I yearned for summers and breaks when I could hunker down at my desk. During the school year, I tried to get up at five in the morning. Hey, I did that when I was in the novitiate or playing blackjack, didn't I? Problem is, I am one of those slow writers who need blocks of time, and it is hard to steal blocks of hours in the early morn. I was envious of the likes of William Carlos Williams, the practicing pediatrician and world-class poet, who would bang out a poem on his typewriter between appointments. Then again, though Williams wrote lots of terrific poems, he also composed a large number of poems that read like they were banged out on a typewriter between appointments.

No wonder John Gardner—the late, great John Gardner whom I met when I was a Bread Loaf fellow—forgave a writer who married the sort of spouse who can help keep the writer going. "But if a writer finds himself living, for honest reasons, with someone glad to support his art, he or she should make every effort to shake off the conventional morality and accept God's bounty, doing everything in his power to make the lover's generosity worthwhile." He explicitly warns against teaching high school, however: "Nothing is more draining, even for a teacher not overburdened by a sense of responsibility." Amen to that. For though University High School was nobody's presumption of an average high school classroom, it was still high school, and I was afflicted by a sense of responsibility.

Internally conflicted as I was and frustrated as I was seeking time, I enjoyed teaching high school. Let me qualify. I did not like teaching classes from eight in the morning till three in the afternoon. I am productive in the morning, but that doesn't mean I like being with people. Yet in comparison to middle school and in comparison to the university, where I taught at various times, high school kids are remarkably open. They don't know what they aren't supposed to think or accomplish. They wear their emotions on their sleeves. They wear their emotions on *your* sleeves, if you're not careful. At the same time, there was hardly one day when I did not laugh, truly deeply honestly laugh over something that happened inside or outside of class. It's not medical and dental and retirement contributions, but that's not a bad job benefit. Here's the other part: My students let me know they cared for me, they respected me. Sure, I had my share of reprobates and smug and borderline kids I don't care to see ever again. By and large, though, I felt their affection, and I worked hard. I could not explain the difference in intellectual content between my eleventh- and twelfth-grade classes and those classes in college where I once ascended to the starry heights of acting instructor, but high school was different. You teach literature in college. In high school, you teach *kids* literature.

Here's the other side of caring about teenagers. You worry about them. I certainly did, a condition that only intensified once my son entered high school. Drugs, alcohol, eating disorders—it was a minefield out there for kids, and for teachers who cared about them, and for teachers kids came to in times of trouble. And back then it was all about AIDS. I had more than a few students whose dads were dead or dying. Life was precarious and immensely sad for these teenagers—and for their teachers, too. Time spent with them as they struggled with the pain was infinitely precious and gut-wrenching.

Perhaps the greatest side benefit of UHS was this: It helped me understand my adolescent son. Before I knew what was going on, my students taught me how to be a father.

★

UHS AWARDED ME A summer travel grant. I was proposing to teach a course on Vietnam. The war had defined my life in so many respects, and the journey to the other side of the world would help me understand more. I became a member of an educational delegation to Southeast Asia.

One day I was whisked to the Institute of Literature in Hanoi to chat about books with Vietnamese professors. My translator was distractingly beautiful and stylishly dressed for the oppressively hot July day. She had a commanding presence among the academics. There was a lot of around and around and back and forth, and it was insufferably hot and stuffy in the conference room that had a portrait of Ho Chi Minh on the wall. It was a rare room that did not feature the official portrait of Ho looking monkish if not beatific. One of the professors had a question for me, the American visitor. The translator said the man wanted to know my opinion of the great American author John Steinbeck. The American visitor finessed an answer, not being a Steinbeck expert despite my youthful enjoyment of *East of Eden*, but being aware that the Vietnamese, like the Russians, adored Steinbeck, along with Jack London and anti-imperialist Mark Twain. I was loaded for bear with regard to Mark Twain, but no question about him was forthcoming.

The translator said that Professor So-and-so had a follow-up question.

"Professor would like to know your opinion of John Steinbeck's classic novel *The Angry Grapes.*"

★

I WAS IN HIGH school when the war began. An American gunboat was supposedly attacked in the Gulf of Tonkin by the North Vietnamese, and the nation was responding. We now know that there was no such act of aggression. At the time, I felt a surge of patriotism, which took the following anemic form. I checked out of the library catalogues for West Point and Annapolis. I imagined myself in dress whites. I passed on the Air Force Academy, figuring I would be slightly limited being a war hero Air Force cadet due to my fear of heights. On this subject, as with others, I have lived a rich fantasy life.

By the end of my senior year in high school, I had come full circle. I still considered myself patriotic even as I was patriotically opposed to the war in Vietnam. In Berkeley, that position was more welcomed than in most other towns, but that didn't mean you didn't walk into arguments. Most of my friends were either neutral or pro-war. And Catholic bishops were largely supportive of the war, unaccountably enough.

The war took a personal turn, as did my opposition, one afternoon at Sara's house. Sara had red hair and was every bit as cute as those Kahlil Gibran–reading girls who would have reminded me of lots of songs on the radio. In terms of running the bases, getting to first base, second, etc., I was on the bench, in the dugout, looking for my trusty bat, which had to be somewhere because every boy had a bat and every self-respecting male was due someday to run bases. We were friends, friends without any benefits of that sort.

She told me she had been in correspondence with a Marine who had recently returned from combat. The Marine lived in the neighborhood, and she explained she was doing a Catholic schoolgirl good deed by letting a soldier know that somebody was sending support his way. This now sounds as naïve as somebody trusting you can buy a Gucci bag from a Times Square street vendor. In any case, Dave was home, and was somewhat illustrious, having published some combat photos in *Life*. He had designs on Sara. The high school boy stays in the kitchen with Sara's parents, while Dave, back from the steaming jungles of Vietnam, where he had seen scenes of incredible and pointless violence, is in the living room, perhaps splitting firewood with his bare hands. The high school student is standing there, for some inexplicable reason, fearlessly.

Meanwhile, Dave has become irate. Sara was *his*, she wrote him letters, she was *special,* they had a relationship. Sara shuttles between kitchen and living room. Her soldier is out there in his khaki uniform. He is an impressive physical specimen, according to the reports. The high school boy is wearing a pink shirt and he has never been an impressive physical specimen except for a brief period in graduate school when the weight room was the place to be for English doctoral students who did not want to be mistaken for wimps. Talk about a losing proposition. The shuttle diplomacy goes on and on, to what end I am not sure. Sara indicates she is trying to placate the Marine.

"What's going on out there?" her mom asks.

"Right now?"

"Yes, right now," her mom says.

"Right now, he's doing push-ups."

"Does he have a gun?" somebody should have asked, because that was the only relevant question.

"I should probably go," the high school boy says.

They suggested I use the back door.

★

DURING MY COLLEGE YEARS, gigantic protests amassed, upstate New York, New York City, D.C. There was a famous National Student Association convention in El Paso. That's where my friend Bob got national press for doing his hilarious Nixon send-up before thousands of hooting delegates as the national protest movement intensified.

One of the campus leaders was named Ronnie, and she drove everybody mad with desire up and down the East Coast— every man, woman, child, and domestic animal. Her long auburn hair swayed, her white teeth shone, and you could track where she had passed by the trail of male bodies strewn in her backlit wake. The two of us had a class together. One night I had a dream about her, duh, and next day couldn't wait to mention this wonderful event. She had a feline, Cleopatrian visage and danced when she walked and her words gleamed like pearls. "What were we doing?" I couldn't wait to tell her and she said, "That's nice." She was wearing a tan fringed clingy suede jacket, so you can appreciate her credibility was off the charts. Class began—I can see my battered, wobbly copy of the *Norton Anthology of Literature* now—and thought about her instead of John Dryden all class long, not a bad trade-off. Was she the most beautiful girl in New York? She only looked that way.

Ronnie might have rattled Richard Milhous Nixon himself. She was there when the president got out of his car to mingle with protestors on the Mall. He looked drunk and shaky. His make-up was running. The Kent State archives include this report from her:

"Somebody would ask him to speak up, he was mumbling at his feet. And that would jolt him out of wherever he was and he'd kind of look up and shake his head around, but then he'd go back to looking at his feet and he was gone again."

★

FOR A WHILE I lived next door to a Vietnam vet named Rick, who became a friend. His arm had been blown off walking point. Rick tried out living in the seminary and becoming a priest, but it didn't click. He wrote a good novel titled *Jesus Who?* that couldn't get published. Rick had a buddy who was a triple amputee vet. The three of us would do lines in the specially equipped van and talk for hours.

"Vietnam, Vietnam, Vietnam"—Michael Herr's last words in his unforgettable *Dispatches*—"we've all been there." You have to be incredibly foolish to subscribe to that belief.

At picture-postcard remove, the Socialist Republic of Vietnam is a picturesque land of lily ponds and lotus blossoms, thatched roofs and coconut groves, fleets of saipans and junks. Lining the roads are coffee trees, rubber trees, palm trees. And everywhere rice fields and rice fields and rice fields. When sun sets, you will be washed over by the perfume of night-blooming jasmine. If you ever saw the mystically beautiful Halong Bay and the gorgeous sands of the Gulf of Tonkin, north of Hanoi, it would be easy to fathom how tourism will have a bright future in Vietnam.

While I descended into Saigon, which is what the people on the ground call what the party officials named Ho Chi Minh City, what I noticed was the languorous and elaborate Mekong River and its tributaries, partitioning the land into a hundred pleasing shades of green. Later, flying into Hanoi, in the north, I could contrast that with the still detectible shadowy patterns left behind by B-52 carpet-bombing. Most of the obvious vestiges of war had been eradicated. The rubble has been carried off, and you have to visit so-called wartime museums to catch a glimpse of a disabled tank. Long Binh, once the American base and the largest military installation in the history of the world, is now nothing more than ghostly green fields rolling as far as the eye can see. In the classrooms and cafés, around seminar tables and bookstores, or on the streets where street urchins with harelips begged, in the overcrowded and under-equipped hospitals, and also one night on a basketball court, other kinds of scars were still visible.

For a long time after the war, Americans were caught up in the aftermath—and I was one of them, and the aftermath was also going to be part and parcel of this course I wanted to teach. The Vietnamese I met did not exactly have the luxury to contemplate the aftermath. They had higher and less abstract priorities. They wanted to move beyond those questions, and wanted to talk about rebuilding their society shattered by thirty uninterrupted years of war. That's how they referred to their war: The Thirty Years' War, a war in which the Americans played but one part.

I recall a basketball game played one hot night, an improbability in a whole series of improbabilities, in a whole journey of unbroken improbabilities. It all began when along with some colleagues I met with a group of Vietnamese citizens who had applied for participation in the orderly departure program. Though it would be difficult to convince the desperate boat people whose grim, heroic tales captured the public imagination back then, the Sixth Party Congress reportedly had made exit visas easier to come by. Still, the visa-pursuer, while not formally a persona non grata, could no longer hold a job in Vietnam.

So we thought we would begin with a slice of café society, Saigon style. I hopped on the back of a scooter driven by a diminutive Vietnamese neurosurgeon who was legally unemployable and who kept up a running conversation in excellent idiomatic English as we drove across town, enduring the glee of pedestrians amused by the sight of the oversized burly American perched on the back of the scooter like a bear on a flagpole. Traffic was crazy (stoplights would have been nice)— Bangkok, Naples, Athens *crazy,* even with the relative paucity of automobiles. We arrived safe and sound at the café. That's where we settled into low chairs at the low tables. Instantly we were surrounded by a cadre of Vietnamese who were friends and colleagues, who gathered regularly to practice speaking English, and who had applied to leave their country. Cigarette smoke curled everywhere in the dim room, which of course featured a faded, fraying poster of Ho out of the line of sight. Fans slowly swirled the heat around and we sipped on black Vietnamese tea. These ten Vietnamese were elated over the prospect of talking English, of sharing the dream of leaving Vietnam.

One young woman wanted my "opinion" about literature. I tried my best to answer. What about Hemingway, she wanted to know. He was grand, I replied. Finally, she let on her literary ambitions, which I had begun to suspect. She planned to write three books as soon as she arrived in America: a book on the subject of Literature, a book on Saigon after the war, and lastly a book, according to her, on The World. This last title on one level was too vague to grasp, but in the moment not really. She was a writer in the making and she wanted to confront the world. I could relate. She was a leader, clearly, because her friends had been held rapt by her disquisition, and if they did not applaud, they might have.

The Vietnamese, yes, were extraordinarily sweet, supremely innocent, and for an American like me, it was possible to relish the pleasures of their nostalgia for the ruined, gone, carpet-bombed world they had no choice but to recall and recall some more.

One other of the ten was a former ARVN—a soldier in the Army of the Republic of South Vietnam. For all his combat experience, he did not appear to be the grizzled vet. He wanted to know what the American thought about *Platoon*, the Oliver Stone movie that had caused an international controversy. Though I suspected that the man would deplore the movie as much as I did, I had taught long enough to recognize a trick question when I heard one, so I waited, knowing the soldier would voice his opinion before long, and he obliged. "I did not like it." He was animated, visibly bitter about the movie. "It portrayed American soldiers unfairly. I never saw American soldiers rape a Vietnamese woman." The whole table was swept up in his indignation, and he took advantage of the spotlight. "Once I was in the re-education camp, I knew why we fought the war. To keep these people out of power." He reported seeing routine executions, of corpses of failed escapees left rotting in the sun for days as a warning. "The Khmer Rouge, they are nothing in comparison." This veteran had spent eight years in a camp. "I love Americans," he testified. "Do you know what the word for 'American' is in Vietnamese?" He was going to remind this American, who had heard the translation. "The word for 'American' is 'My,' which also means 'beautiful.' I love Americans."

It was impossible not to contrast the soldier's circumstances with my own. My struggles over Vietnam had been feeble and boutique in comparison. Would I have had courage like his? Probably not. And what would my take on the Communists have been? Would I have seen them as the agents of darkness and totalitarian rule, as he did, or would my diffuse patriotism have enabled me to view them as the best possible course of action in the name of national liberation from colonizing Western powers? Would I have been seduced by Diem and Thieu and American money, or would I have believed that the Americans were sacrificing their lives for my freedom? As I looked around the table, I caught myself feeling skeptical if not almost critical of them for desiring to leave their country at this crucial time. I am embarrassed to admit that, but more often than I like my student-body-president knee-jerk take-one-for-the-team persona gets the best of me. At the same time, I could also identify with Thomas Fowler, the cynical, romantic foreign correspondent and narrator in Graham Greene's *The Quiet American*, who was both mesmerized and repelled by Vietnam and who could not decide whether to leave or to stay, and so who ended up, in that Graham Greene sort of way, doing both.

"Shall we have a match?" somebody piped up, referring to a basketball game. Soon we were back on scooters heading across town, and in no time after we arrived, we hit the court, and the game was on. A hundred or so spectators had mystifyingly gathered and would have stood along the sidelines of the court, if there were sidelines.

It was twilight and the court gleamed with the illumination of something like forty-watt bulbs. The air was cooler, thankfully. There were no nets on the baskets, and it proved difficult to dribble past the numerous tiny craters and fissures in the asphalt, but so what? You could see nearby scores of martial artists who were in formation, doing some form in unison. The spectators were loud, making mostly appropriate sounds at the appropriate times. The Vietnamese women competed enthusiastically—no sex discrimination on the court here—and they could subtly push off for rebounds that would impress any coach in any hemisphere.

My teammates' shots could have broken the rims. They could not shoot at all, but they loved to do the weave as they pushed the ball up court with a frenzy. If the game had called for swinging through trees or wading through marsh, they would have done it. It was the drive that mattered, not the score. They ran up and down the court like mad. At one point a big fat bug flew into my mouth and before I knew it, it was a chewy ex-bug.

The ex-ARVN had been assigned the task of guarding me, an American, the only American on the court, an American whom he loved. He was taller but about the same age. The two of us squared off, across cultures, across purposes. He smiled beatifically when the American moved out to take the pass on the wing, and we matched up. In my lifetime of a million pickup games, I usually had the advantage of surprise and usually scored first, because I am quicker than I look and a better shooter than might be expected. It's after that first score, when my superior opponent is now pissed over having been shown up by somebody who looks like me, that the game gets interesting—for the other side, anyway.

So there we were, the ARVN and I. The American had the ball. The American had position. The ARVN was wearing boots. The American was in basketball shoes. Instinctively, I gave him a head fake right, drove baseline left, and felt terrible when I heard the cheers rise up in response to the successful layup. Why did the soldier go for the head fake, the oldest one in the books? To this day, I can still see him falling for it, still reaching out for the place where he thought the beloved American was bound to be. The game went on, but I had lost my heart for it, and I was glad when it was done.

A friend of mine said no Viet Cong would have gone for the head fake in Ho Chi Minh City, and maybe he was right.

Americans may never really understand Vietnam. One of those on the list gave me her address after the game. Only later did I realize she believed she lived in a country that no longer existed: South Vietnam.

★

BEFORE I LEFT SOUTHEAST Asia, I visited Tuol Sleng in Phnom Penh, Cambodia, the Belsen of the Khmer Rouge, tillers of the killing fields. It is a sacred and terrifying and humbling place. You can still see in place the instruments of torture. Blood still stains the floors. Here is where guards, who averaged fourteen years old, "interrogated" their prisoners, which included every writer, artist, teacher, and student, every wearer of eyeglasses they could get their fundamentalist hands on. Here is where they extracted written "confessions," which they proudly displayed for their superiors. They had photos of everybody who passed through, and when you visit Tuol Sleng you walk through rooms and rooms of photographs that constitute a museum of, and a shrine to, the victims of the Khmer Rouge. There is a continual hush in the place. Like a church, like a tomb. Once upon a time, nobody should ever forget, once upon a time Tuol Sleng had been a school.

I came back home understanding all over again and in new ways how Vietnam was a tragedy for everyone in my generation. I returned to school to teach my Vietnam course, because that's what teachers do with a tragedy like that: they teach their students and hope against hope that history will never be repeated.

★

I HAVE NOT TAUGHT in a classroom for years now, but it's a rare week when I don't get one or two phone calls or emails from former students. Many of them are immensely successful actors, astrophysicists, authors, artists, cantors, entrepreneurs, doctors, insurance salesmen, investment managers, lawyers, philanthropists, politicians, professors, one professional baseball player, teachers, work-at-home moms and work-at-home dads. It's good to hear from them. More than a couple of these former students I have ceased thinking of as former anything. Some are friends.

I left UHS when I was hired as the assistant head and academic dean of my old high school. My all-boys Catholic high school was going co-educational at long last, and I relished the challenge. True, I had enjoyed an unstable relationship with the institution. For instance, when the twenty-year reunion came around, I saw the roster of alums, and couldn't miss how I was listed:

Joseph Di Prisco, Deceased.

Reports of my demise proved exaggerated, and who was better suited to retool a curriculum that was sealed in amber since before my student days? Maybe we could teach something other than *The Good Earth*, or maybe assign the unabridged *Great Expectations*. And who had more reason to lead a faculty used to teaching only boys on a journey toward teaching girls, too? This was the school where I learned everything I did not know about girls in the first place.

A prophet is not without honor except in his old high school. For one thing, I was in a battle nonstop with the passive-aggressive president of the high school, a Brother who may have been (and I do not say this lightly) the single most unscrupulous person I had ever worked with in a school—or anywhere else. Later, he was drummed out after he allegedly made unpassively-aggressive advances upon some young Brothers.

All that said, I am glad to have worked there. Today I look out my upstairs window down the hill where, a couple of miles away, I can see the school. The campus looks different. It isn't my campus anymore. The eucalyptus trees I once loved have been chopped down, a new gym looms. The school looks beautiful and tranquil in the distance, the way so many important places look, once they are safely in the distance.

★

DURING MY TIME AT UHS, I became friends with a gifted psychologist on staff. Mike Riera and I went on to write two books together about adolescence and child development that were well received. Riera has a genius for working with families and kids, and we did two national book tours. I don't know what it means that somebody like me was interviewed on NPR and many other places about parenting expertise, and that I did a fair amount of public speaking on the subject, but that's the truth. If somebody cares to snicker and invoke the term "ironic," I would be the last to argue. All I could possibly say is that some of us learn our best lessons the hard way.

After UHS and after going back briefly to my old high school for my fair share of abuse as vice principal, I took refuge in my office and wrote. Novels and a new book of poetry were published, and their arrival was met with something akin to the howl of a faraway coyote. My wife suggested maybe I should get out more. At some point, I began to be asked to serve on nonprofit boards devoted to the arts, children's health, education. In the process, I did a good deal of speaking and facilitated gatherings, osmotically absorbing the vocabulary of my altruistic new MBA pals. In fact, I became Chair of the Board of Trustees of Redwood Day School, an excellent institution in Oakland. It so happened that my colleague Riera applied for the job of Head of School when there was a vacancy, and despite his association with the Chair, he was hired and enjoyed seven years of success.

The board chair position, which I held for seven years, an eternity in Board-Chair years, may have been the most interesting, most challenging job I ever had, and one I didn't get paid for. When I told a friend of mine that I learned something every day as board chair, the wise guy couldn't resist: "That bad, huh?" Point taken. Schools and crises go hand in hand. No wonder I felt at home. I also seemed to possess fundraising talent, which perhaps combined skills developed as altar boy and card counter and restaurant manager and teacher—and all right, maybe also college radical and unindicted racketeer. Board chair may have been the work I was born to do.

★

DURING MY SEVEN YEARS at UHS, I was twice elected commencement speaker by the graduating senior class, the most coveted faculty distinction. Would I say that we teachers were overly competitive? As one colleague remarked, if an election were conducted among faculty for teacher of the year, each faculty member would garner exactly one vote. The first time I was elected speaker, in June 1989, was wonderful for reasons that will be obvious in a minute. I was wistful that day, however, because Mario said he wanted to be there but couldn't. He had graduated from the eighth grade and getting ready to matriculate at UHS in the fall thanks to financial aid. He had a big ballgame that day, and he pitched a no-hitter—and lost. There are more life lessons to be gleaned from that experience than Oprah Winfrey and Bill Cosby combined can possibly cover in a commencement address.

The next time I spoke was in June 1993. It was a gorgeous, warm day with a big milky blue sky over the park. Mario was graduating. In fact, he himself had been elected student speaker by the class, and he spoke before me. The last twelve months had been quite a ride for him. He was going to the college of his dreams, where he would go on to play varsity baseball. The underdog UHS baseball team had won the California North Coast Section Championship, and he pitched a dominant complete-game victory in the championship, giving up one unearned run thanks to an error on the part of the right fielder whose dad had recently been awarded a Nobel Prize. In March, my son's rap group, The Age of Gray, performed at the school dance.

"Why are you guys called The Age of Gray?"

"Because, Dad, it's not about black and it's not about white."

He was the only white member of the group, and maybe I had taught him something after all.

On the way home the night of the dance, he fell asleep at the wheel. He woke up as his car was upside down, airborne. The car slammed into the freeway divider and was annihilated. Only a miracle explains why he survived, practically unscathed physically, and he knew it. He has never forgotten it. I will never forget it. These emotions permeated my remarks and his beautiful speech. In the end, it was a perfect day the two of us will always treasure, made somehow more perfect by the fact that we were both here, both alive, to make it happen.

★

Now this is what I call a transcendent experience. Not simply representing the faculty at commencement. And not simply being invited to address this wonderful graduating class. But being permitted to make a few remarks today—that is, after Mario has had his say. Usually, after he's said his piece, I'm accustomed to being all alone in the spectacularly vacated room.

I also cannot resist recalling that the last time I spoke here in this idyllic setting, to the class of '89, something else transcendent took place. A certain Starrs McBurney was graduating, one of the many terrific human beings I've been lucky enough to teach at University High School, and there in attendance with the rest of her fine family was her godmother, a certain Patricia James, whom I had never met. Afterward, at Starrs' party, Patti and I spoke. In a moment, I'll be distributing the photo album because, well, tomorrow we celebrate our wedding anniversary.

In any event, it's time to get down to business. Or, to quote Groucho Marx when, as the lunatic explorer Captain Spaulding in Animal Crackers, *he sang, "Hello, I must be going." Which, as they say while*

*being interrogated in the old detective movies, is my story, and I'm
sticking to it.*

*You know, psychologists, who have names for everything, label this
sort of thing (the "Hello, I must be going" sort of thing, the "Come
here, go away" sort of thing) a double message. Of course, there are
double messages and double messages. Poets depend for their existence
upon double messages, saying one thing and meaning another, but so do
politicians and bureaucrats, saying one thing and doing another. We human
beings must have either a magnificent tolerance or a tremendous need for
such doubleness. If you think about it, any good class is predicated upon
doubleness—discussing one thing while treating another. We are reading
or performing Shakespeare, or studying Vietnam, or the Bible, or American
literature, but we are simultaneously reading, and maybe even performing,
ourselves, simultaneously examining the grounds of our own understanding
of ourselves, our community, our world. Of course, the whole bittersweet
secret to high school is that we're not covering material—books, texts, ideas,
themes, whatever. At the same time we are also discovering, uncovering
ourselves, our values, the sources of our senses of meaning.*

*Even so, this is our common task today, at commencement, to say
in some fashion to each other, Hello, we must be going. In a matter of
minutes we are out of here, some of us for the summer, some of us for
what seems like forever, but in the very moment of disengaging, perhaps
we might find ourselves more engaged than ever before. Perhaps, moving
away from each other, we might find ourselves growing closer. There goes
that doubleness again.*

*But before you graduate, a word or, I guess I should say, two. Isn't
it strange that, though your guardians and parents and teachers have
had you in their care for some time now, we will probably be unable to
resist the temptation to give you just a few more pointers on the use and
misuse of this education, this life, this world?*

*Since commencement speeches should have some high, redeeming
social purpose, I hope to show you how to read the doubleness of these
last-minute exhortations. As you go forth into that wondrous world
beyond high school, you will hear profound thoughts volunteered by*

your family and friends, deep insights into the human condition, learned admonitions, savvy propositions gained at the expense of hard-won experience, such as:

1. Don't leave your clothes unattended in the Laundromat.

Amazing, how otherwise competent people with fascinating stories, inspiring vocations, and intelligently diversified investment postures and social consciences will exhibit an unquenchable interest in the state of your laundry. You may assume that "Don't leave your clothes unattended in the Laundromat" means "Let's not spend any more at The Gap," but actually on another level, translated, this means, and though we wish it weren't true, sometimes the world is a nest of spiders, sometimes people are going to let you down. But if perfect strangers will prove capable of mind-boggling, heartbreaking indifference, cruelty, these same strangers may also exhibit shocking tenderness. Because translated, this means, when you do leave your clothes overnight in the dryer, as you will, who knows, you may return to discover that someone has folded everything crisply, and left you another, more beautiful shirt. Translated, this means, it's okay when you mess up. Be ready for the small miracles and the genuine good luck that may, for no good earned reason, come your way.

2. Don't change a flat tire on the highway. *Translated, this means don't drive your car or anybody's car too fast, too slow, too long without factory-authorized professional maintenance or without fuel. Don't drive in front of, behind, or alongside a truck, a motorcycle, a bike, a bus, or any another moving or stationary vehicle. Don't drive in the first light, or under the noon sun, or after darkness falls, or when it's raining, or snowing, or windy. In fact, if you can arrange it, we'd appreciate it if you didn't drive at all. And while we're on the subject, don't use any form of transportation, public or private. Translated, all this ultimately means is, slow down, what's the hurry, where are you going, take some long walks by yourself, to settle the scores within yourself before you take them up with anybody else. Translated, this means, some risks are worth taking, and some are simply not. Translated, this means, travel far but travel well, remembering occasionally what Thoreau said, about traveling widely, all over a small place known as Walden Pond.*

Translated, this means, sometimes, in the middle of a fantastic accident, hitting the freeway divider at full speed, you wake up in midair, see your life pass before your eyes, float upside down to the asphalt on the wings of what have to be angels, and walk away without a scratch.

3. Please, please, please don't get a dog. *Translation: Soon as you are ready, get a really good dog. I personally recommend a mixed-breed dog in the neighborhood of seventy to eighty pounds, and I suggest naming this dog after a character in a nineteenth-century novel. This will serve as a trusty conversation-starter, and will always remind you of your intellectual roots—though conceivably to your embarrassment.*

Translated, this means, at the same time, that we wish for you just a little bit of loneliness, not so much that you doubt your worth, and not so little that you never experience a test of your character. As a poet once remarked, the only cure for loneliness is solitude. Don't forget, a good dog is very good company in solitude. Translated, in addition, this means, we hope that you will make good and strong friends, that you never take for granted the loyalty and love of your friends.

4. Don't play in a poker game organized by the slowest, but, gee, the nicest guy you think you know. *This literally means, you are about to become the breakfast of champions. Translated, on another level, this means take up an interest others may find esoteric, quaint, or odd as soon as possible, like fly-fishing, billiards, Classical Greek. Become an expert in James Joyce, or roses, or pottery, or Elizabethan poetry, or jazz, or most especially birds, which reward intense interest with supreme, gorgeous apathy, sometimes a necessary thing to endure. Translated, this also means, be suspicious of all received opinion, all the conventional views. Think your own thoughts as far as you are able, make your own mistakes, take your own chances.*

5. Once you get settled in, drop us a line, or call up, anytime, day or night. *Translation: This seemingly obvious one could refer to the subtlest mystery of all. It isn't about keeping tabs on you, it isn't about control. Translated, philosophically speaking, this means, we don't truly know how we're going to get along without you.*

6. Sleep. *Translation: All-nighters are uplifting for the soul. Studying by the midnight oil (whatever that is), or frantically composing papers at the very last minute is very good for the soul, if not necessarily in the short-term interests of the body. I mean, do you care, do you really care to put it all together? This may be something as of yet that you do not know about yourself, and it will be terrific to find out that you care this much, this deeply. But commit yourself to discovering the truth of an idea, to braving the consequences of your desire to master and to explain. There are few things more exhilarating than the pursuit of knowledge. Translated, this means, too, when you stay up all night, take a good look at the sunrise, which has now been somehow earned by you, the bands of pink and grey across the horizon, and notice carefully the way the early air smells of new snow, or fresh rain, or the turning of a season. Despite everything, the world is a beautiful and amazing place, all the more beautiful and amazing for your noticing it, and for your being in it.*

7. Don't meet Professor Peach for a late-night cappuccino. *The precise translation of this is: Don't meet Professor Peach for a late-night cappuccino.*

8. Get ready for number eight, because we always stuff everything in this number eight steamer trunk. *Just pack the warm coat. Play defense with your feet. Eat your greens. Don't argue with a fool. Never make the third out at third base. Don't put on your socks in a dark room. Pay no attention to the man behind the curtain—lions and tigers and bears, oh my. Opposition is true friendship. Learn how to cook perfect scrambled eggs. Death to comma splices. Don't make every assertion end with a rising intoNATION? and question MARK? Live beneath the open sky and dangerously. Sound a barbaric yawp. Hate flattery and flatterers with a pure and constant heart. Don't believe the hype. And, don't forget, take that coat. Translation: We hope we gave you a few clues, we hope we have given you a head start. A head start on what? That would be hard to say. No family is without flaws, and you can't leave any school without taking a few scars. Translated, this injunction has something to do with love, that unmanageable thing. For the world can be a cold and broken place. Translated, this means, fix the prisons. Fix the schools. Fix the cities. Fix the government. Fix the sky, the sea, the earth. Translated, this means, write the strong novel, break the tough story, build the beautiful building, sing the pure song, paint the essential painting, heal the sick, feed the hungry, shelter the homeless, teach the children. Give blood, give your time, give your self.*

9. You sure you're ready for a big-time romantic relationship? *Right. What an altogether useful, sensible piece of advice. As everybody knows, the typical adult has been the paragon of decorum, for the last seven and a half minutes, anyway. But beyond that, translated, number nine means, better a too-serious, committed relationship than the other sorts, because—and we don't know how to take the edge off this, and here goes—because we are terrified of AIDS. And we are more terrified if we don't know that you are a little bit terrified, too. Translated, this also means that we wish you good fortune, that you won't be hurt as much as you probably will be, and we wish that you are capable of being hurt, even if we don't wish that you do feel the knives of this disappointment. Strictly speaking, translated, we still find it impossible to understand how you could love anyone else—but we promise to try.*

Finally, number ten. Be good. *I don't know how to break this, but "Be good" is technically untranslatable. Of course, be safe as you can be without letting life pass you by. Of course, be kind as long as kindness does not enable you to compromise your principles. (And by the way, if you don't have any absolute principles—and absolute principles may seem pretty hard to come by in this monstrously relativistic postmodern moral universe we have created in the twentieth century—try out a few, and practice, practice, practice.) Of course, be great if that's your fate, but if you are doomed to be great you probably can't avoid it anyway. But you know, being good could be tougher than being great. It certainly doesn't mean be recklessly careful, or polite, or conciliatory. Don't be afraid of conflict. If there's no cause, no dream, no person worth fighting for, and fighting over, then who are you? As you can tell, if you get number ten, you can forget numbers one through nine, because number ten is what it's really all about. So be good.*

There's more, but never mind.

You see, at this moment of moving away from each other, we may finally enjoy enough distance to see each other in plain relief. If this experience has not already occurred to you, it may happen today on the lawn of Julius Kahn Park, or at some celebration this afternoon, or across a restaurant table this summer, or at some noisy airport this fall, or in the crowded hallway of some dormitory during orientation—and we will see each other in an altogether new, suddenly much more available light. It promises to be an astonishing moment, even if we've been preparing for this surprise for the last seventeen, eighteen years.

Sometimes, in the middle of a class discussion, you make a point, you share an insight, you ask a question that breaks open everything, and I hear myself spontaneously uttering exactly what I am thinking, which is—I'm glad you came to school today. Even now, right now, I suggest you are giving witness to precisely that kind of insight, asking just such a perfect question, and so—and I mean this—no double message here: Each and every one of you, thank you, thank you, thank you for coming to University High School today.

★

IF I HAD ONE book to choose for my well-deserved desert island banishment, I would choose the essays of Montaigne. As Montaigne says about his own writing, "If my mind could gain a firm footing I would not make essays, I would make decisions." Toward the conclusion of his "Of Experience," he writes: "We are great fools. 'He has spent his life in idleness,' we say; 'I have done nothing today.' What, have you not lived? That is not only the fundamental but the most illustrious of your occupations.... Have you been able to think out and manage your own life? You have done the greatest task of all."

As for the author of this book, I fell off the path from time to time, though maybe some people don't have paths. Maybe some people cannot see them. Maybe for writers like me the trod-upon paths are the ones to be avoided. Remember Robert Frost's two roads that diverged in a yellow wood and sorry he could not travel both and be one traveler long he stood and looked down one as far as he could to where it bent in the undergrowth?

For me, there were always more than two roads. For me, the roads appeared like one of those manic Italian roundabouts, where there are fifty signs, including six different and conflicting pointers to Rome. All roads lead to Rome, so they say, and they are right. I took one road, I took them all, I kept going in circles, often mistaking motion for progress and desire for direction. I don't know exactly how, but somehow I got somewhere.

PART THREE

"The cradle rocks above an abyss, and common sense tells us that our existence is but a brief crack of light between two eternities of darkness."

—Vladimir Nabokov, *Speak, Memory*

This Is As Far As We Go: 2010

M Y EIGHTY-FIVE-YEAR-OLD FATHER IS fading. That's the news. Which isn't. His life winds down, inexorably. With all my jaggedly spliced heart I do despise the word "inexorably," but sometimes it is the only word that will do the trick. On some level, my dad knows what is happening—or knows it to the extent that he now knows anything, which is partially, cryptically, enigmatically, uncertainly. And fine, if you insist, *inexorably*.

His short-term memory is virtually non-functional. He can call ten times a day or more. "I have something important to ask you." This is a typical message he leaves on the voicemail. And when I call back, he denies having called. Or he cannot recall what was so urgent. He turns argumentative. Or takes the offensive. "Why don't you come see me?" He was never one to be reasoned with. Now the difference is that he is often mentally incapable of grasping what you are saying—or what *he* is saying.

"I have lots of problems," he once confided to a caregiver, a non sequitur, in a vulnerable moment. "I'm not too good at finding solutions."

Like father, like son?

That self-recognition of his sounds like thoughtfulness. Such thoughtfulness could have led a man toward wisdom fifty years ago—though I am only guessing, as I myself have merely done flyovers of the land of wisdom. I wish I had witnessed the emergence of that reflective side of his in the past. Today this insight—"I'm not too good at finding solutions"—amounts on his part to the flying of a white flag.

When I am asked by friends what it feels like to cope with his Alzheimer's and congestive heart failure, their question is framed sympathetically. Does it make me fearful of my own fate, the inevitable depletion of my own memory bank? It is more than that, or different. His life is not suddenly a cautionary tale for me. His life was *always* a cautionary tale for me. And I offer that admission recognizing that it is not to my credit.

Now that I think about it, *my* life has served as a cautionary tale to me. Still, as anybody can see at this late stage of my story, I didn't heed all the lessons I should have, which leads me to speculate that cautionary tales are about as useful as the concept of closure—handy as a tuxedo on a surfboard, a knife in a gunfight, hedge funds in a mausoleum.

My father cannot always remember that my mother, his wife, is dead. We go over this ground practically every day.

"Did you hear the news?"

"What news?"

"Nobody told you?"

"Told me what, Dad?"

"My wife is dead!"

Groundhog Day is a great movie, but I wouldn't recommend living in it.

Sometimes, very rarely, he thanks me for helping him. Sometimes, he wants to know: "Am I causing you trouble?" Other times, he seems resentful of any efforts on my part. He is continually agitated and angry, like the time when I commandeered his debit card. His doctor and I realize he has no ability to manage his finances, but he doesn't. How could he? He has dementia.

"It's my money, Joe. Get your own card."

Now that I internalize that he has a mental defect, an illness, I can usually be more patient. I can spend a solid thirty minutes on the telephone guiding him over and over and over on how to use his remote control to get to the football game on television. I tell him the number: "Push seven two four, 724, on the remote control."

"Seven two four," he repeats, and then I hear him putting down the remote control and removing the phone from his ear, while he punches in seven two four—on the telephone keypad. Somehow we navigate to the station with a football game, or failing that, at least basketball. Baseball bores him. He missed the news that the San Francisco Giants won the World Series. He hates the Giants, so this would have been fun for him to complain about.

What lies in store? Decay, like growth, is not linear. He seems to be heading fast for what they euphemistically call the Memory Wing of his assisted-living residence. This is a floor for those with dementia who need constant assistance to get by and whose independence needs to be curtailed for their own safety.

My mother, in addition to Alzheimer's, also had congestive heart failure and numerous other maladies. As for her walker, she spurned it with impunity. She could spurn with impunity like a champ. She didn't like the look of the walker. She preferred to be escorted by the arm. By contrast, my father's physical health is not so terrible for a man his age. The numbers that come in on the tests impress his doctor.

To paraphrase Philip Roth, they say old age is a battle, but they are wrong. It is a massacre, he says. I have seen the results of this massacre on the battlefield of my father's life and it can be terrifying. More than anything I fear becoming a burden to my own son someday. I wonder how I will behave when I lose it—and I don't mean *if* I lose it. For unquestionably it will be lost. I grasp how suicide can appear an appealing option to those in extreme pain and in despair, and I am more than sympathetic. Sometimes I wonder if the Catholic in me will be able to withstand the trusty Siren's call.

My father can ask the same question three or four times in a row, or repeat the same statement, and show no signs of taking in any information—or of retaining the information he seems to yearn for.

A"re you coming here for lunch?" This is something he asks an hour after I leave his residence, after we had lunch.

"How many kids does Mario have?" He cannot register that he has *three* great-grandchildren, one of whom is currently teething. For their part, sweetly enough, the great-grandchildren are very kind to their Bisnonno, their great-grandpa. At their young age, they sense there is something not quite right, and they are sympathetic. But let's not be silly. The boys, three and five, are not mini-mendicants. They are bright and calculating enough that, when Bisnonno is especially forgetful, they can get him to fork over a second ice cream from the freezer if they play their cards right.

"I need to go to the bank."

"Who pays my rent?"

"I need $20,000. Why? To buy a car."

"I need a razor. I need toothpaste. I need toilet paper. I need to go to the drug store for a prescription." All his physical and domestic and medical needs are already taken care of, however. There came a day when he refused to go to a doctor's office. For one thing, the doctor was a male, and my dad needs to be the alpha. For another thing, he was sensing that the doctor and I, by extension, were zeroing in on his dementia. He didn't like the questions he was being asked. So he said he wasn't going back to the guy. Hence he has a concierge doc, who is a woman. He gets along better with women, and his union pension benefits makes personalized medical attention possible. I used to tell him long ago that one day nobody will enjoy the kinds of benefits he takes for granted. That never stopped him from complaining. "They are all tryin' to clip ya." That was his catchall counsel: "Don't get clipped."

These days my dad is fortunate that he doesn't need to worry about cleaning his apartment, or paying a bill, or going to the pharmacy, or organizing his meds. And I am fortunate that I don't have to worry about him trying to do any of that. He has asked me a hundred times where his checkbook is. He wants to pay his bills. I tell him I am paying the bills. He doesn't like this arrangement. Once or twice, he expressed resignation if not quite acceptance when he said to me, "Guess you're a pretty honest guy." Despite all his questions and worries, he always has plenty of toothpaste and razors and toilet paper, and the staff picks up and dispenses his meds. He is covered. Too bad he cannot enjoy that.

★

"WHAT HAPPENED WHEN THE FBI took you back to New York?" I have asked him before, more than a few times over the decades. Time's wingéd chariot is drawing nigh, what's to lose? My father mulls anew what he is going to say. And also what he is not going to say.

I had cause to revisit the topic. Recently I received in the mail a fat packet from the FBI containing materials related to him. I had made a request under the aegis of the Freedom of Information and Privacy Act (FOIPA), Title 5, United States Code, Section 552/552a. It took four months of correspondence before they delivered. They reviewed *eighty* pages pertaining to him. They were releasing *seventy*. They cited exemptions on the basis of Federal Rules of Criminal Procedure pertaining to privacy, law enforcement procedure, and confidential informants.

The pages pertained not to the flight from Brooklyn and the return trip to testify, and not to the bookmaking, but to an FBI Strike Force investigation of sweetheart Teamster Union deals that allegedly occurred when my dad was the chief executive officer of a local. Details in the documents were few and far between, but the financial stakes in play seemed absurdly trivial—especially if the risk entailed federal prison time. Near as I can tell, they were investigating whether or not he was receiving something like $500 a month under the table, thereby absconding with union dues. I recall my father lamenting a certain nemesis, a former colleague turned disgruntled foe. He contemptuously spoke of him as a rat, so I am guessing this fellow was a confidential informant with a paranoid imagination or a zeal for revenge. Let's not be naïve. He possibly had the goods on my father, though honestly, I have my doubts. In the end, my father was investigated for over three years by the FBI Strike Force and no charges were filed: "Subsequent investigation has revealed no specific evidence of criminal activity based upon these allegations." In 1993, the case was formally closed.

The ten denied pages likely contained some material I had hoped to find. I have no confidence I will ever pry loose from the FBI the information pertaining to the Brooklyn episode, but I will keep trying. If I were a betting man, to quote my father, I would wager that the FBI will ultimately contend that hands-on recordkeeping from the early 1960s, before the age of the computer, was spotty or incapable of being accessed anymore. I have retained a D.C. attorney to push back.

I had also formally filed for my own records from the FBI. After multiple communications, they wrote that they could not uncover any pertaining to me. I have filed an appeal here as well. Personal friends who have had high-level experience in federal law enforcement say that the chances of there not being records about me approximate zero. To quote my mother's handy phrase, "We'll see."

★

IT WAS DECEMBER 2010, and my father appeared to be having a lucid moment, so I thought I would make one more attempt to press for details. We were in his apartment after Christmas

Eve brunch, during which he had spoken hardly a word, as usual, but he seemed otherwise alert. Every time I am around, I observe how his fellow residents greet him in a friendly manner, though this hardly ever occasions any exchanges. He does like the employees, or at least he shows interest in their work. Maybe he is hoping to organize a union.

My father and Patti and I are sitting across from each other in his room and he is reminding us that his wife died.

"Yes, Joe," Patti picks up the ball, "Kay died a year ago. But you will see her again in Heaven."

The two of them talk about the afterlife. Patti is devout. She believes. His forehead wrinkles as my father conveys doubt as to Heaven's existence, but it is a tentative, measured doubt, almost as if he realizes there is no downside in subscribing to the belief.

An opening: "Dad, what happened in New York? You recollect anything?"

"Yeah?" Question to answer a question: the default Brooklyn reflex.

"When you went back to New York, you remember what happened with the FBI?"

His words seep out slowly, sap from a tree. "They took care of me. They were protecting me."

"Who were they protecting you from?"

He stares at me, suspiciously. I've seen that look— "Whaddayou, writin' a book?"—a thousand times.

"You were testifying, corrupt cops, remember?"

"Possibly." Possibly equals a yes in his glossary.

"You had information, you told me."

"Yeah, possibly."

He recalls the time he was arrested for bookmaking when he was a teenager, and how the judge threw out the case because he figured out the kid was taking the pinch for the real big fish. That story has stayed the same over the years. I remind him we are speaking of a different episode.

"But what happened when you went back to New York with the FBI?"

"They were *protecting* me."

He's used that word before, and it has always confused me.

"What were they protecting you *from*?"

"Why you keep asking me?" Now his eyebrows rise, and he scowls.

I say, "I'm just trying to remember."

"Yeah, well, I'm trying to forget."

In the instant, *protecting* becomes clear. How could it have taken so long for me to figure this out? It wasn't just the FBI he was running from. No, he had squealed on the wrong guy. He ran from Brooklyn because there was a hit put out on him.

★

I COULD BE WRONG, of course. What are the possibilities? He made up out of whole cloth the basis of the drama that cast him into exile from Brooklyn? Though he is a gifted, prodigious liar, this seems unlikely, if not impossible. Too many wheels were set into violent, irreversible motion when he was a young man with a young family. They wouldn't have been set into motion without significant impetus. Too many clues litter the landscape of our lives. On the other hand, maybe he was humiliated by the role he played. Being a snitch, if that was what he was, would constitute a dishonorable reputation to live down for the rest of his life, and maybe somebody really did plot to kill him. I get it. After all, I am the equivalent of a snitch, the author of this memoir.

An old man in the gathering twilight has a right to forget. I cannot argue. There is another possibility. Maybe there *was* a big criminal drama, and maybe he played no role whatsoever. Maybe there were no dirty cops involved. Or maybe he was another small-potatoes street-level guy who wasn't trusted with enough information to endanger anybody in power. I suppose there are a few other possibilities, too. He has no concept of what happened to him. *Something* happened, he senses, but what it was he still does not understand. Or maybe he has simply forgotten everything by now, all the facts lost in the blizzard of his dementia. Or maybe he is repressing his remembrances. Finally, maybe he does not want *me* to know. Why trust a snitch like me? Again, like father, like son.

I concede I will never know as much as I would like to know.

I keep seeking the absent predicate for the Brooklyn exile. Am I also doing a sort of exegesis—studying the family texts, as it were, looking for the original sin of the father, the transgression that gets us thrown out of the Brooklyn garden that was no Eden in the first place? And what is the purpose of such exegesis? It's not like I don't have plenty of my own transgressions to keep me occupied.

Beyond that, I have read and written enough books to wonder how little we know about anybody. How much is knowable about a life, including by the person who is living it? So my search necessarily shifts the focus onto the searcher. Naturally the narcissist in me is pleased, if only momentarily. What does this quest disclose about me? Why can't I be content to live with the mystery that is my father and my family? I wish I knew the answer to that question. I keep looking for a key, and I find a hundred of them, and just as many locked doors that no key can open. What difference does it make for me what happened to him, or what sort of people my parents were, or what kind of family mine was, or the fact that we all took that subway to California? Maybe the ultimate mystery is the everyday, ordinary mystery I relentlessly, restlessly pose to myself about my own life. As my handy old *Baltimore Catechism* put it so hauntingly, "a mystery is a truth which we cannot understand."

Is it all too obvious? I had crazy, indubitably sociopathic parents. I am hardly alone in that respect. I myself made insane choices, destructive choices. Again, who doesn't? The work I was good at doing I resisted for as long as I could. Who doesn't need a career coach? I published some books that stumbled along or went nowhere. Take a number, buddy boy. I was a poor excuse for a father for a long time, and I strive every day to make up for lost opportunity. Now, here comes this little book of mine that is in your hands, in which I am trying to connect some dots. Aren't we hardwired to connect the dots? If I had the ability to add footnotes, this book might never end. Perish the thought. The same might be said for anybody's memoir, anybody's life.

★

My dad's delusions disturb me, almost as much as they rile him.
"Have you talked with my wife lately?"
"Is she going to be here for Thanksgiving?"
"Why didn't anybody tell me what happened to her?"
"She died? How come nobody sent me a letter?"
"Is John coming by?"
He asked me that last question the other day. That was a first. "Is John coming by?" That was one moment when he left me speechless. I didn't have a clue what to say. This question shook me. It forced me to admit it's one question I also catch myself asking when nobody else is around. *Is John coming by?*

The progression of my dad's dementia has been fast, cruel, and unrelenting. Only months before he was conferring with his lawyer without me in the room and meeting with his doctors and—much to my grudging admiration—making cagey decisions to work around me, pitting staff against me when it worked to his advantage, managing transportation to the bank to take out some cash (which he once managed to accomplish despite having no personal identification), before I cut off the flow of funds armed with my power of attorney—the power he legally bestowed upon me in what must have been a rare moment of lucidity, not to mention trust.

For a while, he was pushing to go to the racetrack on Sundays, and, after lots of back and forth between us, he persuaded me to take him.

This new social commitment put a different spin on my East/West Sundays. I had my routine. Between eight and ten on Sunday mornings, I was in Qigong class. If you ever see throngs in China doing a form of ritualized exercise in the parks and plazas, half of them are doing tai chi, half Qigong. To the uninitiated, the forms would look indistinguishable. The latter literally means Qi practice, and it is, essentially, a less martial version of tai chi. I had difficulty mastering the form, and never came close to achieving it, but it was invigorating to try. At eleven I went to Mass.

Our church is a small, spare, unassumingly beautiful Dominican parish in North Berkeley, a few minutes from home. The patron saint is a woman from whom Jesus cast out seven demons. Her name is Mary Magdalene, once assumed to have been a penitent ex-prostitute. Biblical scholars argue there is no evidence of such a professional résumé. The legend obstinately persists, however, demonstrating again how a tarred sexual reputation, though undeserved, is tough to live down. As John's gospel tells the story, after Jesus is crucified Mary goes to the tomb and sees that the rock that barred entry has been removed and that He is nowhere to be seen. His burial linens are on the ground. She suspects that somebody has stolen the body. She weeps. Then she notices angels inside the tomb where His body had been placed. Jesus materializes and says to her, "Woman, why are you weeping?" Men have asked of women such a question since the dawn of time, but never anybody like Jesus, who rose from the dead, and never with such plangent power. Afterward, she runs to tell the disciples, though it is hard to understand how she found the voice for these astonishing words: "I have seen the Lord." They believe her and the world has never been the same since.

The parish priests are sophisticated, literate, and philosophically inclined. The Dominican School of Theology is located up the hill, not far from the church. Dominicans have a deserved reputation for being excellent preachers, and the parish priests live up to their billing. The Catholic professors are in Sunday attendance if they don't opt for Newman Hall near Cal. Czeslaw Milosz, the Nobel Prize–winning poet, was a parishioner till his death. As important as anything else, the parish choir is first-rate. As the eminent rabbi Abraham J. Heschel said, "The only language that seems to be compatible with the wonder and mystery of being is the language of music."

When we were kids, my brother John and I used to leave our house early dressed in coat and tie and walk a couple of miles to attend nine o'clock Mass at Saint Mary Magdalen. When John died, I was touched that the pastor of the parish came and said a few words of consolation at the memorial service.

As for my own religious practice, there have been many years when I did not go to Mass, and years when I went all the time, including early morning weekday Mass. As I said before, my son had something crucial to do with my return. My ongoing, fitful, often tense conversation with Catholicism continues to this day.

The great writer Evelyn Waugh was the author of *Brideshead Revisited* and many other terrific books, and many regarded his professed Catholicism with wonder if not skepticism. Once he responded to a denunciation of his character—he seems to have been a son of a bitch—by saying, "You have no idea how much nastier I would be if I was not a Catholic." I take his sarcastic point to heart. He speaks to me. I wish I could explain my mind on the subject of Catholicism. But my mind has nothing to do with my Catholicism, and I don't find it to be a subject. It is a way of life. A way of my life.

I am no so-called cafeteria Catholic and no so-called cultural Catholic. Both of these half-baked, dated terms of disparagement have been cooked up by the Catholic right wing whose tastes run to ad hominem argument, at which they excel. They prefer the language of dismissal to confronting the legitimate differences embraced by their Catholic kin.

Maybe it is embarrassingly simpler than that. I have discovered, sometimes to my chagrin but as often to my delight, that I can't live with Catholicism and I can't live without it. If I am honest with myself, sometimes that's the best I can do by way of explanation. This is not much to offer, I realize, in the way of *apologia pro vita mia*. And it's not exactly Pascal's wager, is it? (To grossly simplify and paraphrase Pascal, the genius of probability theory: I can't prove God exists, but if I wager that He does exist and that turns out to be true, then I gain everything, and if He doesn't exist, even if I subscribe to His existence, then I lose nothing.) Pascal treats the question as if the answer were a coin flip, fifty-fifty. As somebody who dabbled a while in the fine arts of applied probability theory in the casino, I would have to say it is never a smart thing to wager everything on a coin flip. The larger problem with Pascal and his wager, of course, is that he treats the question as if it were a rational proposition. If belief were rational it would not be belief.

What did Flannery O'Connor say? "To discover the Church you have to set out by yourself." So maybe I am not very far off whenever I set off by myself. If there is an afterlife, we can work it out there. Once in the afterlife, I will also take up with the proper party the issue of skunks. Whose bright idea was *that*?

I realize there are those under the impression that Catholicism is the refuge of sap-headed weaklings. Supposedly we are consolation freaks unable to embrace the truth that we live in a godless universe. We should take our medicine. I understand that point of view, I do. I once held it myself. But if people think Catholicism is a path to easy comfort and a cure-all for the terror of mortality, they are sorely mistaken. All they would have to do is read Saint John of the Cross or

Gerard Manley Hopkins or George Herbert or John Donne or... The list goes on, and one main takeaway from these great poets is that only a fool thinks God gives you a crutch. Faith means living on fire.

My hero Garry Wills is the devout Catholic author who makes the most sense to me on what it means to be a Catholic today. He is the Church's most comprehensive, enlightened critic. He can masterfully contextualize the historical vagaries and inconsistencies of patently politicized Church practice and dogma. Whatever its divine genes, the Church is also an all-too-human institution, flawed and wrong about such matters as an all-male celibate priesthood, contraception, and homosexuality, and that's just for starters. Yet this is an institution that serves the poor around the world with unstinting care, and has bravely stood toe to toe with dictators, terrorists, and tyrants of all stripes. But let's not forget that nasty period when the Church unconscionably played footsie with Hitler, because this abomination is nothing to gloss over. Over and beyond everything, though, there are the sacramental rituals, which are not mere ceremonies. For me, these rituals inform and transform every crucial experience, from birth to the grave.

That last sentence calls for a tome's worth of reflection. Unfortunately, I am not capable of writing such a book.

In time the Church will change. The Vatican has always asserted otherwise—though the new Pope Francis has certainly been shaking things up and challenging assumptions. I take the long view. When we talk about institutions and the long view, we normally mean ten, twenty, fifty years out. When it comes to the Church, the long view encompasses centuries. In the meantime, the Church languishes in a dark phase, no question. The pedophilia crisis is only one aspect, but what a horrible aspect. That was an abject, indefensible failure on every level of accountability, legal, moral, and spiritual. Maybe one day there will come to be an American Catholic Church—I cannot predict and I won't be around to care. But I do know when Wills says that ultraconservative popes like Benedict XVI, God's Rottweiler, are irrelevant, I say hallelujah.

I am no longer the altar boy in my Greenpoint parish. Nor am I the novice Brother. But I am also not the college student who couldn't be bothered. And also not the guy who nosed around for meaning in the streets and along the darkened byways I followed during my twenties and thirties.

One of my favorite parables of Jesus is this one: "The Kingdom of Heaven is like yeast that a woman took and mixed in with three measures of flour until all of it was leavened" (Matthew 13:33). Without a parable, says the evangelist, Jesus "taught them nothing." As I read it, Jesus's sly leavening in the bread of the Church is working secretly over the course of history. And sometimes, on the good days, I can almost feel the leavening working its miracle and power within me. Those are pretty good days indeed.

★

GOLDEN GATE FIELDS, IN Albany, California, is a ten-minute drive from my home. I can see it from my upstairs windows. The racetrack gleams like a jewel on the sparkling shore, not at all like how it looks up close—seamy and rundown. For months my dad and I would go there on Sundays. For him, it was like watering a thirsty plant. He would handicap the races with wordless excitement, and as recently as last spring he was sharp. In silence, he would work through the algorithms of his decision-making. Then he would hobble to the higher-limit betting window and put down good money. Based on what I could see, he was more than holding his own. One Sunday I got lucky and picked five winners. He crowed to perfect strangers: "My son picked five winners." Though he had to add for my benefit, "Don't get too cocky."

I didn't. I never picked five winners again. By the way, where he got his money, I have no idea. He always seemed to have ready cash. Maybe he had brought a stash with him from Florida. Once the staff at his assisted-living facility found a couple of thousand dollars in hundreds in his pocket. It is not a good thing for an old man with dementia to be walking around with cash like that. That's too much temptation for people. So one day when he had a doctor's appointment, I searched his room. I spent an hour going through every drawer, every pocket, every piece of luggage. I found nothing. Against my better judgment, I was impressed. The man still had his chops.

When he brought home a winner, he would slip me some money, a few twenties. I felt like I was ten years old again, but not in an altogether bad way, and I saw no way to turn down the money without hurting his feelings. One Sunday racing day, it dawned that, since he returned to California, I had spent more time with him in the last months than I had my entire life.

This racing ritual of ours was going well and mostly pleasantly for a couple of months till it unraveled at the end of May. He suddenly grew furious all over again about my taking away his ATM card. He would not be calmed and we had to leave the track. I drove him back to my house, and I myself lost my temper. He was perseverating about the card and he was making eccentric connections.

"You can get your own credit card, give me mine," he kept saying. "And you protested Vietnam, and I am going to get help from the Veterans' Administration."

That day, I watched him struggle up the stairs from the garage, and I determined not to assist him, knowing full well he was going to have trouble at the top. And when he reached the uppermost stair, he fell in a heap, or perhaps he tripped. He skinned his knee. Fortunately, he did not crack his head or break a bone. But I had no reserve of sympathy when I lifted him up from the landing. It was a low moment for me.

★

THERE WAS ONE TRACK experience with him I will never forget, and that had to do with the Kentucky Derby, May 1, 2010. We sat in the track's restaurant while the flashy throng bustled and buzzed with expectation, many decked out in their finest and floppiest millinery, sipping on their mint juleps. For his part, he was in his regulation short-sleeve knit shirt, his track uniform, marking up his Racing Form.

Being at Golden Gate Fields always reminded me of a scam by my brother John many years before. He was maybe twenty years old at the time and not yet strung out on opiates. He lived on a hill, close enough to the track that he could watch the races through binoculars from his roof. He was placing action with a very dimwitted bookmaker. John would time it such that, when the race went off, he would be on the phone with his slow book, and he would make an instant assessment as to who was coming out of the gate with a vengeance. And before the bookmaker knew the race had gone off—remember, this was back in the day, pre-computers—John had lots of information. Then would he get his money down. Sometimes when he was brazen, he bet the race *after* the horses crossed the finish line. He prospered till the book told him to take his action elsewhere. Johnny laughed when he told me, and he conceded that the dummy had figured him out, probably because he got greedy. It was nice while it lasted. Story of my younger brother's abbreviated life.

On that Derby day in 2010, my dad and I were discussing the field for the big race, the principal jewel in the Triple Crown.

"Who you like?" he asked. He wasn't always curious.

I told him I liked Sidney's Candy, ridden by Joseph Talamo. Good value, odds at five to one, sensational horse, stylish jockey— that was my reasoning. Talamo had brought in a few winners for me.

But Sidney's Candy? My dad was dismissive. He screwed up his face, not loving this pick, and shook his head sadly, pitying me.

"How come you don't like Sidney's Candy?" I honestly wanted to know.

"Not my horse. He's a good horse, but he's not my horse." He never could explain himself to my satisfaction, so this was nothing new.

"OK, so who do *you* like, Dad?"

Obviously he didn't like Lookin at Lucky. Lookin at Lucky was the favorite.

"I like the 4," he said. That was his horse. The 4 was ridden by the great jockey Calvin Borel.

"He's at nine to one," I said.

"Sounds right."

I hustled to the window and bet the 4, too, for old times' sake. I got my money down at 3:23. At 3:24 the race went off far across America in Kentucky bluegrass. There the two of us were in California, father and son, a mere couple of miles from where we first lived when we arrived here from Brooklyn. Throughout his fifty years in California, in whatever rented apartment or house, my father always managed to live within minutes of Golden Gate Fields. My mother grasped that the location of their various domiciles was no coincidence. Well into her eighties, she was still calling her husband a "degenerate fucking gambler."

We followed the race on the huge television screens. It was raining heavily in Kentucky and the track was sloppy, and with twenty horses, the field was crowded and the horses were a trial to manage. It was an electrifying race, and there were extraordinary performances by great horses in the muck and mud. Then, seemingly in a flash, the Derby was history. My early pick and first bet, Sidney's Candy, finished way out of the money, as did the betting public's overwhelming choice, Lookin at Lucky.

As for my dad, he won. He may have been suffering from Alzheimer's, but unlike me and millions of others he had picked the winner of the Kentucky Derby. His horse, the 4 horse, proved to be the class of the field. The 4 came in first by several lengths, guided brilliantly by Borel. The horse's name was Super Saver.

Of course, Super Saver would have to be the name of my father's horse. That's what he had been seeking for as long as I could remember.

"Great pick, Dad."

"You get down on the 4?"

"I got down on the 4."

I wondered if *we* should collect *our* winnings now.

"The money'll still be at the window." He meant the betting window, but still, windows and money always connected for me. Some fifty years before, what did he tell my brother and me? "Don't count your money in front of no windows."

"Thanks for the pick, Dad. How'd you know?"

It was his horse. End of story. But he didn't say what he used to say to my childhood queries: "Whaddayou, writin' a book?" It's hard to believe he knew one day I would be doing exactly that, but he fooled me many times before.

After that day, from time to time I would ask if he wanted to go to the track on Sunday. For a fleeting moment he would look pleased and seem to entertain the idea. But then he begged off. "I don't know." On one occasion he managed to articulate a reason: "I lost the interest." Once upon a time, I used to hate how, from my superior point of view, he had wasted his life at the track. On this occasion, though, when he said he didn't want to go to the races anymore, I felt nothing but sadness and regret. Sadness for the life he had led and the life he had not, regret for the choices he had made and not made.

My father lost the interest. The horses would not charge out of the starting gate for him anymore. His race began more than eighty years ago, well before he jumped behind the wheel of his 1951 Ford and fled Brooklyn and the FBI agents and whoever put out the contract on him. Now he was approaching the finish line far from where he started, here in California. It would not be long before he would be lost in the blizzard inside his brain, when he would say to nobody things like:

Is the boat here?

The gate is open.

The cops are coming.

We're losing more than we're winning.

That day of the victorious Kentucky Derby was different. He still had the interest. He was a winner, not a loser. That day when he won the biggest race of the year, when I let him know that I thought he was a hell of a handicapper, he responded with a shrug. But that time, he also allowed himself to smile. That crease on his mouth was not an everyday sight. It came more rarely than Christmas.

Then he slipped on his eyeglasses and painstakingly flipped the pages of his Racing Form. He was handicapping. Popey was in his element. That's when he began to analyze the next races going off all around the country—Golden Gate Fields, Belmont, Hollywood Park, Churchill Downs, Santa Anita, Pimlico. There's always a good bet to make, if you happen to know what makes a good bet *good*.

On that Derby day, as the 4 horse was being crowned with roses in the Winner's Circle, I opened up my Racing Form, just like my father. I was middling my life once more, searching for a Super Saver of my own, taking no shit from nobody.

Epilogue

G IUSEPPE LUIGI DI PRISCO, a.k.a. "Popey," died on July 3, 2012, in California. My father was eighty-seven.

His death took place on the Feast of Saint Thomas, who is called the Doubter, because he wouldn't believe that Jesus had risen from the dead until he could stick his own hand into the wounds.

Father Shane performed the last rites.

For the eulogy I read the speech my dad was unable to deliver at his Teamster retirement dinner.

He and my mother are buried beside each other, and alongside my three brothers, overlooking Brooklyn.

Acknowledgments

The author is deeply grateful to many, especially:

Mario Di Prisco.
Elizabeth Trupin-Pulli, JET Literary Associates, his literary agent.
Pat Walsh, his editor.
Tyson Cornell, publisher of Rare Bird Books.
Julia Callahan, Alice Marsh-Elmer, and Angelina Coppola of Rare Bird Books.
David Poindexter, the late publisher of MacAdam/Cage.
Dorothy Carico Smith and Sonny Brewer of MacAdam/Cage.
Regan McMahon.
Katharine Ogden Michaels.
Laura Cogan, editor-in-chief of *ZYZZYVA*.
Michelle Dotter.
Katherine Palermo. Jennifer Palermo Bobe.
Anne Rosenthal.
Tricia Palermo.
Hospice Foundation of the East Bay.
His former students and (most of) his former colleagues.
Redwood Day School, Oakland, California.
The late Edwina James.
Patricia James, who makes it all possible and worth doing.